ANNALS OF THE DELHI BADSHAHATE

ANNALS OF THE DELHI BADSHAHATE:

BEING A TRANSLATION OF THE OLD ASSAMESE CHRONICLE PADSHAH-BURANJI, WITH INTRODUCTION AND NOTES

S. K. BHUYAN

GYAN

Published by

Gyan Publishing House
5, Ansari Road
Daryaganj, New Delhi-110002
Phone: 011-47034999, 9811692060
E-mail: books@gyanbooks.com

Distribution Network
gyanbooks.com
India, USA, Canada, UK, Australia

ISBN: 978-93-6920-000-9 (PB)

First Published, 1947

2nd Impression 2025

Printed at: Gyan Press, Delhi.

ANNALS OF THE DELHI BADSHAHATE
Author: S. K. BHUYAN

ANNALS OF THE DELHI BADSHAHATE

BY THE SAME AUTHOR

English :

1. An Assamese Nur Jahan, Queen Phuleswari Devi. 1926.
2. Report and Conspectus of the Assam Research Society. 1927.
3. Early British Relations with Assam. 1928.
4. Preliminary Report on the Agency Records of the Assam Government, 1823-1874. Printed in Assam Secretariat Office file. 1930-31.
5. Bulletins of the Department of Historical and Antiquarian Studies in Assam, Nos. I, II and III. 1932-36.
6. Tungkhungia Buranji, with Glossary, Index, etc. 1933.
7. Assamese Literature : Ancient and Modern. Printed in Assam Secretariat Office file. 1936.
8. Dr. Francis Hamilton's Account of Assam. 1940.
9. Lachit Barphukan and His Times. 1947.
10. Anglo-Assamese Relations. Thesis approved for the Ph. D. Degree of London University. *In the Press.*
11. Military System of the Assamese People. Prativa Devi Memorial Lectures, Fourth Series, 1941. *Ready for the Press.*
12. Atan Buragohain and His Times, 1662-1681. *Ready for the Press.*

Assamese :

1. Gopal Krishna Gokhale. 1916.
2. Nirmali, poems. 1918..
3. Ahomar Din. 1918.
4. Jaimati Upakhyan, poem. 1920.
5. Anundoram Borooah, Sanskritist. 1920 and 1924.
6. Rabindranath Tagore. 1920.
7. Barphukanar Git, old historical ballad. 1924.
8. Panchami, short stories. 1927.
9. Jonaki, lives of eminent men. 1928 and 1938.
10. Chaneki, lives of eminent women. 1928.
11. Asam Jiyari, Assamese women of history. 1935.
12. King Rajeswar Singha, 1751-1769. *Ready for the Press.*

Assamese chronicles, edited with Introduction in English :

1. Assam Buranji by Harakanta Barua. 1930.
2. Kamrupar Buranji. 1930.
3. Deodhai Asam Buranji. 1932.
4. Tungkhungia Buranji. 1932.
5. Asamar Padya-Buranji. with a Synopsis in English. 1933.
6. Padshah-Buranji. 1935.
7. Kachari Buranji, with a Synopsis in English. 1936.
8. Jayantia Buranji, with a Synopsis in English. 1937.
9. Tripura Buranji. 1938.
10. Assam Buranji, S.M., with an Analysis in English. 1945.

ANNALS OF THE DELHI BADSHAHATE

Being a translation of the old Assamese chronicle Padshah-Buranji, with Introduction and Notes

BY

S. K. BHUYAN

Rai Bahadur, M.B.E., M.A., B.L. (Cal.), Ph.D. (Lond.),

Director of Historical and Antiquarian Studies in Assam.

Published by the Government of Assam in the Department of Historical and Antiquarian Studies, Gauhati.

1947

First Edition, 1947

TABLE OF CONTENTS

ANNALS OF THE DELHI BADSHAHATE

PREFACE

The compilation of the present book *Annals of the Delhi Badshahate* owes its origin to the encouragement of three eminent scholars, alas, who are now no more !

In December 1927, Professor S. Khuda Bukhsh, historian, philosopher and humanist, visited Gauhati as President of the Assam Students' Conference, when I acquainted him with the contents of the *Padshah-Buranji*. He was greatly interested in the chronicle, specially in the description of the Nao-roza festivities of which I had prepared a translation for him. He asked me to write a few articles introducing the book to scholars so that they might know of the existence of such a valuable source of information about the Muhammadan Period. He also assured me that he would get my articles published in some magazine.

I had the privilege of being Professor Khuda Bukhsh's student at the University Law College, Calcutta, in 1915-1916, and he left upon my youthful mind a very powerful impress of his personality, and of his "sweetness and light" which ideal he followed throughout his life. His suggestion was of the nature of a mandate to me, and I put my heart and soul into the work, and soon completed writing a series of articles, entitled *New Lights on Mogul India from Assamese Sources*.

I despatched the articles to Professor Khuda Bukhsh in the middle of January 1928, and he transmitted them to Mr. Marmaduke Pickthall, Editor of the *Islamic Culture*, Hyderabad, Deccan. Mr. Pickthall welcomed the articles in the pages of his journal, and they were published as a serial in four parts in the issues of July 1928, October 1928, January 1929, and October 1929. The first two articles have since been revised, enlarged and rearranged, and incorporated in the present book in the Introduction and the Appendices.

On November 20, 1928, I had the good fortune of meeting Sir Muhammad Iqbal, poet and philosopher, at the tea-party given to the delegates of the Fifth All-India Oriental Conference at Shahdara Gardens attached to the mausoleum of Emperor Jahangir at Lahore. Sir Muhammad referred to my articles in the *Islamic Culture*, and expressed a desire to see the entire *Padshah-Buranji* in English.

As a preliminary step, I collated the Assamese text from the available manuscripts, and arranged the chapters in chronological order, and then translated the whole chronicle into English.

This translation, entitled *Annals of the Delhi Badshahate*, was submitted to Mr. Pickthall for publication in the *Islamic Culture.* Mr. Pickthall whose scholarship and catholicity were well-known, and who had won an undying fame by his translation of the Holy Koran, welcomed the *Annals of the Delhi Badshahate* as well in the pages of his journal, and it was published in five parts in the issues from January 1933 to July 1934.

So late as August 1941, Dr. M. A. Mu'id Khan, M.A. (Osmania), Ph. D. (Cantab.), D. Litt. (Cairo), Secretary, Editorial Board, *Islamic Culture*, was good enough to remind me of my old connection with the paper. The encouragement given to me by Professor Khuda Bukhsh, Mr. Marmaduke Pickthall, Sir Muhammad Iqbal, and the authorities of the *Islamic Culture*, constitute an unforgettable chapter of my life redeeming the arid exertions of a historical researcher in this lonely corner of India.

The Assamese text of the *Padshah-Buranji*, edited by me with Preface and Introduction in English, has been published by the Kamarupa Anusandhan Samiti, Gauhati, in 1935, with the aid of funds placed at the Samiti's disposal by Maulavi Abdul Hamid, then Education Minister of Assam. It is gratifying to note that the articles published in the *Islamic Culture*, mentioned above have been included in Professor Sri Ram Sharma's *Bibliography of Mughal India*, and in a similar bibliography compiled by Reverend Father H. Heras, S. J., of Bombay.

From the Buranjis which have hitherto been published, and from the use made of them by Sir Edward Gait and Sir Jadu Nath Sarkar in their monumental works on the history of Assam and Aurangzeb, the scholarly world has been well acquainted with the wealth of Assamese historical literature. The Buranjis deal mainly with the political events of Assam, and its relations with the neighbouring tribes and races.

But there is a class of chronicles like the present one which deal with peoples outside Assam, and they were compiled for the purpose of general enlightenment, and as a measure of political necessity to furnish the background of Assam's relations with those peoples. The *Tripura Buranji*, compiled in 1724 by two Assamese ambassadors, throws new lights on the history of Tipperah and of Mogul India as well. The Assamese chronicles of the class of *Padshah-Buranji* and *Tripura Buranji* therefore break new ground, and I am confident that a vigorous and systematic search for Buranjis will be rewarded by the discovery of other chroicles of trans-Assam interest, which are bound to contain a large mass of unexplored source materials of Indian history, both general and provincial.

As for my Assamese countrymen, I only wish that they should become conscious of the untold wealth lying buried in the folios of their dilapidated manuscripts, some of which are in a state of preservation in domestic and monastic archives, while many others have disappeared owing to neglect, and the ravages of floods to which Assam is frequently exposed. As for myself, I would quote the words of William Irvine, the historian of the Later Mughals,— "May my reward be, as an Oxford historian phrases it, that some Gibbon of the future may throw me a word of thanks in a footnote."

I take this opportunity of expressing my thanks to the following gentlemen for their help in many ways in the compilation and publication of this book: to Srijut Madhab Chandra Baroowa and Srijut Umesh Chandra Talukdar of the D.H.A.S. staff; to Maulavi Sayid Murtaza Ali, B.Sc., Additional Deputy Commissioner, Kamrup; to Maulavi Abul Fazl Sayid Ahmed, M.A., Assistant Director of Public Instruction, Assam; to Maulavi Muhammad Abdul Hye, M.A., and Srijut Prafulladatta Goswami, M.A. of the Cotton College, Gauhati; to Maulavi Sayid Abdul Quddus, Teacher, Cotton Collegiate School Gauhati; to Srijut Suryya

Kanta Barpujari, M.A., of the Handiqui Girls' College, Gauhati; to Srijut Bhupendra Kumar Hazarika, M.A., Historical Research Scholar of the Government of Assam; to Maulavi S. Z. Ahmed, Merchant, Gauhati; and to Mr. H. Ghosh of the Indian Press Limited, Allahabad, for the promptness with which he has executed the work of printing.

GAUHATI, ASSAM,
1st *March* 1947.

S. K. BHUYAN.

ANNALS OF THE DELHI BADSHAHATE

INTRODUCTION

A.—ASSAM'S CONTACT WITH THE MUSLIM WORLD

Wars and conquests have always contributed to the enrichment of historical literature as well as to the expansion of the intellectual horizon of different nationalities. The contact of European nations with the Saracens through the medium of the Crusades led to the interchange of Arabic and European culture, and was responsible for the Earlier Renaissance which first dispelled the gloom and stupor of the mediaeval ages. This is nowhere truer than in the conflicts of the inhabitants of the eastern frontier of India with the Muhammadâns.

In the fourth century of the Christian era, Shankal, king of Kamarupa, overthrew Kedar Brahmàn, king of Northern India, and founded Gaur or Lakhnauti which remained the capital of Bengal for more than one thousand years. Peeranweisa, the generalissimo of Afrasiyab, the great king of Turan and Scythia, met the army of Shankal near Ghoraghat. The Mongols of Afrasiyab were completely defeated: but Afrasiyab himself now appeared on the scene with his invincible legions, and compelled the Kamarupa monarch to offer his submission. Shankal was carried off by Afrasiyab to Turàn, where he remained for some time being àfterwards slain in action by Rustom, the Achilles of Persia and the slayer incognito of his son Sohrab.[1]

Muhammad Bin Bakhtiyar, a Turk of the Khilji tribe, invaded Kamarupa about 1205 A.D. He crossed a stone-bridge and advanced into the interior of the country. But the Kamarupa Raja in the meantime marshalled his forces, destroyed the bridge and besieged the army of the invaders, who in their hasty retreat rushed into a river which they found fordable to some distance, but deep and rapid in the middle. The whole army perished in the river, except Muhammad who escaped with a few hundred horsemen. The destruction of the hostile forces in *saka* 1127 or A.D. 1205, is recorded in a Sanskrit couplet inscribed on a rock at North Gauhati.[2]

Ghiyasuddin Iwaz-i-Husain Khalji, Sultan of Gaur, invaded Assam in about 1226, but he was defeated and compelled to return to Gaur.[3]

Ikhtiyaruddin Yuzbak Tughril Khan invaded Assam in 1256-57 A.D., and achieved a victory over the Assam king, which he celebrated by erecting a mosque.[4] It is said that he got possession of 1,200 hoards of treasure left in Kamarupa by Gustasib who had marched through that territory on his way from China to India. But when the rains set in, the king of Kamarupa fell upon the soldiers of Ikhtiyaruddin and inflicted upon them a crushing defeat. Yuzbak was killed, and of his army only a few could return to Bengal.[5]

It is recorded in the *Alamgir-namah*, that the Delhi monarch Muhammad Shah, son of Tughluq Shah, despatched against Assam in 1332-33 an army of 100,000 horses, " but the whole army perished in that land of witchcraft, and not a trace was left of the army." Another army was sent but they could not go beyond the frontiers of Bengal.[6]

Ibn Batutah travelled from Sadkawan (Chatgaon) for the mountains of Kamru, with the object of meeting a saint named Shaikh Jalaluddin Tabrizi. *Kamru* was the name of Kamrup, by which it was known to the Islāmic world, being adopted by Alberuni as well. Ibn Batutah was in Assam in about 1350 A.D. The travellor Ibn Batutah records in his *Turbat-nuzzar* that he stayed at Tabrizi's hermitage for three days. Some amount of confusion has arisen between this saint visited by Ibn Batutah, and Shah Jalal, who died in 1189 A.D., and whose *Dargah* or mausoleum at Sylhet is still visited by pilgrims.[7]

Sikandar Shah, Sultan of Bengal, launched an attack on Kamarupa about the year 1356. The off-shoot is not precisely known, though it is evident that he conquered the whole or a part of the kingdom, from the fact that he issued coins from his camp in Kamarupa, arsat Kamru.[8] Other names for Kamrup, by which it was known to the Islamic world, were *Kamrud* and *Kanwru*.

In the reign of Rukunuddin Barbak Shah, Sultan of Bengal, 1457—1474, Shah Ismail Ghazi, "a descendant of the family of the prophet," and born at Mecca, invaded Kamrup in about 1460, then ruled by one Kameswar. Barbak Shah had previously despatched several expeditions against Assam, which had all met disastrous defeat in the land of witchcraft, and so the generalship fell this time on Ismail Ghazi, evidently a saint, who had formerly defeated Gajapati, king of Orissa. Kameswar, the king of Kamarupa, "who was one of the greatest heroes of his time and possessed good military talents" offered the invaders a very stubborn resistance. The Raja was ultimately brought to bay by the diplomatic manoures of the Muhammadan commander, and made his "voluntary submission" to the latter. The title of "Bara Larwaiya," or a great fighter, was conferred on the Raja. Sultan Barbak suspected Ismail "to have entered into an offensive and defensive alliance with Kamrup with the object of setting up an independent kingdom." He was beheaded on January 4, 1474, and his head is buried at the *Dargah* or shrine at Kanta-duar, Rangpur. The faquir in charge of the

Dargah had, in 1874, a Persian manuscript, entitled *Risalat-ush-Shuhada*, or Book of Martyrs, which contains a full description of Ismail Ghazi's life and career.

Sir Edward Gait has not attached any credence to this invasion of Ismail Ghazi " as it is wholly uncorroborated " and " as it does not occur in any Assam chronicle or tradition." But as the above manuscript was composed by Pir Muhammad Shattāri on the testimony of the keepers of the tombs in Kantaduar and Jala Maqam in 1663, who prayed for " the correction of mistakes and rectification of errors by the learned of the time," we are unwilling to dismiss the episode as entirely untrustworthy. In the *Padshah Buranji*, one Masalanda Gazi is mentioned as an invader of Assam: and as the title Ghazi is somewhat rare, this name might be the Assamese version of the original Shah Ismail Ghazi. James Prinsep in his " Useful Tables " refers to the invasion of Assam by Masalanda Ghazi about 1498.[9]

About 1498 Alauddin Husain Shah, Sultān of Gaur, invaded Western Assam, Kamata and Kamārupa, and subdued Nilambar, king of Kamata, and other chieftains, *viz*., Rup Narayan Pola, Kumwar Gora, Lakkhan and Lachhmi Narayan. Dāniel, his son, was left in charge, but he was defeated and killed, this time evidently by the Ahom king of Upper Assam. Hussain Shah's coins embodied his victory over Kamarupa and Kamata in the following legend,—" The Sultan-conqueror over Kamru and Kamata." In the Fathiyya-i-ibriyyah, written by Shihabuddin Tālish, who accompanied Mir Jumla in his Assam expedition we read: " Once Husain Shah, a Sultan of Bengal, entered Assam with 20,000 foot and horse and numberless boats, and the Rajah leaving his kingdom fled to the hills. Husain Shah then returned to Bengal, leaving his son with most of his troops to occupy the country. When the rainy season arrived and the roads became closed, the Rajah came down from the hills to the low country and surrounded Husain Shah's son with the help of his subjects who had professed submission to the latter. And that unfortunate Prince and troops, soon becoming weak through lack of food, were slain or captured."[10]

A Muhammadan commander of Gaur named Turbak invaded Assam in 1532, and the Ahom general after a war lasting for three years defeated the invader, and extended the sphere of Assam's influence up to Cooch Behar and Gaur. This was the war in which the widow of an Ahom commander displayed unprecedented bravery, and where guns were used for the first time. Turbak is described in an Assamese chronicle as the adopted son of the Padshah of Gaur, and as having been killed by the Ahoms by a stratagem.[11]

Kalapahar, the commander of Sulaiman-i-Karrani, Sultan of Bengal, invaded Assam in the middle of the sixteenth century, but failed to achieve any permanent result. Kalapahar is called Pora-Sultan or iconoclast in Assamese chronicles, and is associated by tradition with the destruction of numerous images and temples in Kamarupa, including those of Kamakhya and Hazo.[12]

During the reign of Jahangir, Mukarram Khan, governor of the Eastern Koch kingdom, the country taken from Parikshit, deputed in 1614 Sayyid Hakim, Sayyad Abu Baqr and Satrajit to invade the Ahom territories. Abu Baqr and his son Ghiyasuddin were slain in the battle. Satrajit's son was sacrificed to the goddess Kamakhya. The body of Ghiyasuddin, who was a highly devout Muhammadan, was buried at Hazo, and his tomb is still visited by pilgrims, though a claim is made on behalf of another Ghiyasuddin, who was the successor of Daniel, son of Hussain Shah, in the Fauzadarship of Hazo. The pilgrimage at Hazo is known as "Poa-Macca," literally, "one-fourth Mecca." A shrine on "the hillock of Sultan Ghiyasuddin Auliya" near Hazo is mentioned in the *Baharistan-i-Ghaybi*, in connection with the wars of the early seventeenth century.[13]

During the reign of Shah Jahan, Islam Khan Mushhedy governor of Bengal, despatched in 1636 Shaikh Mahiuddin, brother of Abdus Salam, the Fauzadar of Koch Hazo, with a large army, to intercept the activities of Satrajit, Thanadar at Pandu, who had joined the Darrang Raja Balinarayan.[14] The invaders met with a crushing rebuff, and a fresh reinforcement was despatched from Jahangirnagar under Allah Yar Khan. Satrajit was captured, taken to Dacca and executed. After a protracted contest the invaders cleared Koch Hazo of the Assamese, and the boundaries of Assam and Bengal were fixed in 1639 in the treaty terms drawn up by Allah Yar Khan and Momai-tamuli Barbarua. The great Ahom king Swargadeo Pratap Singha actively participated at times in the protracted campaigns of the period.[15]

In continuation of the campaign against Prince Shuja, Mir Jumla invaded Assam in 1662, partly on the provocation offered by the Ahom king Jayadhwaja Singha, and partly on his own initiative as a preliminary step towards the conquest of China.[16] His action was subsequently confirmed by Aurangzeb. The Ahom Raja fled to the hills, and though the invaders faced unprecedented disasters and hardships, they ultimately succeeded in compelling Assam to enter into a treaty favourable to the Moguls, by which they imposed a heavy indemnity on the Ahom monarch and an annual tribute. Jayadhwaj Singha had to part with his only child Ramani Gabharu aged about six, as a present to the imperial harem.[17]

After the departure of Mir Jumla, the Ahom king Chakradhwaja Singha, successor of Jayadhwaja Singha, preferred war to perpetual subservience to the Moguls. He mobilised a large army and attacked and reoccupied Gauhati, the Ahom army being led by Lachit Barphukan, son of Momai-tamuli Barbarua. Aurangzeb deputed Raja Ram Singha of Amber to invade Assam in the beginning of 1668, as a punishment for his connivance at the escape of Shivaji and the Sikh Guru Teg Bahadur. Ram Singha, evidently broken-hearted, his dissatisfaction being aggravated by reports of his son's maltreatment at the hands of Aurangzeb, was defeated by the Ahom general Lachit Barphukan in the battle of Saraighat, which being the greatest of all the Assam-Mogul contests is held by the Assamese as their Marathon and Thermopylae. Ram Singha retired to Rangamati in April 1671, and paid his respects to the Emperor in June 1676, his long stay in Eastern India being evidently a punishment for his alleged remissness.[18]

Assam's preoccupations with these frontier wars with the Moguls led to internal troubles. Laluk Sola Barphukan, the brother and successor of Lachit Barphukan, offered to Prince Azam Shah, also called Sultan Azamtara, governor of Bengal, that he would surrender Gauhati, on condition of the prince's promise to help the Barphukan to become Raja of Assam. Azamtara despatched Mansur Khan, who occupied Gauhati in March 1679, and lived there as Fauzadar for more than three years. The Barphukan performed a bogus coronation ceremony at his own residence and became Raja wearing the regalia stolen from the royal store, but he was assassinated soon afterwards. The Emperor Aurangzeb rewarded Sultan Azamtara with costly presents for this "conquest". The prince had already married Ramani Gabharu, newly named Rahmat Banu, the daughter of the Ahom monarch Jayadhwaj Singha.

The continued occupation of Gauhati by the Moguls brought back the intriguing ministers to their senses, and they placed the powerful prince Gadadhar Singha on the throne of Assam. He attacked the Mogul garrison at Itakhuli or Gauhati. Mansur Khan and his troops offered some resistance, but they were defeated towards the latter half of 1682. Jayanti Singha, a Mogul commander, displayed unusual bravery, but he was captured by the Ahoms. Mansur Khan escaped to Rangamati with Satmal Sli Akbar; and his other generals Indramani Jal Singha and Kabir Khan deserted their camp and fled. The Ahoms obtained in this victory a very large quantity of provisions and supplies including guns and horses.[19] The battle of Itakhuli is the last contest between Assam and the Moguls. The river Manaha became from that time the western boundary of Assam which continued as such till the termination of Ahom rule in 1826.

King Rudra Singha, 1696-1714, who is believed to be the greatest of the Ahom monarchs, resented the humiliating overtures of Murshid Kuli Khan, governor of Bengal, who used to send to the former presents of *khelats*. It is said that the Mogul forces attacked Gauhati, but they were defeated after a few engagements. Rudra Singha planned to march to Bengal, with an army of 4,00,000 soldiers, to restore to Assam its *Pauranic* limits which had extended from the confines of Sadiya to the Karatoya river.[20] He also sent embassies to the rulers of Delhi, Amber, Tripura, Bihar, Burdwan, Nadia, Pangia, and other Nawabs and princes of Bengal. But his plan was frustrated by his death which occurred during his stay at Gauhati. It is recorded in old Assamese chronicles that the object of Rudra Singha's embassies was to organise a confederacy of Hindu Rajas against the Moguls who, according to reports received by him, had proved unfriendly to Hinduism.[21]

The death of Swargadeo Rudrà Singha occurred seven years after that of Emperor Aurangzeb. The disruption of the Timurids, which followed the death of that great Emperor, prevented all thought of a military expedition to the extreme north-east corner of India. The germ of decay also ate into the vitals of the five-hundred years old Ahom Government. Assam, which combated successfully against the repeated efforts of the Moguls to incorporate it within their territory, ultimately succumbed to the internal depredations of a mere religious sect; and the inhuman hordes despatched by the Avanese monarchs of Alompra dynasty gave the final sword-thurst to the province, which was already gasping in the throes of death consequent upon its self-exhaustion and inanity.

During all these conflicts the foreigners could never acquire a permanent footing in Assam.[22] Its unexpected floods, its pestilential airs, its rugged hills proved a serious handicap to soldiers accustomed to fighting in the plains of Northern India. Besides, the invaders had to ply their boats upstream and come over long distances which compelled them to bring only their minimum forces and provisions. The banks of the Brahmaputra were studded with high rocky hill-tops which served as natural fortresses, on which the Assamese mounted their cannon and garrisoned their army. The unsuccessful soldiers dinned into the ears of the Delhi Emperors stories of magic and witchcraft in Assam to which they attributed their repeated ill-fate and disaster. According to the *Khulasatu-i-Tawarikh*, the people of Kamarupa were supposed to "build houses, by the force of magic, with pillars and ceilings made of men, who remain alive without having the power of breathing and moving; with the help of black arts they transformed men into quadrupeds and birds, so that these men got tails and ears like those of beasts."[23] The stories of black arts supposed to be practised by men of Assam were carried back to Mogul India by the soldiers who accompanied and survived the numerous expeditions, and the result was that in the imagination of the people of India, the magic of Assam excelled that of Egypt, and the only thing with which Assam was associated was its formidable sorcery and witchcraft.[24] Ram Singha brought with him the ninth Sikh Guru Teg Bahadur, and five Muhammadan pirs, Shah Akbar, Shah Bagmar, Shah Saran, Shah Sufi and Shah Kamal, to undo the effects of Kamrupi black arts.[25]

Apart from the natural disadvantages which the invaders had to confront, and the alleged potency of Assamese magic, the prowess and strategy of the Assamese people were also not of an inferior order. Their legions had fought in the battle of Kurukhsetra; with them, King Bhaskaravarma served in the campaigns of his friend Emperor Harshavardhana, and extended his sovereignty over Karnasuvarna, and subsequently helped the Chinese general Wangheuentse in his invasion of Nepal;[26] with them, King Harshadeva, the father of Rajyadevi, consort of Jayadeva, the Lichchavi king of Nepal, made himself the lord of Gaura, Odra, Kalinga and Kosala.[27] Their valour and courage were a wonder to the Kashmir invaders Muktapida Lalitaditya and Jayapira. Their repeated success in stemming the tide of foreign invasion was not the eccentric gift of fortune or of fate; it was the outcome of the supreme efficiency of their internal organisation, their unparalleled patriotism, their capacity to subordinate personal interests and ambitions to the higher demands of their motherland.[28] The indigenous military system was made equally efficient under the organisation of the Ahoms who had conquered Assam in the thirteenth century. Besides the regular forces the Ahoms kept ready for service a standing militia, composed of all the secular adult male members of the country, and conscription was in the very blood of the normal system of government, under which an army could be mobilised at a short notice, its number being determined by the exigency of the situation.

The espionage system of the Assamese was highly efficient. The commanders entrusted with the conduct of military engagements could never be bribed or won over to the hostile camp. There are instances of voluntary desertion to the enemy's side by men like Baduli Phukan and Bejdoloi Phukan, but it had no effect upon the course of the war, as the heart of the general mass of soldiers was sound. Ram Singha made repeated attempts to win over Lachit Barphukan and his captains, but here Mogul-Rajput strategy failed, while it had succeeded in many other parts of India. After the defeat of Ram Singha, Lachit Barphukan ordered his soldiers in the following words not to tarnish the fair name of their country by pursuing the remnant of the vanquished army and seizing their properties and war-materials. "Being unable to achieve any success during a contest lasting for one year the enemy is now retreating in utter disgrace and shame. Why should you bring discredit upon the reputation of our victorious sovereign and his ministers by seizing the goods of the fugitives?" Important military commands are said to have been given by the Ahoms to Assamese Muhammadans who fought for their land of adoption with zeal and patriotism.[29] Mir Jumla's chronicler said with regret.—"As for the Mussalmans . . . . their hearts are more inclined towards mingling with the Assamese than towards association with the Muslims."[30]

The Assamese legions were composed not only of the Aryan settlers in the Brahmaputra Valley, but also of the primitive tribes living in the neighbourhood with some of whom war and bloodshed were a daily recreation, among whom social rank and prestige were determined by the number of human skulls each member of the phratry could collect.[31]

The Mogul wars of Assam represented a clash between the strategy and strength of the Timurid Turks, miscalled Mongols, settled for generations in the enervating atmosphere of Northern India, and of the Mongoloid tribes of the Brahmaputra region, who inhabited the inaccessible defiles and recesses of the Assam mountains, and whose undiminished primitive vigour was marshalled to the best advantage by the subtle military organisations of their intellectual neighbours.

With the adoption of Hinduism by the Ahoms, attended by their natural desire to acquire posthumous bliss in supersession of the benefits of this mundane globe, dissipated their martial ardour; and their spiritual preoccupations were followed by continued neglect of state duties, which led to the inevitable relegation of kingly powers to ministers and potentates, which in its turn led to unremitting jealousies between rival clans and families. It is curious to note that the ascendancy of the Muhammadans in India synchronised with Shan supremacy in the Brahmaputra Valley. Both dragged on a faineant existence during the eighteenth century, and had ultimately to succumb before a culture and strategy of a new order.[32]

The invincibility of the Assamese during the period of Muhammadan conflicts has led a writer to remark,—"The Assamese were to the Moslems what the Numidians and Mauritanians were to the old Romans—*genus insuperbile bello.*"[33]

The Muhammadan historian, Muhammad Kazim, wrote in his *Alamgir-namah*.—"The Rajas of Assam have never bowed the head of submission and obedience, nor had they paid tributes or revenue to the most powerful monarch; but they have curbed the ambition and checked the conquests of the most victorious princes of Hindustan; the solution of a war against them has baffled the penetration of heroes who have been styled Conquerors of the World." Shihabuddin Talish wrote about Assam: "In short, every army that entered the limits of this country, made its exit from the realm of Life; every caravan that set foot on this land, deposited its baggage of residence in the halting-place of Death. . . . And as no one who entered this country, like visitors to the realm of Death, ever returned, and the manners of its natives were never made known to any [outsider], the people of Hindustan used to call the inhabitants of Assam sorcerers and magicians and consider them as standing outside the human species, and enter the name of this country in [their] spells and counter-spells. They say that whosoever visits this country is overcome by charms and never comes out of it."[34]

Ram Singha in the thick of the battle of Saraighat where his plans were frustrated by the forethought and strategy of the Assamese generals had exclaimed in a fit of rapture,—"Glory to the King! Glory to the Counsellers! Glory to the Commanders! Glory to the Country! One single individual leads all the forces! Even I, Ram Singha, being personally on the spot have not found any loophole and opportunity."[35]

The conflicts of Assam with the Muhammadans have been recorded for all ages in Persian chronicles. The descriptions are made more valuable by the light they throw on the social and political condition of Assam in those days. The most comprehensive account of Assam is given in the *Fathiyah-i-Ibriyah*, compiled by Shihab-ud-din Talish, who accompanied Mir Jumla's expedition. The book deals with the causes which led to the invasion, the route which lay in the journey, the occupation of the country, the conclusion of peace, and the return of the general and his death near Khizirpur. The second part contains a description of Assam and the Assamese, and of the aboriginal tribes in Eastern and Southern Assam. The author inserted in his chronicle some portion of a Persian *qasida* on Assam, composed by his companion Mulla Darvesh, "who had explored the Persian tongue more than the Arabic tongue."[36]

One indirect result of Assam's contact with the Muhammadans through the medium of war was the expansion of her horizon of experiences and possibilities, though history affirms that she was not outside the pale of the formative influences which acted and re-acted on the civilisation of Aryavarta in the pre-Muhammadan period. There was frequent interchange of embassies between the Ahom and the Mogul courts. The Assamese government appointed very skilful Brahmans in their diplomatic service who were expected to properly safeguard the interests of their country. Though they were primarily political emissaries, they also served as the medium through which foreign customs were introduced into Assam. King Rudra Singha created two new orders in Assamese society, the Khaunds and the Bairagis, whose chief function was to visit important centres in India, and import beneficent foreign customs into their own country.[37] Ahom princesses flaunted along in the halls and corridors of the imperial palaces of Delhi and Agra, and the *Maasir-i-Alamgiri* records the marriage of Rahmat Banu, the daughter of the king of Assam, to Prince Muhammad Azam on May 2, 1668.

The Ahom monarch maintained in his court a

large number of Muhammadan offiicals who deciphered Persian correspondence received from outside, and drafted letters to foreign sovereigns and potentates. The royal mint was under the superintendence of a Muhammadan officer, and several Assamese kings and queens struck coins with Persian legends engraved on them.[38] The Persian or Urdu language was not absolutely unknown among the mass of people and a witness in a criminal trial of about 1775 reproduced the exact words of the conversation which had been carried on by the accused in "Farsi". The nucleus of the present Muhammadan population of Assam was formed during the period of Muhammadan conflicts, the main stock being strengthened from time to time by fresh immigration and conversion.

The esteem and reverence in which Muslims were held in Assam can be illustrated from two contemporary records. In September 1780, an Assamese Muslim, named Anwar Hazi Faquir, of the guild of Parsi-parhias or Persian translators, met King Lakshmi Singha after his return from his pilgrimage, obviously to Mecca. The king became highly pleased by his conversation with the Faquir, and granted him revenue-free lands in Kamrup together with the necessary number of servitors, as well as the perquisites of the following *maqams* or *darghas*,—Shah Madar Bar-maqam in Bausi perganah, Shah Faqir's maqam in Barnagar perganah, Panch-pirar maqam in Khettri perganah, and one-fourth share of the Bar-maqam at Hazo. It was laid down that "Anwâr Hazi Faqir Parsi-parhia will enjoy the above in perpetuity, down to the days of his sons, grandsons and their descendants on the male line, wishing for the welfare of the king. He will also be the head of the above-mentioned maqams, and maintain his religion thereby". The above grant was embodied in a royal *farman* inscribed on a copper-plate. Anwar Faqir is the founder of a distinguished Assamese Muslim family the members of which have attained eminence in various spheres of activity at present. A search for similar grants will lead to the discovery of numerous instances of the Ahom monarchs' patronage of Muslim worthies.[39]

Dr. John Peter Wade who stayed in Assam from 1792 to 1794, as the Surgeon attached to Captain Welsh's expedition, records an instance of the respect shown to Muslim priests at the court of the Hindu kings of Assam: "A Mussleman of the name of Newas was gooroo-general of his persuasion in Assam, from about the time of Roodur Singha. He had numerous attendants dressed in the high Mussleman fashion. He resided at or near the capital and frequented the durbar; and the Swargadeos used to despatch him to pray at Hadjoo after the Mussleman fashion for their prosperity. He was usually succeeded by his nearest relations. He and his family disappeared at the Swargadeo's flight (during the Moamaria disturbances). The latter had no pooja since at Hadjoo. He was indulged with the privilege of riding on horseback, but not in a palki-dolah. Three or four priests always remained in attendance at the palace. The moment the king came forth to take the air, they called down the blessing of God on him with elevated hands. Whenever the Surgee sent this man to perform pooja at Mokam Hadjoo, he always sent considerable presents to the temple, but they had no regular establishments from the kings".

Muslim *maqams* or *darghas* are scattered in the Assam Valley and their maintenance was encouraged by the state as we know from the assignment of the perquisites of a number of *maqams* in Kamrup to Anwar Hazi Faqir, and the custom of despatching annual presents from the court to the Poa-macca shrine at Hazo. An examination of the *maqams* in Assam is bound to add to our knowledge of the careers of eminent Muslim saints who came to this country from outside to minister to the spiritual needs of the people. The religious songs composed by Assamese Muslim pirs, known as *Jeekeers*, are heard even till this day.

During the occupation of Gauhati and Kamrup by the Moguls from 1639 to 1658, and from 1663 to 1667, Muslim rulers interested themselves in the improvement of mosques, and also in the patronage of Hindu priests. The shrine of Sultan Ghiyasuddin Aulia at Hazo was perhaps destroyed or damaged; and an inscription on the wall of the present mosque records the fact that during the reign of "Sahebe-querane Shani Shah Jahan Badshah Ghazi", and the governorship of "Abul Ghazi Shujaa-ud-din Muhammad Shah," the foundation-stone of the mosque at Shujaa-bad (Hazo) was laid by Lutfulla Shiràji, on the occasion of the planting of the flag-post in honour of "Sahebe Sabyeen". The construction of the mosque was completed by Lutfulla's son Niamat-ulla in the month of Ramzan, 1067 A.H., June 1657 A.D.

From a document in possession of a priest of Kamakhya it is learnt that the gift of two *bisas* (bigha?) of land in Mauza Turukpara, Sarkar Dakhinkul, was confirmed in the 9th year of Emperor Aurangzeb's reign, in the month of Rabi-ul-awal, 1078 A.H., June 1667 A.D. The grant had been made originally by Allah Yar Khan and Hasan Kandahari Khan, Fauzadars of Gauhati; and the grantees were two Pujaris or priests of the Kamakhya temple, Sri-ballabh and Prananath. It was a grant in perpetuity in the system of tenure known as *Madammas* or *Brahmottar*. The land was exempted from the payment of the usual taxes, and the grantees from the customary personal service to the state. The grantor's name is not mentioned, but it must be Syed Firoz

Khan, who was the Fauzadar of Gauhati immediately before the reoccupation of Kamrup by the Ahoms in November 1667.

From a *sanad* issued by "Badshah Ghazi Aurangzeb Salar Khan", in the 9th year of his accession in the month of Safar, Aswin 1074 Bengali era, September 1667 A.D., it is learnt that two Pujaris of Umananda temple at Gauhati, Sudaman Brahman and his son Kamdeb, were granted two portions of land in Bangeswar, pergana Pandu, and Sarkar Dakhinkul.

The price of the land was rupees thirty. The two priests were also granted the sum of rupees twenty for the expenditure of the high and low lands. The sum was to be met from the collections of the abovementioned land. The Emperor laid down in the *sanad*: "It should be noted that the cash allotment is given on condition of their (Sudaman and Kamdeb) being alive, and holding both the portions separately in their possession, so that they may utilise it simply for what is necessary for their maintenance, and may engage themselves in prayer for the continuance of the kingdom, and on condition that they should not put any hindrance to the assessment of the surrounding lands and the crops of the Devaloi". Sekara and Itakhuli are mentioned as the mauzas where the lands were situated.

The secular section of the Assamese Muslims were mainly employed in the professions in which they possessed special skill, *e.g.*, embroidery, engraving, wood-carving, cannon-casting, sword-making and similar fine works. Muslim artisans and craftsmen were incorporated in the *Khanikar khel* or the guild of artisans, under a superintendent known as Khanikar Barua. Muslim ladies have still retained their skill in artistic weaving.

The greatest landmark in the age-long contact

between Assam and the Islàmic world is, however, the gorgeously illustrated Assamese manuscript *Hastividyarnava*, compiled by Sukumar Barkaith in 1734 A.D., under the orders of King Sivà Singha and his chief queen Maharani Ambika Debi. The book is a treatise on elephants; but in illustrating the different types of elephants, the author has mentioned their characteristics as far as their reactions or the fortunes of the monarch are concerned. For example, when the author inserts the picture of an elephant of the docile class which is a suitable animal for the king to ride upon, he àctually places King Siva Singha on the howdah of the elephant to illustrate his theme. Similarly, elephants which bring prosperity to the king are illustrated by a continuous stream of boxes of presents from foreign courts as they are being delivered to the monàrch. An obstinate and untameable elephant is depicted as being turned out of the royal presence.

Having thus prepared the canvas the author inserts in the book a large number of pictures depicting the king and the queen, their son Ugra Singha Tipam Raja, junior queens, maids and attendants of the palace, nobles, officers, subjugated chieftains, processions, Hindusthani musicians and dancing girls and wrestlers. He also inserts the portraits of eight kings who have heard the fame of King Siva Singha. Opposite every picture of the Ahom court there is a painted scene of the portals of à Mogul palace with the Nahbat-khana and other attendant details, inserted as a set-off to the Ahom counterpart. Mogul costumes were introduced into the Ahom court during the reign of Ṣiva Singha's father King Rudra Singha, 1696—1714, and the Ahom king and his nobles are shown in the pictures of *Hastividyarnava* as wearing the Mogul head-dress. Occasionally a fully blossomed rose is inserted in the hand of the monarch in the fashion of Mogul portraits. The drawings are the handiwork of two painters Dilbar, a Muslim, and Doshai, a Hindu; and their own portraits are inserted to illustrate the occasion of Sukumar Barkaith's delivery of the manuscript to the two artists for illustrating the book. Dilbar was obviously employed to furnish the Mogul setting. Similar paintings in the manuscripts of the period of Siva Singha's reign, like the *Dharmaparan* manuscript in the British Museum, bear indelible marks of the influence of the Mogul school of painting.[40]

The wars with the Moguls focussed the attention of the Assamese on the affairs of the capitals Delhi and Agra, on the personages who were making and unmaking history in Northern India, on 'the cloud-capped towers and gorgeous palaces' under whose roofs the Mogul Badshahs held their courts near the sprouting fountains of jasmine and of rose; on the Rajas, Mansabdars and Nawabs to whom only the waving of the imperial finger was necessary to march their redoubtable legionaries of Jat and Sawar cavalry against a frontier chieftain who had not yet sought the protection of the Chaghatai arms. Nor could they forget the rose-perfumed Begums in whose enviable companionship their own princesses were listening to the unpremeditated harmony of the bulbul which had been presented to some fortunate denizen of the imperial harem by the Sultan of Samarkand or Bokhara, in the neighbourhood of vine-groves which had been reared on soil transported in boatloads from Kashmir and Kabul.

Whether through the tales of Assamese sojourners at Delhi, or through the visitors to Assam from Northern India, the Assamese were introduced to a world of splendour hitherto unknown, and the historical instinct which had distinguished them from other races of India led them to record their impressions and knowledge for the enlightenment of those who had not the opportunity of seeing first-hand the magnificent towers and mausoleums of Delhi and Agra. The spirit of enquiry, thus kindled, moved apace, and we have in the picturesque words of our chroniclers the history of the rise and progress of Muhammadan power in India. Besides, as the Moguls were a constant menace to the solidarity and independence of Assam, an intimate knowledge of the history, customs and war-methods of the enemy was essential for success in military operations.

We have accounts of the activities of Muslim commanders and Mogul generals as far as they have any bearing on the history of Assam; there are interspersed in Assamese chronicles dealing with the events of the Ahom period. We will cite a few examples of this source of information:—

(a) This is how the story of the renegade and iconoclast Kalapahar, who is known in Assamese Buranjis as Pora-Sultan, Pora-Kuthar, Kala-Sultan and Kala-Jaban, is recorded in an Assamese chronicle,—

" A Brahman of pure descent living at Benares had a son born to him. The astrologers calculated his stars and made the following prediction,—' This boy will in future be fallen from his caste and religion by carrying on liason with a Jabani or Muhammadan woman, but he will be wealthy, virtuous and learned. The boy after attaining maturity, and being fully cognisant of the ordinance of his stars, visited several places of pilgrimage, and made offerings to the gods and did acts of piety to propitiate his stars. Ultimately he came to Gaur, where, as pre-destined he saw the daughter of Hussain Shah Padshah of Gaur, and became mad for her love. He forgot the prophecy, and became fallen by secretly gratifying his sexual instincts with the princess. The Begum reported the matter to her lord the Sultan, Hussain Shah, who was pleased to learn that the offender was a Brahman of pure blood and summoned him to his presence and said,—" Why did you commit this act?"

The Brahman,—" Thus it has been enscrolled in my Book of Fate: this has been caused by my predestination."

Hussain Shah,—" Would you agree if I offer my daughter to you in marriage?"

The Brahman,—" Yes, I am willing."

" The marriage took place accordingly, whereupon the Sultan conferred on the Brahman a mansab of 10,000. After sometime the Brahman became disgusted with himself and thought,—" I have not been able to avert the decree of my fate. So one's destiny always reigns supreme. All our attempts to undo it are in vain." Thus saying he descended into the Ganges and solemnly discarded his penance, prayers, incantations, the Gayatri and his sacred thread.

" After this he proceeded to destroy Hindu temples and domes; some were demolished and others were burnt. He also destroyed the temple of Kamakhya. He climbed to the summit of the Garurachal Hill, [the Poa-Macca Hill at Hazo], and surveyed therefrom his own land of Gaur, and he also saw Letai Dhubuni washing her clothes. Fearing that the enemies of Gaur might reconnoitre the land from that hill-top with hostile intentions, he kicked the earth thrice with his feet and depressed it by three fathoms. He died there and was buried according to Muhammadan rites. Shah Shuja, son of Emperor Shah Jahan, while at Rajmahal, made endowment of paiks and lands for the maintenance of worship at his tomb, which is still continuing. This renegade iconoclast is known as Pora-Sultan in view of his desecration and burning of Hindu temples and shrines."[41]

(b) Mir Jumla, during his march to Bengal in pursuit of Prince Shuja had not received any official order to invade Assam, which was an after-thought caused by the Ahom king's aggressive raids in Mogul territories. The terms of the treaty between Allah Yar Khan and Momai-tamuli Barbarua were violated by the Ahoms, and Kamrup was wrested back by Jayadhwaja Singha, who according to Charles Stewart, " sent an army down the Brahmaputra which had plundered and laid waste the country as far as Dacca." Mir Jumla wrote to the Emperor from Dacca,—" Assam has occupied Kamrup, and is contemplating to invade us. My scheme of subduing the country of the Maghs cannot be completed within a short time. So in the meantime I propose to invade Cooch Behar and Assam. I am awaiting the orders of the Emperor." Aurangzeb replied as follows,— " I want you to invade Cooch Behar and Assam and to consolidate our supremacy there." This is supported by the *Riyaz-us-Salatin*.[42]

(c) In 1663 two Assamese envoys, Chandrakandali and Sanatan, were despatched to Delhi at the head of an embassy to represent to Emperor Aurangzeb the violation of the treaty terms fixed as Ghilajharighat on the termination of the invasion of Mir Jumla. The Mogul Dewan arranged for their residence on the bank of the Jumna where they were supplied with regular food provisions from the Mogul durbar. They were taken to the court after eight days, and what they witnessed there is graphically recorded in an old Assamese chronicle: "The Padshah was sitting on the throne. Below the imperial dais at a descent of three steps there stood Jafar Khan Dewan on the right with a golden staff, and the Uzir on the left.

After them were the Rajput Rajas on the left headed by Jasomanta Singha, as well as other Ranas and Haros of the rank of twelve thousand and seven thousand. The Chai-hazaris came next, followed by the commanders of five, four, three, two and one thousand in due order of precedence. There was also a vast concourse of ministers, elephants, horses, sepoys, musketeers, shieldsmen, archers, equipped with the five weapons, presenting a gala and picturesque appearance. The fort, the lanes, and the platforms were all made of red and orange-coloured stones of numerous varieties including marble and translucent stones, and men were busy in their work sitting under roofs with golden streamers fluttering above".[43]

(d) During the campaigns of Ram Singha in Assam, there was a hitch between Nawab Rashid Khan and the Rajput general. The Nawab was a commander of 5,000, and though officially subordinate to Ram Singha as far as that campaign was concerned, he refused to regard the Raja as his superior, at least in matters of precedence and formality. This is how the incident is recorded,—"Ram Singha blew his *Nahbat* five times a day. The same was done by Rashid Khan. Then Ram Singha said,—"Rashid Khan's *Nahbat* should not be beaten in the same manner as mine. If I blow it twice, he will blow it only once." Rashid Khan replied,—"I have been deputed by the Emperor as well as Ram Singha. Why should I not blow my Nahbat?" This is one cause of their misunderstanding." This incident is interesting as indicative of one of the reasons which led to the disastrous defeat of Ram Singha's forces in Assam.[44]

(e) A very interesting document is the letter written by Sultan Azamtara's Assamese consort Rahmat Banu Begum to her maternal uncle Laluk Barphukan, the Ahom viceroy of Gauhàti, who had planned to become king of Assam through the instrumentality and assistance of the Padshahzada. The letter is preserved in several Buranjis in both Assamese and Persian versions, the Persian original being written in Assamese script. Rahmat Banu, known in Assam as Ramani Gabharu and Nangchen Gabharu, was the only daughter of the Ahom king Jayadhwaj Singha who made her over to Nawab Mir Jumla in fulfilment of the terms of the treaty of 1663. She was married to Azamtara in May 1668 when her name was changed to Rahmat Banu. No one in Assam had ever made any enquiries about her well-being and health till 1677 when her uncle Laluk Barphukan sent epistles and presents to her, with a request for her mediation in obtaining the assistance of Azamtara, then governor of Bengal. Her reply runs as follows:

"May God in His mercy raise the height of the shadow of your glory and fame, and may you, under the protection of that shadow, rest on the bed of peace and happiness till the hairs of your head become all white. You are well aware how I, a child of yours, have been living in a distant land. I am always longing for countless blessings from you; this is my prayer, and it is mingled with my salutation.

"My second message conveys the news that we are all well here in this place. I pray day and night for your physical welfare and the accompanying increase of your glory and fame.

"This is what I have felt,—I was sent away from home at the age of six as a present to the Moguls. Now I am nineteen years old; and you have not made any enquiry about my miserable self on any day, on any occasion, and in any month.

"You know well what friends and relatives I have in Hindusthan. Some six years ago Moina brought some news from my poor uncle through Adam, and it was during our stay in Hindusthan. Since our arrival in Bengal from Hindusthan, through the will of Khoda, I have not been favoured with any message or present from you.

"The envoys mentioned in your letter arrived at the Saheb's court with your messages of friendship and good-will. The articles you sent to me as presents together with the news of your well-being were received here in a favourable moment and in the presence of the courtiers and nobles. This fact has given pleasure to the hearts of the men of Hindusthan.

"One year has now elapsed since we arrived in Bengal from Khisarabad [Khizirabad]. The four elephants with their trappings and caparisons, which you had sent to me and the Begum, have been duly received. Through your blessings I am not short of any article. Still then, on account of the presents sent by you, your name and fame, as well as our praise, are shining forth in all quarters. I am surprised to learn that the presents I sent to you through Madhabcharan and the other envoys did not reach your hands; these articles were in addition to those mentioned in the list.

"And so I implore you to take Moina from here by some means or other if you cherish any affection for me. He will be able to tell you all about me and about this place. The Padshahzada in a fit of vexation had confined the envoys sent by you. It was this very Moina who came to the inner apartments and disclosed the news to me. I interceded with the Padshahzada and procured the release of your messengers. I also arranged the allotment of two thanas to the envoys by making a similar request to the Padshahzada.

"You should send your daughter's son to this place. You should postpone definite action till Moina arrives at your place. You should commence action only when you receive full particulars from the lips of Moina.

"The rest of the message will be communicated to you by Madhab Brahman who has seen and heard everything here.

"You should so arrange that I remain in constant receipt of news about your welfare and health. What more could I write? 1599".[45]

B.—ASSAMESE HISTORICAL LITERATURE

While many other races of India are groping in darkness for materials to construct the history of their past ages, the Assamese have ready-made chronicles compiled by contemporary eye-witnesses and historians. These chronicles are known as *Buranjis*, a word of Ahom or Shan origin, literally meaning a store of useful knowledge. The chronicles dealing with the events of the Ahom rule, 1228 to 1826 A.D., are systematic and complete, but we have also chronicles of the Hindu or pre-Ahom period, though of a fragmentary and desultory character. Assam came in contact with Kashmir the only Hindu kingdom which can boast of any historical production, through Meghavahana, Lalitaditya and Jaypira who came to Assam on friendly as well as belligerent missions. The Shans are noted for their historical instinct which manifested itself in the Burmese *Azawins* and the Siamese *P'ongsawadans*. It has not yet been decided whether Assamese historiography owes its origin to these Kashmirian visitors or to the Shan conquerors and settlers.

The Assamese regarded historical knowledge as an indispensable accomplishment of a gentleman, and this was necessary in a country which had no written constitution, where the government with its numerous branches had to be conducted on precedents gleaned from history or tradition. The supreme importance which history played in Assam attributed to it the sanctity of scriptures, and in certain quarters it was looked upon with esoteric veneration. Oaths were taken by touching handwritten chronicles, and occasionally, the recital of a few pages from history was an inseparable function in an Ahom royal marriage. We may quote here the testimony of Sir George Grierson,—

"The Assamese are justly proud of their national literature. In no department have they been more successful than in a branch of study in which India as a rule, is curiously deficient. The historical works, or *Buranjis*, as they are styled by the Assamese, are numerous and voluminous. According to the custom of the country, a knowledge of the Buranjis was an indispensable qualification to an Assamese gentleman."[46]

Existing chronicles.—The number of existing chronicles which I have myself seen and of which I have heard or read comes up to nearly one hundred and fifty. To this number should be added those, which are lying untraced in family archives. During the reign of the Ahom king, Rajeswar Singha, 1751—1769, his chief executive officer Kirtichandra Barbarua destroyed a large number of chronicles which were suspected as having references to his ignominous descent. The depredations of the Moamarias, of the Bengal burkenduzes and of the Burmese which preceded the British occupation of Assam in 1824, had led to the disruption and depopulation of the country, which were responsible for the loss of many chronicles and other valuable manuscripts and treasures.

The existing chronicles may be roughly divided into the following classes:—

(1) *Chronicles dealing with the events of the Ahom period*, or extending up to several decades of British occupation. They are written in Assamese prose, or in the now obsolete Ahom language—the language of the Shan conquerors of the province. Some of them were also written in verse. We have here side-lights on the activities of Mogul generals and Emperors as far as they have some bearing on Assamese history.

(2) *Chronicles narrating the history of other countries besides Assam.* We had chronicles of Burdwan and Kashmir, of whose existence we have the testimony of reliable men, but they have not been recovered as yet.[47] We have chronicles dealing entirely with the affairs of Muhammadan India. As far as we know all of them are in Assamese prose. The object of the chroniclers was the enlightenment of their countrymen about neighbouring and remote territories. A chronicle of Tripura, written in 1724, has been published by the Assam Government from a manuscript deposited at the British Museum, London.[48]

(3) *Fragmentary chronicles.*—Dealing with particular episodes, events, tribes, something like what we mean at present by monographs, for example, the desultory history of ancient Kamarupa; of the Kacharis, Chutias, and Jayantias; and the metrical history of the Rajas of Darrang. We have also a manuscript containing an account of the tribute paid to Mir Jumla.[49] These manuscripts are in Assamese, and are generally tagged on to chronicles of the first two classes.

(4) *Kataki Buranjis*, or chronicles of diplomatic embassies, dealing with the foreign relations of Assam. They contain, besides other facts, accounts of recep-

tions accorded to the ambassadors of Assam and of foreign courts in their places of deputation. They contain copies of diplomatic epistles, though these letters are also occasionally inserted in other Buranjis to illustrate the context.

(5) *Vangsavalis or family chronicles.*—Most of these families were of considerable influence and importance, and their family history throws ample light on the general political history of Assam. The Vangsavali of the Baniya-Kakati family contains several references to the activities of Raja Ram Singha in Assam.

(6) *Satria Buranjis*, or chronicles of the various religious monasteries, or histories of their founders and prominent pontiffs. They are highly interesting as their relationship with the kings, under whose patronage they were usually established and maintained, have a significant bearing on the political history of Assam.

Compilation of Buranjis in Assam.—The Buranjis were compiled primarily under official supervision with the help of court-minutes and despatches of local governors, and of commanders engaged in military operations. Families of distinction managed to take copies of the above, and supplemented and brought them up to date with the help of materials at their own disposal. Self-importance, family animosity or tribal jealousy were occasionally responsible for undue emphasis, elaboration, or omission. So the bare nucleus of information obtainable in the various chronicles is generally the same, and their multiplication can be justified only by the fact that some contain more details on particular subjects, while others dismiss the same in a line or two. One Buranji, for example, devotes only ten lines to Mir Jumla's invasion of Assam, while another elaborates the theme in ten folios. The undue brevity in the former might be due to the family's having other chronicles in its possession which did full justice to the Assam campaign of the great Mogul general. We scarcely come across two palpably contradictory statements regarding the same event, leaving aside scribal mistakes which can be easily detected. Dates are recorded at frequent intervals to their day, hour and *danda*. The accuracy of Assamese *Buranjis* has been a matter for wonder and amazement. Their correspondence to each other, and to other independent accounts left by foreign visitors only points to the fact that historiography in Assam was really a branch of the sacred scriptures, where wilful misrepresentation was not only a crime but a sin. Their value as great monuments of a racy Assamese prose-style,[50] belonging to an age when no prose work could be found in Bengal, and their conservation of the customs, manners, ideals, feelings and aspirations of the people place them in the highest category of representative national literature.[51]

C.—PADSHAH-BURANJI MANUSCRIPTS

The Assamese chronicles which are primarily devoted to the history of the Badshahate of Delhi are known as *Padshah-Buranjis*, or chronicles of the Padshahs. They abound in episodes and accounts which are not found in other histories of the Muhammadans in India. They no doubt indulge in gossip and gasconades, but their value as exhibiting the inner life of Delhi and Agra, left out by the average historian, is supreme and unquestionable, while their general tone and spirit are in agreement with those of the contemporary Persian narratives. The facts recorded in the Padshah-Buranjis are materially corroborated by other accounts.

Of the *Padshah-Buranjis* preserved by the Assamese I have had access to four, while I have positive knowledge of the existence of two others. The four manuscripts which I have personally examined and used for the purpose of the present translation are:

Manuscript A.—This manuscript was recovered several years ago by Sir James Buckingham, sometime Superintendent of the Amguri Tea Estates Limited in Upper Assam, from an Assamese villager. After the death of Sir James, this manuscript along with others collected by that enterprising tea-planter was despatched to England for being preserved in the family library. Colonel C. Simkins, a successor of Sir James in the Superintendenship of the Amguri Tea Estätes, arranged a loan of the manuscript in 1923 for Srijut Benudhar Sharma who prepared a copy for the Kamarupa Anusandhan Samiti or the Assam Research Society at Gauhati. The original manuscript was afterwards returned to Lady Buckingham. Unfortunately, Mr. Sharma did not note down the number of the folios and other necessary particulars. The manuscript, as I learn from the transcribed copy in possession of the Assam Research Society, is incomplete. The last page ends abruptly in the middle of the letter addressed by the Adil Shahi Sultan to Emperor Shah Jahān. There is also a page missing between the two divisions of the chapter devoted to the enumeration of the allies of Sawai Jai Singha of Amber. The chapters are not numbered or named, but we have the usual marks adopted by all Assamese writers and copyists to indicate the termination of one chapter and the commencement of another. The book has thus seventeen distinct divisions, each dealing with a separate theme, and we have called them Chapters.

This chronicle constitutes the main bulk of the text from which the present translation has been compiled. Out of the nineteen chapters of the *Annals of the Delhi Badshahate*, only the two chapters, II and V, relating to the rise of Timurlane and Jahangir's conquest of Secunderabad, are not to be found in this manuscript.

Manuscript B.—This manuscript was discovered by me in May 1925 in the godown of the American Baptist Mission at Gauhati along with several others, some of which are general chronicles of Assam. The *Padshah-Buranji* forms the third part of the manuscript which is written on *sanchi* bark with the usual fast-coloured Assamese ink.

The *first* part of this manuscript, Folios 1 to 56, deals with the history of Assam, with special reference to its conflicts with the Muhammadâns. It ends with the defeat of Mansur Khan in 1682, during the reign of the Ahom monarch Gadadhar Singha. A portion of this chronicle was published in 1853 in the first Assamese magazine, *Arunodai*, which served as the organ of the American Baptist Mission of Assam. On Folio 55-a, we have the copy of a letter written by Prince Azam to Laluk Sola Barphukân, appointing the latter Raja of Assam in return for his surrender of Gauhati. The page is illuminated with gorgeous borders, with reproduction of the seal and *panja* or hand-impression of the Emperor's son. The Assamese chronicler or scribe, not being able to read, or thinking it unnecessary to reproduce the original benedictory verses in Arabic, points out the places where they occurred in the epistle with this note in Assamese, "Here was Arbi," and "Here also Arbi was written."

The *second* part, from Folios 57 to 68, contains eighteen letters that passed between Ahom monarchs, generals and plenipotentiaries and Mogul representatives. The letter-writers and addressees include among others Allah Yar Khan, Momaitamuli Barbarua, Jayadhwaj Singha, Emperor Aurangzeb, Mir Jumla, Ram Singha, Lachit Barphukan, and Nawab Dilir Khan. The language of these diplomatic epistles is curiously cosmopolitan. We have the usual strings of Sanskrit epithets, even in letters addressed by and to Mogul generals. The main text of the letters is written in a mixture of Hindi, Persian and Assamese and the uninitiated copyist has played havoc with the vocabulary. Letter No. 18 purports to explain several Persian words, *e.g.*, rif'atbuland, hawali, manjil, ezhar, etc. This letter is reported to have been brought by one "Captain Fing," evidently a Firinghee captain, in Saka 1715, or 1793 A.D., who was possibly one of the lieutenants of Captain Welsh, the head of the British contingent deputed to Assam in the previous year.

The *third* part of this manuscript, from Folios 69 to 78, contains a *Padshah-Buranji* in four chapters, Nos. II, V, VII and VIII, dealing respectively with Timurlane, Jahangir's conquest of Secunderabad, Jai Singha's subjugation of Eastern India and Shah Jahan's interview with Prithivi Shah of Kandor. Of them, Chapters VII and VIII are also to be found in Manuscript A; while Chapters II and V are found *only* in Manuscript B. The common portions seem to be reproductions of the same original; there are textual variations here and there which may be due to scribal idiosyncrasy.

The first part of this manuscript has been published by the Department of Historical and Antiquarian Studies in Assam with the title *Kamrupar Buranji*, under the editorship of the present writer. The letters mentioned in the second part are incorporated in the text in their appropriate places.

Manuscript C.—It was obtained in 1931 by the Department of Historical and Antiquarian Studies from the Ahom Juvak Sanmilan through the late Srijut Anandiram Gohain who was an enthusiastic worker in the field of Assamese historical research. The manuscript has 61 folios, each having two pages. It contains a number of short chronicles some of which are independent and complete even though the narratives concerned are of an episodical character; and the rest are fragments of larger chronicles.

The subjects dealt with are: The origin of the Nara, Mantara, Ahom, Jayantia, Cachar or Heramba kings, mostly of the legendary period; the rulers of Cooch Behar, Biswa Singha, Naranarayan, Chilarai, Raghudeb, Lakshminarayan and Parikshit; brief sketches of the reigns of the Ahom kings from Sutupha to Suhumpha Dihingia Raja; Princess Garama, daughter of the Padshah of Gaur, and consort of Kamateswar, Herambeswar and Dihingia Raja; invasion of Cachar and Assam by the Gaura commander Turbak; diplomatic correspondence between Swargadeo Jayadhwaj Singha and Raja Prana Narayan of Cooch Behar; Swargadeo Ramadhwaj Singha and Debera; the amours of Ramadhwaj Singha's daughter; some events of Gadadhâr Singha's reign, Miri rebellion, troubles on the Assam-Bengal frontier, repairs of the fortifications of Gauhati; Rudra Singha's relations with Raja Rup Narayan of Cooch Behâr; and a list of Ahom kings with dates from Sukapha to Purandar Singha. Some of these narratives have been laid under contribution in collating the text of 45 paragraphs of *Deodhai Asam Buranji*, published by the D.H.A.S. in 1932.

Folios 2 to 5 of this manuscript contain a list of the kings of Delhi from the accession of Chitrasen Raja on the 21st January 475 to the 18th January 1662. The latter date is described as marking the termination of thirteen months' reign of Emperor Aurangzeb. The Rajas prior to Chitrasen were obviously inserted on Folio 1 which is unfortunately missing.

The list of Delhi kings is followed by the account of the conquest of Delhi by Rukundin Padshah of Nako, which constitutes the first chapter of the present book *Annals of the Delhi Badshahate*. The episode ends on the second page of Folio 10, after which commences an account of the legendary rulers of Jayantia.

Besides the above, there are two significant features in this manuscript. On the first page of Folio 48, which is virtually blank, we have three lines in Arabic script, with the words *Raja-katha* and *Harisaranam* in Assamese characters noted on the margin, perhaps to indicate that the scribe was a Persian-knowing Hindu. The two words mean respectively, annals of kings, and one whose shelter is Hari or God. The Persian passage is supposed to be written in *Nastaliq* and *Sikast* characters of a cryptic nature; and its decipherment and interpretation have presented considerable difficulty. It is curious how this Persian passage intermixed with Urdu, could find its way into an Assamese manuscript. It undoubtedly proves that knowledge of Persian formed an essential part of Assamese scholarship in those days.

The account of the ancestors of the Ahom kings, on the second page of Folio 48, is preceded by an invocatory preamble in five lines of Sanskrit verse, which give vent to a historian's consciousness of his limitations and difficulties when he has to draw his materials from scattered sources. The passage when translated stands as follows: "After due salutation at the lotus-feet of Srikrishna, which are drunk by the righteous like so many honey-sucking bees, the origin and deeds of the kings sprung from the line of Indra are here described. Oh, learned ones! In the recital of the history of these kings who are credited with varied and brilliant achievements one is not to be an object of laughter [if mistakes and discrepancies creep in] as the accounts exist in diverse places, and in their unification whose powers are not strained?"

Manuscript D.—It is in the form of a transcript obtained by the Department of Historical and Antiquarian Studies in 1929 from Srijut Krishnanath Barua, then a student of the Cotton College, Gauhati. It contains a miscellaneous account of Kamarupa dealing with its history and topography. This portion has been inserted as an appendix to *Kamrupar Buranji*, published by the D.H.A.S. in 7930.

Another portion of the book contains a list of the kings of Delhi from Judhisthira to Aurangzeb, followed by an account of the establishment of Muhammadan supremacy in Delhi by Rukundin Padshah after the defeat of Pithor Raja. In the list, however, Raja Udayamalla takes the place of Pithor Raja as the last Hindu king of Delhi. The narrative of Rukundin's conquest of Delhi is thus found in Manuscripts A, C, and D, with slight textual variations here and there. Srijut Krishnanath Barua claims this book to be the work of his father Srijut Sarunath Barua of Chamata, who was reputed for his interest and enthusiasm in historical pursuits. A claim to the authorship of the book was made subsequently on behalf of the late Srijut Devicharan Chaudhury of Bàihata in Kamrup District.

In the interlude between the list of the Delhi kings and Rukundin's conquest it is stated that the Ahom viceroy of Gauhati Gargayan Sandikoi Phukan, appointed scholars to compile the list and the episode from the materials in possession of Muhammad Ali who was reputed for his learning and who had been the tutor of the sons of Nawab Mansur Khan, the Mogul Fauzadar of Gauhati from 1679 to 1682.

Of the manuscripts about which I have heard and read, the first one was in possession of the famous Bakhar Bara family of Sutargaon in Nowgong District. The late Srijut Kashinath Barua a direct descendant of Bakhar Bara, a distinguished officer of the reigns of Swargadeos Lakshmi Singha and Gaurinath Singha, 1769-1795, used to recite to me several stories which he had read in the manuscript when it was in possession of his family. They bear a striking similarity to the episodes recorded in the four *Padshah-Buranji* manuscripts. A certain gentleman of Upper Assam borrowed the manuscript from the Bakhar Bara family some thirty years ago, but he failed to return it to the original owners.

The second manuscript was discovered by Pandit Srijut Pratap Chandra Goswami in the Rangpur District in Bengal during the course of a search for Assamese manuscripts undertaken at the instance of the Assam Sahitya-Sabha. The Padshah-Buranji found by Mr. Goswami contained about a hundred folios, each measuring 12″ by 5″. The manuscript is in an extremely dilapidated condition, and the folios crumble to pieces when some one attempts to detach a piece from the bundle.

Mr. Goswami however succeeded in rescuing the text of a portion though with a considerable number of lacunas; and he published the same in the Assamese magazine *Avahan*, Volume IV. The extract deals with the murder of Sobha Singh Raja by his own consort who happened to be the daughter of one Jagat Rai. After committing the murder the Rani stabbed herself to death, and her lifeless body lay by the side of her husband's corpse. Modan Sing Dewan gave out that the Rani had died as a result of snake-bite, and her body was accordingly thrown into the Gàjrai river. The Raja's body had meanwhile been cremated during the dark hours of the night. The conspiracy appears to have been engineered by Modan Sing Dewan, apparently with the assistance of Jagat Rai, for the benefit of Sobha Sing's brother Himat Sing, who now occupied the vacant *guddie*. The miscreants took advantage of the absence of Maha Sing who was then at Baddhiman together with his force. Mention is also made of Barada as the capital of Sobha Sing's territory. It is not difficult to identify the persons and places mentioned in the extract as fuller details are available in other sources.

The above events refer to the rebellion of Sobha Sing Raja, zemindar of Chetwàh and Bardah in Burdwan district, when Nawab Ibrahim Khan was the Mogul viceroy of Bengal. Sobha Sing killed Raja Krishna Ram of Burdwan, and with the exception of his son Jagat Rai, seized his fàmily and all his property. With the help of Sobha Sing's Pathan allies under Rahim Khàn, the rebels plundered the villages and occupied Hugli. Among the captives taken in Burdwan, writes Charles Stewart, "was à beautiful virgin, a daughter of the Raja whom the zemindar (Sobha Sing) kept in confinement until an opportunity should offer of sacrificing her to his lust. The time was now ārrived, when he thought he might gratify his vile passion with impunity; he secretly entered her apartment, and endeavoured to obtain by force what he could not obtain by flattery and entreaty; but when he folded her in his arms, the girl drew from her clothes a sharp knife, which she had concealed for the purpose, and stabbed him in the belly; she then turned the weapon against herself, and, with mistaken heroism, but high sense of honour, pierced her own heart. The wretch lived but a few hours; and was succeeded by his brother Himmut Sing, who exerted himself to the utmost in ravaging and plundering all those persons of opulence who would not join in the rebellion". After the death of Sobha Sing, the Pathan leader Rahim Khan, now known as Rahim Shah, continued the depredations, and occupied the whole country from Rajmahal to Midnapore, yielding a revenue of sixty lakhs of rupees. Aurangzeb replaced Ibrahim Khan by his own grandson Sultan Azim-ush-shan in the governorship of Bengal. Rahim Shah was first defeated in 1697 by Zàbardast Khan, son of Ibrahim Khan; but he again raised his head, and he was finally defeated and slain in 1698 in a pitched battle led by Azim-ush-shan in person. It was during these disturbances that the Europeans, with the permission of the Mogul rulers, fortified their factories at Chinsurah, Chandernagore and Chuttanati (Calcutta), and the English obtained further concessions in their trading activities. It was also during this period that the foundation of Calcutta was laid, first under Job Charnock who died in 1692, and then under his successor Mr. Ellis.—*Vide* Stewart's *History of Bengal*, Calcutta 1910, pp. 359—375; *Riyaz-us-Salatin;* and Manucci's *Storia do Mogor*, tr. Irvine, II, pp. 318 and 323.

D.—A BIRD'S-EYE VIEW OF THE CONTENTS

The main bulk of the present text has thus been obtained from Manuscript A, to which we have added Chapters II and V from Manuscript B. Chapters VII and VIII are found in both Manuscripts A and B; while Chapter I is found in the three Manuscripts A, C, and D. The chapters have been arranged by us in chronological order. A bird's-eye view of the information derived from the *Padshah-Buranji* can be presented as follows:

An ambitious Muhammadan sovereign, the inheritor of fabulous wealth and resources, marches with his hordes towards India, and defeats the Rajput Prince Pithor Raja. The victorious adventurer occupies the throne of Delhi which was in the hands of Hindu sovereigns from time immemorial, and thus inaugurates Muhammadan supremacy in India. Though unwilling to introduce any radical change in the social and religious customs of the conquered people, the new Padshah of Delhi organises his army on the *mansabdari* system, fixes the divisions of his palace, and allots different functions for the different days of the week. During the reign of his successors Timur marches from Central Asia and conquers Delhi. His descendants, Babar, Humayun, Akbar, Jahangir, Shah Jahan and Aurangzeb consolidated their powers by friendship with Hindu chiefs. Refractory rulers were subdued and fresh additions were made to the Mogul Empire from time to time. The Hindu adherents of the Mogul Emperors were pitted against disloyal Hindu rulers, and Man Singha whose valour resounded from one end of India to the other grumbled because the Emperor did not give him any respite from war, thinking that being disengaged from war abroad he might organise a Rajput clique against the sovereignty of the Moguls.

Strategy was not an uncommon feature of the military operations of those days, and it was resorted to whenever direct warfare held no prospect of success. The ultimatums issued to hostile rulers were written on the supposition that enemies might one day become friends, and friends might one day become enemies. Victors in war were honoured with rich presents and titles. The age of chivalry had not entirely gone: two

Rajput warriors rush to a mortal combat in the presence of two eminent sovereigns.

The Begums of the period display their wares, personal splendour and precious gems to the only and the greatest customer of the age—the Emperor of Delhi. Fatima Begum, the irresistible daughter of Sultan Shuja, spreads her bewitching charms over the gallant heart of her father's enemy and nephew Prince Muazzam. Gulmukhmal enters into the seraglio of the diplomatic Siliman Padshah of Farrang who deputes to Secundrabad warlike spies and soldiers in the guise of peaceful merchants and citizens. Military conquests dog the steps of commerce, and Secunderabad finds itself under the vassalage of Farrang. The motherly heart of the world-famed queen, Arzumand Bano Begum Mumtaz Màhal, pines at the thought of the inevitable fratricidal conflict of her spirited sons, and puts an end to her life.

Aurangzeb after sitting on the throne of his ancestors prepares a list of the rulers who had not yet offered their submission to the authority of which he was now the accredited symbol. Sewa-raja's reply to the Emperor's threats would have cost him his life but for the intercession of Ram Singha, the son of Mirza Raja Jai Singha Kuchchwa of Amber. Sewa-raja escapes from captivity, and his custodian Ram Singha naturally incurs the wrath of the Emperor. The Rajput prince makes himself unworthy of any further imperial confidence by loosening the bonds of the imprisoned Sikh Guru. So off to Assam, ànd the novious airs and waters of the witchcraft-laden land of Kamrup! Shaista Khan offers the Raja of Amber a reception which is an object-lesson pointing to the possibility of Hindu-Muslim friendship in the past, in the present and the future.

The young 'barbarian', Prince Azam, the unworthy son of a puritanical father misuses his powers in Bengal, and the Nestorlike Shaista Khan is dragged from his patriarchal repose to guide the destinies of that most troublesome territory on the Lower Ganges. The forces of disruption begin to work as soon as the strong hand of the Great Mogul is withdrawn from the scene. Sawai Jai Singha, the Raja of Amber, creates a colossal confederacy with his Hindu allies, including Mulahar Rao, and strikes at the very root of Muhammadan supremacy in India.

The book is of interest to all students of Mogul history; but its primary importance to Assam can never be questioned. Assam, in those critical days of war and foreign invasion, wanted to know the forebears of Mir Jumla, Ram Singha and Aurangzeb who were so vitally connected with her own destiny. Assam demanded knowledge of Mogul strategy and warfare the efficient counteracting of which alone could safeguard her well-being and independence. Assam wanted to know the rules of courtesy and docorum then adopted by the Moguls, which was necessary for her success in diplomatic missions. Assam wanted to know the position of the important centres of activity in Mogul India, so that her ambassadors and agents might travel from place to place to trace the movements of generals and commanders who were to be sent against her.

E.—THE AUTHOR

Anonymity is the rule of Assamese Buranjis. That was an age when chronicles served the same purpose as newspapers and journals do at the present, *viz.*, the recording and communication of current events, with retrospective surveys of past affairs for those to whom they were necessary. Faithful narration of facts was always accompanied by the risk of provoking the animosity of men who thought their prestige, personal or ancestral, was jeopardised thereby; chronicles had to deal with good deeds as well as bad, and the position of the contemporary historian was always an unenviable one, specially in view of the absence of any protective legislation safeguarding bonafide narration and fair criticism of facts. So the chronicler was driven to anonymity, except when chronicles were compiled under royal commission in which case all responsibility was transferred from the individual writer to the state. In the preamble to an Assamese Buranji dealing with the history of the Tungkhangiya Dynasty, 1681—1806, the writer solemnly prohibits the disclosure of the facts stated therein to any one but to a trusted friend, not even to one's son if he was of an unreliable character, adding that betrayal of trust amounts to an indecent gesture shown to one's mother.[52] When we remember that even in English journalism, anonymity was generally superseded by the system of signed articles only in the latter half of the nineteenth century, we are not surprised at the almost universal absence of the chroniclers' names in the precious Buranjis they have left to posterity. No chronicler ever dared to touch even the fringe of publication in view of the spirit of uncritical retribution which was to be seen everywhere in old Assam. All this led to the multiplication of Assamese Khafi-Khans.

Though the author of the *Padshah-Buranji* was free from even the remote possibility of any individual retribution, as his theme concerned personalities who could never know what he had written about them, yet he could not extricate himself from the influence of the time-spirit. Any proof of his historical proclivities would have landed him in trouble even though he was personally innocent. It would have been certainly interesting to know who this man was who unfolded the romance of Delhi and Agra to his unsophisticated countrymen. But internal evidence helps us to form some idea of the abstract personality of the author, of his equipment and of his sources of information, which in the domain of historical scholarship is certainly superior to the cravings of idle curiosity.

F.—THE AUTHOR'S SOURCES OF INFORMATION

The materials at the disposal of the author were of two distinct classes, oral testimony, and written records.

(A) ORAL TESTIMONY

The author makes positive references to his sources of information when it was derived from the lips of persons whom he had met, as distinguished from information obtained from written records. By mentioning the names of his informants, he allows his readers to judge the value of the narratives, and he shrinks from any attempt to give the impress of authenticity to hearsay evidence.

(i) *Muhammad Ali of Secunderabad.*—Chapter VI dealing with the strategic conquest of Secunderabad by Siliman Padshah of Farrang ends with the following remark,—" From that time till now Secunderabad has continued to be the territory of Siliman Padshah. The son of Siliman Padshah was entrusted by his father with the government of Farrang. From this territory of Siliman Padshah, Delhi is situated at a distance of three months' journey. Muhammad Ali is a Mogul of that place. He is a very great scholar, and knows all the *logat*s or languages, Arabic and Persian. He taught the sons of Mansur Khan, and for this he received a remuneration of full rupees one hundred per month. The above narration is taken from his mouth."

Nawab Mansur Khan was deputed in 1679 by Prince Azam, then Governor of Bengal, to occupy Gauhati from Laluk Sola Barphukan, and remained in Assam as the Fauzadar of Gauhati for more than three years, till his forces were defeated by King Gadadhar Singha in 1682, after which Gauhati was reoccupied by the Ahoms. It was a custom with Mogul governors and generals to take learned men and *aulias* with them wherever they went, and Muhammad Ali stayed with the Nawab at Gauhati imparting education to his children. Our author might have come in contact with him during the course of some diplomatic mission to the Fauzadar's court, or even after the defeat of the Nawab's forces as post-war friendship between former belligerants is not of infrequent occurrence. As we have said, it is specifically stated in manuscript D that after the reoccupation of Gauhati by the Ahoms in 1682, the viceroy Gargayan Sandikoi Barphukan appointed scholars to take down from Muhammad Ali facts about Mogul India.

About Mansur Khan's stay in Assam, our own Buranjis supply the most authentic information. Laluk Barphukan, brother of Ram Singha's redoubtable antagonist Lachit Barphukan, handed over Gauhati to Mansur Khan, who had been deputed to take delivery of the same by Prince Azam. The only condition imposed by Laluk for this bloodless surrender of his charge was the prince's promise to place him on the throne of Assam. A chronicle contains the following statement,—"On Wednesday, the 14th of Phalgoon, 1600 *saka*, Nawab Mansur Khan came with his forces and occupied the fort of Gauhati; and he remained in possession of that place for three years and five months. The Ahom king and his nobles, after mature deliberation, despatched an army to reoccupy the fort of Gàuhati in the month of Ashar, 1604 *saka*.'' We have a feeling that Muhammad Ali, the declared narrator of the story of the conquest of Secunderabad by Siliman Padshah, was also associated with the Assamese versions of some other stories as well, for example, the stories of Rukundin's conquest of Delhi and Jahangir's conquest of Secunderabad.

(ii) *Gakulpuri*.—The story of Shah Jahan's interview with Prithivi Shah, forming Chapter VIII of our present book, is given in full in Manuscript A. It also occurs in Manuscript B where some details regarding the presents interchanged between the two sovereigns are omitted. The name of the narrator is mentioned in Manuscript A, but is omitted in B. This omission is however compensated by the insertion of the stories of Timurlane's ascendancy and Jahangir's conquest of Secunderabad which we do not find in Manuscript A.

The concluding words of Chapter VIII are as follows:—"The two monarchs Shah Jahan and Prithivi Shah met each other with their soldiers and retainers, which were as large as the sea. But there did not occur any hitch or misunderstanding for which the masters of the ceremonies belonging to the two monarchs were praised by all. Here is finished what was said by Gakulpuri.''

But who was this Gakulpuri? The author does not mention his name, and Gakulpur is a place-name in India. Toponomous personal names are not uncommon in India and elsewhere, *e.g.*, Lahori, Shiraji, Ardastani, Jodhpuri, Aurangabadi, etc. And in Assam the original names are generally omitted, being replaced by toponomous appellations, *e.g.*, *Guahatia* Barua, *Abhaypuria* Rajkhowa, *Dihingia* Raja, and so forth.

But our chronicler whose desire for citing his sources of information is manifest, would never have left us uninformed if he had not known that the word *Gakulpuri* would mean no body else but one particular individual, *e.g.*, the phrases *French Tiger*, *Bengal Tiger* and *Ultimatum Romanarum* could signify no one but Clemenceau, Sir Asutosh Mookherji, and Brutus, respectively. Besides, as we shall see at present the name of our Gakulpuri was not known even to his own contemporaries.

The great Gakulpuri of Assamese chronicles hailed from Brindaban, and his career in Assam had enormous political significance, culminating in the dethronement and murder of King Udayaditya, 1670-1672, during whose reign the Mogul forces under Ram Singha were completely defeated. Gakulpuri came to Assam as a Sannyasi, and lived first at Hazo and then at Kamakhya, where by his religious observances and alleged power to work miracles, he gathered round him a large circle of enthusiastic devotees. Hearing reports of the Sannyasi's personality, King Udayaditya took him to his capital at Gargaon, and constructed for him a monastery, and the Ahom monarch himself became the first disciple. The Sannyasi exercised such a hypnotic influence upon the credulous king, that he pressed the highly venerated abbots of ancient Assamese monasteries to receive their intiation from the Sannyasi "whose name, caste and origin were unknown." A reaction set in under the leadership of the king's brother who murdered Udayaditya, and himself occupied the throne with the name Ramadhwaja Singha. The first act of his reign, was the execution of the thaumaturgic Sannyasi.

Assamese chronicles are unanimous in saying that the name and origin of the *Bairagi* or Sannyasi of Gakulpur Brindaban were never known, which aggravated the irritation caused by the infatuated monarch's abnormal devotion to the stranger, specially at a time of ceaseless hostility with foreigners. So our chronicler's inability to mention the name of his Gakulpuri informant is excusable. In a manuscript Buranji presented to me by a descendant of Lachit Barphukan the name of this Sannyasi has been specifically mentioned for the first time as Parmananda. So in our opinion, the Gakulpuri of our author could be no other than Parmananda Bairagi of Assamese history whose hypnotic personality brought about the disastrous downfall of his royal devotee and patron.

(B) WRITTEN RECORDS

From the detailed character of the narratives given in some of the chapters, we can not but infer that the author had before him written records and documents. He gives the length of the periods intervening between the reigns of Judhisthira and Jahangir in Chapter VIII. The facts connected with the eastern campaigns of Man Singha and Jai Singha are stated elaborately. We have specifications of the distances between the Mogul capitals and other important towns and localities. The allies of Jai Singha II of Amber are named with the number of their soldiers, horses and camels. All this could never be possible if he had not before him ready-made documents or inventories. The author himself refers to existing chronicles of Mogul India in the preamble to Chapter IX:—

"After the death of Jahangir, his son Shah Jahan sat on the throne in an auspicious moment. The events which took place during the first eight years of his reign are recorded in other books; only the events which took place after the lapse of eight years of his reign will be found in this book",

Of the information derived from the two classes of sources we have noticed one distinction. The stories narrated by Muhammad Ali and Gakulpuri are of a somewhat general character, not without some flavour of romance, characteristic of orally transmitted episodes. The narratives of the second order are marked by congestion of details and subordination of sensationalism to facts. But each of the narratives or chapters is of the nature of a historical idyll, artistically conceived and executed, with the constituent parts linked together by a unity of purpose and design. As we shall see, the description of the Nao-roza has been inserted only in connection with the annual *pesh-kash* which Cooch Bihar had to transmit to the Emperor during its celebrations. The description begins with the query,—"What is Nao-roza?", which the author anticipated invariably from his reader. The history of Timurlane has been given in order to introduce us to Jahangir.

As to the source-books of the author, we are absolutely in the dark. But we would venture to remark that in addition to the existing literature in Assamese, he had access to Persian and Urdu sources. This will lead us to the question of the author's equipment as gleaned from the language of the book.

G.—THE DICTION OF THE BOOK

Maulana Muhammad Ali whose great scholarship, specially his proficiency in Arabic and Persian won for him the munificent patronage of Nawab Mansur Khan, did not certainly narrate his story in the language of the Assamese people; nor did Parmananda Bairagi whose stay in Assam could not be of a very long duration. To carry on conversation in

Assamese is one thing, and to tell a sustained story with all the thrill and picturesqueness of details is quite another matter. They must have used Urdu or Hindi which was easily understood by our chronicler, the most assiduous member of the junto that sat on a moonlit night to listen to the romantic adventures of Rajas, Omras and Padshahs. That the author was fairly acquainted with Urdu or Persian is evident from the large admixture of words of Islamic parlance used in the book. These words have been inserted not merely to impart to his narratives an atmosphere of *Badshahi Khandan*, but they came naturally to the writer which may be due to his long contact with Hindi-Urdu-Persian-speaking people and literature. We have read other chronicles of the period, but though they have an archaic *naivete* of their own, they do not indulge in such an abnormal use of a vocabulary of non-Assamese or non-Sanskritic origin. The author of the *Padshah-Buranji* uses the inevitable phrase which Muhammadan speakers or writers would employ in the same context. This betrays his wonderful knowlege of the ceremonies, formalities and customs in vogue among Muhammadans. A few examples will illustrate our point,—

Akhun	... Muhammad Ali is a *very great scholar*.
Amal	... The Wazir informed Jahangir that he had lost *sovereignty* over a number of chiefs and territories.
Argaja	... Rose-water, attar and *argaja* waters are sprinkled on the decorated floor. *Argaja* is originally a Hindi word meaning a kind of perfume.
Arzahi-Arzhah	... On Sundays and Wednesdays, Rungaddin sits at the Roz-Adawalat, and decides the *petitions of complainants*.

Baghal	... Man Singha boasted that he had carried in his *armpit* dozens of Padshahs like Hussain Shah.
Behaya	... Prince Muazzam hearing of a beautiful maiden, and himself being of an *amorous* disposition, could not resist the temptation.
Dil-asa	... Sher Shah retained the officers of the older regime by giving them *hopes and assurances.*
Doa-sepasi	... Sher Shah says that he has become the Padshah of Delhi through the *blessings* of all.
Fatiha	... The Qazi advises Humayun to hold a *feast* where the Nawab's attendant would be pointed out.
Ghairahu	... The Wazir advised Jahangir to take up the subjugation of the neighbouring territories first, and then to despatch invading forces against Hussain-abdal, Piran Maluk *and others.*
Gor	... Shah Jahan's consort prefers to court *burial* with the name of Khuda instead of seeing her sons' fratricidal conflicts.
Haramkhor	... Aurangzeb said to his Wazir,-" "Please tell me which of the principalities have now become *disloyal* to us."
Haramzada	... Shah Jahan wrote to Jai Singha,—"The Rajas and Zamindars of Bengal and Orissa are *very troublesome*".
Inam	... Jahangir gave to Raja Mandhata a *reward* of three lakhs of rupees for eating pan and betelnut.
Jin-paṇjal	... Sultan Azamtara presented to the Waqayanavis at Dacca a horse with *saddlery* of the value of one thousand rupees.

Keramat	... Shah Jahan became somewhat perturbed seeing the *influence and power* of Jai Singha.
Khuda	... On Fridays, the Padshah goes to the mosque to say his prayers to *Khuda*.
Lalach	... Raja Mandhata said to Jahangir,—"Hussain Shah does not entertain any *solicitude* for his life".
Loghat	... Muhammad Ali knows all the *languages*, Persian and Arabic.
Mahalli	... Shaista Khan advised Ram Singha not to *admit* the women of Shujanagar into his *residence*.
Mehmani	... Shah Jahan said to Jai Singha,—"You should take me to your state, and show me due *hospitality*".
Muzra	... Mir Jumla *greets* Nawab Shaista Khan.
Nazdagi	... The door-keeper called a *near-by* attendant of Shaista Khan, and sent information through him of Mir Jumla's solicitation for an interview.
Nikah	... Muhammad Jahan, the brother of Shah Jahan, *marries* the widow of the Turki Sultan.
Padshah-Hazrat	... Prince Khurram wrote to his father,—"This is known at the two feet of the *Padshah-Hazrat*".
Qabul-qarar	... Sewa Raja said to Ram Singha, "You brought me here with *assurances and promises* of safety".
Saf	... Shah Jahan said to Jai Singha,—"Bengal has always been *subdued* by your family; and so you should proceed there".

Sambhal	... Sher Pingal said,—"I could not *manage to take due steps* when I faced the crisis of an armed conflict".
Shabash	... Rungaddin said to Sarbabhaumchandra, "*Well said*, Pandit, your words are wholesome to me".
Shabhaz	... Shah Jahan wrote to the Adil Shahi Sultan,—"My *royal falcons* will tear to pieces the kites of the entire world".
Shitab	... Sher Shah wrote to Humayun asking the latter to return *immediately* to Delhi if he agreed to the terms proposed.
Sulaiman Paigambar	... Prince Khurram wrote to Jahangir,—"Did *Sulaiman Paigambar* receive any injury at the hands of the ants?".
Sufarish	... Raja Baris-sal informed Ise Khan that he had *spoken well* of him to Raja Mandhata.
Takhth	... Shah Jahan after sitting on the throne despatched an admonitory letter to the Adil Shahi Sultan.
Takid	... Mir Jumla solicited *quick* leave from Nawab Shaista Khan.
Tamam	... Jai Singha is a great hero; he has subjugated the *whole* of Bengal.
Vilayat	... Jai Singha was then despatched to the *Province* of Kashmir which had become disloyal to the Emperor.
Waqaya dakhil	... Man Singha returned to Dacca after having *submitted a report* to Delhi on the recent campaigns.
Zabah	... Aurangzeb *decapitates* his brothers Dara and Murad.
Zahar	... Mumtaz Mahal uttered the name of Khuda, and put an end to her life by swallowing *poison*.

The author has maintained throughout the book a precise distinction between a Nawab, a Raja, a Padshah and a Padshahzada. Other words of the official vacubulary are also used in their correct sense and bearing, *e.g.*—

> Ahudi, Amir-ul-Omara, Am-khash, Badshahi Gaj-mohar, Beldar, Darbar, Dewan, Dewan-khash, Dui-tarwali, Farman, Harol, Hazur-navis, Khan-khana, Khan-sama, Khitmatgar, Panch-hazari, etc., Qazi, Roz-Adawalat, Roz-Dewàn, Saranjam, Sika-bardar, Sipar-salar, Sirpao, Waqaya-navis, Wazir, Zulus.

The correct use of words of Persian origin in their appropriate context and the extensive knowledge of Islamic history and formàlities which the book betrays, sometimes tempt us to think that the author might have been a Muhammadan scholar, to whom the words and ideas came spontaneously as they do even now. Hindu writers and speakers very rarely use those words and phrases, unless they insert them consciously and artistically to impart to the narratives a realistic tinge. The knowledge that there were Muhammadan writers connected with the Assamese literature of the seventeenth and eighteenth centuries will be a discovery of the highest importance. Against this presumption there is the use of the benedictory phrase in the beginning of each chapter, " Glory to Srikrishan," which a Muhammadan would never use, unless we take it as a mechanical interpollation by subsequent Hindu copyists. At the same time the fundamental Sanskritic ring of the vocabulary and construction which is in consonance with the Assamese Vaisnava works of the period will encourage some to believe that the author could not be a Muhammadan. But we know that there were learned Muhammadans in Assam in those days, some of whom were appointed in the Persian department of the Ahom government, who could very easily acquire a mastery of Assamese prose style. Of the Muhammadan officers of the Ahom Court, there were 16 Dewans, 1 Nawab-Deka, 2 Persian readers, and one engraver, "who were supported by the State according to the old custom in Assam," and our author might be one of them. There were also learned Hindus, accomplished in Persian, which was an indispensable symbol of culture, and an easy passport to official preferments specially in diplomatic service. The letters exchanged between Jahangir and Prince Khurram must have been translated from the original Persian by an erudite scholar, as the Assamese rendering is redolent of the aroma of Persian traditions, and reminiscent at the same time of the prose of the Vaisnava classics, *Gita* and *Bhagavat*.

Of the Hindus, conversant with Muhammadan history and culture, there were the ambassadors of Assam whose ingenuous retorts stupefied distinguished Mogul generals, and whose training and accomplishments were viewed with jealousy by fellow-plenipotentiaries of other nations.[53] The idea of compiling the *Padshah-Buranji* might be conceived and executed by one of them. So the question regarding the identity of the author will remain ever open, until we come upon new and independent evidence, or we read the chronicle more critically from this standpoint than has yet been done.

H.—DATE OF COMPILATION

The last two events mentioned in the *P.B.* are,—*first*, Prince Azam's deputation of Nawab Mansur Khan to occupy Gauhati, which occurred in 1679; *second*,—the formation of a Rajput-Mahratta confederacy under Jai Singha II of Amber and

Malaha Rao Holkar which, according to Irvine, took place sometime between 1719 and 1731. While in other chronicles dates are recorded to the minute, the *P.B.* is curiously deficient in this respect, except on one occasion when the overthrow of Pithor Raja, the last Hindu king of Delhi is mentioned, rightly or wrongly, to have taken place in "the year 843 of the era of Sakaditya." The purpose of the chronicle was to supply general information, while the chronology has been roughly maintained by the sequence of the monarchs which is stated with precision.

The two dates 1679 A.D. and 1719-1731 A.D. do not provide any indication of the exact date of composition. The chapter on the Nawabs of Dacca where the episode of the first date occurs, and the other on the allies of Jāi Singha II, might be subsequent additions to the main chronicle, while the story heard orally from Gakulpuri must have been put in black and white not later than 1673 A.D., in which year the Sannyasi was executed. Muhammad Ali remained in Assam during the Fauzadarship of Mansur Khan, 1679-1682, during which period or soon after, his story must have been recorded. The different chapters might have been compiled at different periods, and may also be by different authors.

The habit of putting together separate works on the same subject, though by different authors was not uncommon in Assam. We have come across chronicles which end in the events of 1681, but they contain a list of Assamese kings up to the year 1826. A single manuscript sometimes served the purpose of a modern shelf of books, and the combination of several works of the same interest eliminated the necessity of preparing separate thick wood-covers which generally enclose each Assamese manuscript. The date of transcription does not give us any clue to the date of composition besides fixing the latest date for the same.

The language of the book is in keeping with that of other chronicles of the seventeenth century. The necessity for such a compilation dealing with the antecedents of Mir Jumla and Ram Singha, and the previous history of the monarchs of Delhi, was most acutely felt when the Mogul generals were knocking at the gate of Assam threatening to destory her independence and solidarity. So taking all things together, we may easily surmise that the main bulk of the book was compiled between 1663 and 1685 A.D., and the copy of Manuscript A. was made later than 1731 A.D. Manuscript B could not have been copied earlier than 1793 A.D. The character of the script and the present condition of the ink further support such a conclusion.

I.—HISTORICAL VALUE OF THE PADSHAH-BURANJI

Scholars who have devoted their life to the unfolding of the history of the Delhi Badshahate, or who have access to an extensive library of books and manuscripts on Mogul India, will be better judges of the value of the *Padshah-Buranji* as a source-book. But as I do not belong to either of these categories, I offer my remarks in a tentative manner, with the hope that my more fortunate fellow-workers stationed in livelier centres of historical culture will excuse the observations of a man who lives in a place, where generals were sent by the Great Moguls as a good riddance or as a punishment for delinquency in imperial duties, a place which abounds in mosquitoes but not in books, where the atmosphere is surcharged with germs of lingering diseases and death, but not with indomitable and widespread zeal for learning and scholarship.

I am not in a position to say what will be the total output of new information derivable from the *Padshah-Buranji*. But the value of a historical document is never judged by the amount of fresh revelations which it contains. Facts already accepted or settled as incontrovertible gain additional meaning and force when they are confirmed by statements recorded in an independent historical work, compiled in a detached corner under a curious juxtaposition of circumstances, where the author had access to sources which might now be lost. This confirmation from independent quarters guards the so-called settled facts from future dislodgement and refutation. When material corroborations are accompained by occasional discrepancies on minor points from the synthetic reconstrutions of academic historians, the disagreement only points to the possibility that our author had materials which are now lost or forgotten, and that all our settled facts would not have been recorded as such if access to the lost materials would have been attainable. Of facts of a confirmatory character we have many in our *Padshah-Buranji*. Besides, there are numerous discrepancies, which instead of detracting from the value of the book, only serve to open a new line of enquiry; they also give us a glimpse into the mass of materials which are now effaced through the influence of time, and to which our author had evidently some access.

Chronicles are compiled everywhere on the basis of information gathered from written documents, as well as from verbal reports of reliable eye-witness and other informants. Several Persian chronicles of the Mogul court were indebted to the testimony of oral reporters. The evidence of learned scholars like Muhammad Ali and Gakulpuri would have been utilised by Muhammadan chroniclers if such an opportunity was ever found, and it would not have been discarded as utterly untrustworthy. Here for the first time we have in the pages of the *Padshah-Buranji* the unexploited factlore stored in the minds of these two not absolutely negligible personalities which would have been welcomed in the illuminated *nastaliqs* of Muhammad Qasim Hindu Shah Firishtah and Muhammad Amin bin Abu'l-Hasan Qazwini.

ANNALS OF THE DELHI BADSHAHATE

CHAPTER I

Muhammadan Conquest of Delhi

1. *The birth of Rungaddin.*—Mazitpur is a city in the province of Nâko. There ruled a Padshah named Muhammad Shah of Alâmanja. He had no son. Once he feasted some *faquirs* and *pirs* with great cordiality and earnestness, and prayed to them as follows, "I have three hundred wives, but still I have not been blessed with a son. Please consult the scriptures and tell me what I am to do."

The faquirs and pirs replied,—"What means shall we suggest? There is one pir named Marda Sher Khan Ali who wanders about in disguise from city to city on an Irâqi horse. If you can recognise him when he comes to your city, you should pray to him for a son, and he will fulfil your desire."

As luck would have it Sher Khan Ali halted at the city, and the Padshah honoured him and offered the saint large quantities of food articles. The pir asked the Padshah, "I hope you are perfectly happy?"

Padshah: "I have everything complete, but I am unhappy having no son. I have three hundred wives, but still no son has been born to me."

Pir: "In your previous life you had stolen the son of another man, and sold him to a degenerate infidel who must have killed and devoured the child. For this sin you have not been blessed with a son. Now, if you, desirous of a son, offer one lakh of golden pieces to Mecca you will surely have one."

The Padshah did accordingly and got a son, who was named Rungaddin.

2. *Nako, a land of wonders.*—The beasts, birds, fish, men and serpents of that country are of huge dimension and stature. The Padshahs rest under the shade offered by the wings of the bird *Hurma* which lives on rhinoceros and elephants. The bird has a horn on its back.' Some time before its death the bird goes about with an elephant pierced through the horn. The elephant dies afterwards, and maggots breed on its carcase which enter the entrails of the bird and eat them up. The bird dies in consequence. *Sarol* is another bird of that place. The grandees make hubble-bubbles of the eggs of these birds. The price of each egg comes up to rupees one hundred or two hundred. *Sha-Morog* is another species of bird found in that country. Before its death it flaps its wings on the ground in quick succession; the friction produces fire in which the bird is consumed to death. There is another bird named *Sereng* which assumes a white colour in the morning, crimson in the afternoon and black at night; and they are kept by the grandees for their amusement. There is another bird named *Murtaskhor*. It swallows live charcoal of burnt fuel, wood, and bamboos, without scalding its mouth. The rats and mice of that place are very sweet-scented. The nobles of the land use coats and garments made of their skins which they sew and convert into dresses. Their

pillows are also made of the same stuff, and they become cool in summer and warm in winter. Their price ranges from one hundred to two hundred rupees. Diamonds are also found in that country.[54]

3. *The munificence of Rungaddin Padshah.*—After some time Alâmanji Muhammad Shah Padshah died, and he was succeeded by his son Rungaddin. With regard to his own kingdom he enquired: "How long have we been Padshahs of Nâko?" He could trace the date of origin to the wars between the Kauravas and the Pândavas and not further than that. Nobody could say how long they were wielding the sovereign power. The Padshah ordered the articles in the royal store to be counted, but the counting could not be finished.

Rungaddin Padshah said to his Wazir, Farteijang Khân, and his Kârzi, Sul Mardâ-dâdullâ,—"I investigated into the antiquity of our dynasty of Padshahs. The records testify to its existence at the time of the war between the Kurus and the Pândavas. No date could be traced earlier than that armageddon. The articles of the royal treasury were also computed, but the counting could not be finished. So I ask you both to give me such advice as will conduce to my well-being in the life to come as well as in the present life, so that my soul may be blessed."

The two ministers said to the Padshah, "Make more liberal presents to Mecca and to other holy places with due discrimination. Bestow gold, silver and clothes on faquirs, pirs, beggars and the poor. If this is accomplished you will earn blessings in afterlife. Arrange and reconstruct the city in the proper order. Keep more soldiers, so that you may subjugate the frontier Rajas and Padshahs and exact tribute from them. Find out a kingdom greater than Nâko: invade and occupy it, and become its Padshah. If this can be done, you will earn fame and glory in this world."

Accordingly, the Padshah made more liberal presents to religious places, exercising proper judgment and discretion; gifts of gold and silver and apparel were made on a more extensive scale to faquirs, beggars and the indigent. The wives of mendicants wore bracelets and anklets of gold and silver. The city walls, the fort and the forum were constructed with marble stones.

4. *Rungaddin's war-equipments.*—The Padshah then commanded Farteijang Khân to recruit and maintain officers and servants, which was done accordingly. There were 30,500 officers consisting of Wazirs, Dewans, Nawabs, Bukhshis and Mansabdars; a cavalry of 700,000 soldiers using Iraqi, Arbi, Sujarnis[55] and Turki ponies, 3,500 elephants; 42,000 cannon; 84,000 muskets; 28,000 *chandravans*; 100,500 beldars, and innumerable merchants, shopkeepers as well as camels, bullocks and asses.

5. *Rungaddin's expedition of conquest.*—After subduing all the Padshahs and Rajas on the frontiers of his kingdom, Rungaddin marched against Sher Pingal, king of Rum. Before storming the entrenchments and garrisons of Sher Pingal Padshah, Rungaddin halted at a distance of three days' journey and despatched

messengers to the king of Rum with a letter to the following effect,—"I am the Padshah of Nâko, and my name is Rungaddin. How dare you rest in peace after having heard my name? Have you not received reports of the invincibility and splendour of my soldiers and my arms and weapons? Even now there is time for you to come and make friends with me by offering due submission; otherwise be prepared for war. If you lack in war materials, just ask of me, and I will send them to you. Anyhow, I demand war." The above message formed the subject-matter of the letter which was delivered to the Padshah by a courier.

6. *Sher Pingal's reply.*—Sher Pingal became furious on the receipt of the letter and said,—"My name is Sher Pingal, which denotes a tiger. Why should an ordinary human being brag before a tiger? Why should I supplicate you for war-equipments? The splendour of your army has led you to utter these words of pride and disdain, which will be humbled at the sight of the magnificence of the forts of my kingdom. I have three fortresses, one of copper, another of iron and the third of stones; if you can come after passing these three citadels I will then ask you for supplies of war."

To this the Ukil made the reply,—"Have you not heard the name of Rungaddin Padshah? He has humbled numerous Padshahs and Rajas. The three forts of which you have just spoken will not stand you in good stead. Man has constructed them, and man will demolish them. So, do not remain in peace by counting upon their impregnability. Go and offer your homage to him, everything will go well. If you oppose nothing will be saved. Your assertion that Sher Pingal means a tiger is inauspicious, as elephants, rhinoceros and tigers are all killed by men."

After having said so the Ukil was turned out of the Padshah's presence, and he reported the whole matter to Rungaddin Padshah, who presented the Ukil with a pony and ten thousand rupees, saying, "Well done, Ukil."

7. *Crossing of the invincible forts.*—After this, the Padshah despatched Farteijang Khan, a senior Nawab and a commander of twelve thousand, at the head of twelve Nawabs and a large army. At the sight of the copper fort, the general placed in the van large sheets of iron to serve as walls for the soldiers who marched under the shelter thus afforded, unhurt by the showers of arrows and bullets. The cavalry riding on Iraqi and Sujarnis ponies then reached the foot of the copper fort, when they crossed the fort and went over to the other side. The inmates of the fort perished or took to their heels. The copper fort was destroyed by Farteijang Khan. The invaders then attacked the fort of iron. Here also they posted the iron screens in front. The *poladars* served as screens for which they could not assail the fort. The *beldars* or sappers cut open a path with thin steel hoes through which the sepoys, the elephants and other men passed, and occupied the fort. After this the invaders stormed the stone fort. There was a Nawab who had once been wronged by Sher Pingal; he now came and made friends with Farteijang Khan. The general gave him large presents and asked the methods

of successfully attacking the iron fort. The Nawab replied—" There is a secret passage; and horses and elephants cannot pass through it as it is very narrow. A hundred or two men only can pass through the passage."

Some two hundred soldiers versed in magic were then requisitioned for service. They entered the royal apartments by a stratagem, and transported Sher Pingal Padshah bodily with his bed-stead, and handed him over to Farteijang Khan, who in turn despatched the captive monarch to the presence of Rungaddin Padshah.

8. *Sher Pingal offers submission.*—Rungaddin Padshah then brought Sher Pingal to the durbâr and said,—" Well, Sher Pingal, you did not consult men proficient in the ways of the world, nor did you act as one should do when he is in danger and misfortune. Hence you are now facing all this misery."

Sher Pingal replied, " O Padshah, I bow to thee. What you have said is proper and reasonable. You have heard what sort of a man I, Sher Pingal, am. Even Jungam-Shâhân Padshah could not stem the tide of misfortunes;[56] what am I to say now? Do as you think proper."

Rungaddin then said, " Well, Sher Pingal, do not be afraid in the least. I shall leave this place after seeing that you are properly established."

Having said so, Sher Pingal was allowed to dine at the royal banquet, and to attend the assembly of the Wazîr and the Dewan. The elephants, horses and other spoils seized by Farteijang Khan after destroying the three forts were taken with him. He left two Nawabs in charge of the place and proceeded to the presence of the Padshah. Sher Pingal took his oath in accordance with the injunctions of the Musalmans, and Rum became bound to pay an annual tribute of five crores of rupees. Sher Pingal was presented with a *sirpao* or robe of honour, after which he was allowed leave to go. The son of Farteijang Khan was appointed *Subha* or governor of the place.

Rungaddin Padshah said to Sher Pingal, " I assure you there is no cause for alarm. Pay the stipulated sum of money annually to the Subha," To this Sher Pingal replied, " Padshah, *selamat*, you have bestowed a second life upon a dead person. I will act as you have commanded me."

Farteijang Khan was rewarded with presents of elephants and horses, and a purse of one lakh of rupees ; the twelve other Nawabs were also rewarded according to their desert.

After the subjugation of Rum, Rungaddin Padshah encamped on the bank of the river Narmadâ, where Nasir Beg blew the nahbat.

9. *Pithor Raja of Delhi.*—Rungaddin's spies then went far and wide to survey the countries. A messenger returned from Delhi and reported to Rungaddin Padshah, " Pithor Raja rules at Delhi. He is a powerful chief, and his kingdom is a prosperous one. All the commodities wanted by the Padshah are available in his territories. In ancient times it was the kingdom of the Kurus and the Pândavas. It is inhabited by men of all castes, Brahmans, Kshattris, Vaishyas and Sudras, and other Hindusthanis. That place is fit for the establishment of your throne."

10. *Rungaddin marches against Delhi.*—Having heard this the Padshah asked the Wazir for his opinion. The Wazir replied, " I hear Delhi has insurmountable fortresses, great warriors and diplomats. Still, if you resolve, you can occupy the throne of Delhi."

The Padshah then despatched Jambur Khan by the route through the Maru river at the head of one lakh of sepoys, while Harjubar Khan proceeded by the way through Rachanpur in command of an army of one hundred thousand soldiers consisting of Rohellâ-Pâthâns and others. The Padshah went in the middle. Bahlol Khan Nawab marched at the head of a large force of thirty thousand sepoys a journey of six *dandas* in advance, Rungaddin Padshah marching in the rear.

11. *The Rajputs prefer war to submission.*—The general of Rungaddin Padshah captured some forts within the jurisdiction of Pithor Raja's territories. The soldiers stationed at those forts reported to Pithor Raja, king of Delhi, " The powerful sovereign Rungaddin Padshah, son of Muhammad Shah of Alâmanja, king of Nâko, whose capital is Mazitpur, has come with a large army and is marching towards this direction after capturing our garrisons."

Then Pithor Raja conferred with the Rajas of Amber, Bandhab, Hâro, Rânâ Raja, Gar-chitor, Jharkhand and other powerful chieftains, when he said " Rungaddin Padshah is a very mighty prince. After subduing numerous rulers he is now coming to invade our kingdom. Please advise whether we should offer our homage to him."

The Rajas assembled replied in one voice—"We are Kshattriyas and Rajputs. We are not prepared to derogate our name for fear of our lives. Besides, the Raja of Delhi has never submitted nor paid his homage to any other prince. Death in battle is preferable to submission. So make preparations for war, and we shall fight."

12. *Embassies between Rungaddin and Pithor Raja*—In the meantime Rungaddin Padshah's Ukil arrived at the court of Pithor Raja with a letter containing the following message, "I am the son of Muhammad Shah Padshah of Alamanja, and my name is Rungaddin Padshah. Have you heard or not of the magnificence of my army and of my subjugation of the Rajas and the Padshahs of the territories through which I have passed? You should now come and establish friendly terms with me, and I will go back after having settled you in your territories, and you will live in peace by paying me presents and tribute. If you do not submit I will invade Delhi and take possession of the same, and you will be deprived of a great opportunity."

Pithor Raja, king of Delhi, sent the following retort: "The Padshah is a great man to himself, what is that to me? He is the Padshah of a kingdom and I am also the Raja of mine own. He should not have written like this."

The Ukil then said: "What you have said and written betrays indiscretion. Everyone has heard of the prowess and strength of Rungaddin Padshah. Now that you have spoken like this, you will have no loophole to escape."

13. *Clash between the Muhammadans and Rajputs.*— The Ukil reported the whole matter to Rungaddin Padshah. The Padshah marched to the battle, and so did Pithor Raja. The Raja despatched the Rânâ-raja with a numerous army to meet the forces of Jambur Khan, while the Raja of Gar-chitor marched at the head of a large contingent of soldiers and chieftains against Harjubar Khan, Raja Pitholdas was sent with another detachment, six *dandas* in advance. Pithor Raja himself marched to the eastern front personally to conduct the battle against Rungaddin Padshah. Then the advanced guards of the Raja and the Padshah caught sight of each other. The emissaries of the two sovereigns sent report to their respective lords.

The battle commenced at a distance of seven days' journey from Delhi. There ensued a terrible encounter between Jambur Khan and the Rânâ-raja with heavy casualties on both sides. Jambur Khan and the Rânâ-raja were engaged in a duel on horse-back, and they both perished by their swords. This was followed by a furious contest between the Raja of Gar-chitor and Harjubar Khan. On one side were ranged Rajput sepoys who were of very hard mettle; they would never retreat even at the cost of their lives; on the other side were the Rohellâ-Pâthâns, riders of Sujarnis horses; they would perish by the sword, but would never yield. There was terrible slaughter on both sides.

The Raja had a brother named Surat Singha. A Nawab was fighting from the back of an elephant. Surat Singha crept under the elephant and speared the

Náwab to death. The remnant of the Nawab's army fled and joined the forces of Rungaddin. After slaying Hurjabar Khan, Unmatta Singha joined the ranks of Pithor Raja.

14. *The death of Pithor Raja.*—Then ensued a terrific contest between Maharaja Pithor and Rungaddin Padshah. It commenced with the firing of muskets from both the hostile camps, which was followed by a battle with bows and arrows. Then came the battle of the elephants, and horses, which was followed by that of spears, swords and daggers. Thus the struggle continued for one full year in which varieties of weapons were used. Then the Rohellâ and Pâthân cavalry of Rungaddin Padshah, riding upon Arabian and Sujarnis horses, destroyed the elephants and horses of the Hindu Raja, whose men were also killed by thousands. The Raja from an elephant's back hurled his own *chandravan* (discus ?) which fell back on himself and killed him. After his death, the cries of his subjects crossed the barriers of heaven. The Raja's brother Rana Singha and his son Kumud Singha burnt the dead body of the Raja on a pyre made of aloe-wood. The queens of the Raja who numbered 120 accompanied their lord. Several hundred pitchers of ghee were poured upon their bodies, and the fire reached the summit of the sky. Ten crores of rupees in gold and silver and ten thousand cows, as well as clothes, were presented to Brahmans and Vaishnavas for the spiritual wellbeing of the deceased sovereign.

15. *Rungaddin's victorious entry into Delhi.*—Adam Fartu Khan, brother of Rungaddin Padshah, and Shah

Adil Khan, his son, met the Raja's brother Rana Singha and his son Kumud Singha in a serious combat. All the four perished by their swords. Thus ended the war between the two armies. Rungaddin Padshah won the day, while Pithor Raja encountered a defeat. The remnant of the army of Pithor Raja surrendered to Rungaddin Padshah who inspired them with confidence and good-will. The victorious Padshah then proceeded towards Delhi. On an auspicious day and moment he made his entry into the walls of Delhi. All the gold and silver and other articles that belonged to Pithor Raja were plundered and seized.

The prince who had been left behind by Rungaddin Padshah in his native land was known as Sultan Muhammad Mâzum. The Padshah now sent to him presents of precious articles of Hindusthan, as well as a sceptre and umbrella with the command appointing him Padshah of Nâko. Rungaddin retained two lakhs of sepoys with him, and sent back the rest to his own kingdom of Nâko, after having presented them with gold, silver and clothes. With regard to the two lakhs of sepoys kept by him, he doubled the number of mansabs. Pithor Raja's crown, worth three lakhs of rupees, was presented to Farteijang Khan. Others were also amply rewarded. The Rajas and chieftains of various ranks who fought on the side of Pithor Raja either perished in battle or survived. The brothers and sons of those who were killed were appointed Rajas. They were all given presents. Further, they were assured of his support, and allowed to live in their old dignity and rank. He enquired into the respective status of his subjects, and allowed them to retain the same.

16. *Rungaddin's respect for Hindu traditions.*—Rungaddin Padshah invited Sârbabhaum-Chandra, the family priest of the late King Pithor Raja, and said: "This Delhi was ruled by Hindu sovereigns for a very long time. I was the Padshah of Nâko at a distance of six months' journey from Delhi. The Almighty God has now placed a Musalman Padshah to rule here in place of the Hindu Rajas. You should advise me in a manner which will lead to the continuity of our rule here."

Then said Sârbabhaum-Chandra: "O Padshah, what shall I say? You are yourself acquainted with all laws and traditions. God has created the nations of the earth in separate groups, each different from the other; and He has not provided uniform customs and religions for all. If the different castes and creeds are protected, God will protect you also, and you will be able to remain at Delhi without any trouble or fear."

Rungaddin Padshah then said: "Thanks very much, Pandit. You have given me wholesome and salutary counsel." The Padshah presented to the priest rewards and four thousand rupees, and made the following declaration: "The laws and traditions which existed before will remain unaltered."

17. *The organisation of Mansabs.*—After this Rungaddin Padshah ordered Farteijang Khan: "We have two lakhs of horses of our native kingdom, and four lakhs more recruited in this country, coming up to a cavalry of six lakhs strong. Now you should proceed

to group them under Nawabs, Mansabdars and Fauza-dars." Farteijang Khan accordingly created Nawabs with various grades of Mansabs, such as haft-hazari, chai-hazari, pânch-hazari, chari-hazari, tin-hazari, dui-hazari and ek-hazari. Mansabs were also created with eight hundred soldiers and five hundred guns, and Fauzadars with three hundred, and one hundred and fifty respectively. The new system was recorded on paper and communicated to the Padshah. Farteijang Khan was further commanded to despatch soldiers to different localities, the number being proportionate to the exigency of the place, and to make gifts to all the people. Then all the inhabitants of this country were given a sufficient quantity of gold, silver and clothes irrespective of their castes and classes.

18. *Divisions of the palace.*—The Padshah then enclosed his compound with ramparts built of stone, and commenced the construction of his quarters. First came the *Mardana-mahal* where the Padshah sits and reclines or confers with the males, so it is called Mardana-mahal; then came the *Zanana-mahal* where the Padshah sleeps and amuses himself with the begums, where males have no access; then came the *Dewan-khana* where the Dewân holds his court, superintends his affairs and communicates to the Padshah when necessary, so it is called Dewân-khânâ; then came the hall of the *Khan-saman* on the north, where is situated the store for the articles of the Padshah, hence it is called Khân-sâmâ; on the west is the *Roz-dewan* where the Padshah receives reports of affairs of countries far and near, and issues his orders and decisions with

regard to places as occasion demands. In front of the hall, there is a place enclosed by gold railings, with two pillars of gold, near which the two Wazirs take their seat; the Dewan sits within the enclosure. After this we have the silver enclosure with twelve pillars of silver against which lean the commanders of seven thousand and six thousand. Then comes the copper enclosure meant for the panch-hazaris and chari-hazaris; then the brass enclosure intended for the tin-hazaris and dui-hazaris; and last, the iron enclosure for the ek-hazari Nawabs. On the south is situated the Roz-âdâwlat where the Padshah enquires into the petitions of complainants.

19. *The Padshah's weekly routine.*—The Padshah proceeds to the durbar when ten *dandas* have elapsed, and rises when there are two *dandas* for the commencement of the second *prahar*. On Mondays and Saturdays he conducts affairs of the state sitting at the Roz-dewan; on Sundays and Wednesdays he decides the applications of complainants; on Tuesday he enquires into the income and expenditure of the royal treasury; on Thursday he holds his court at the Hall of State called *Khirnavat* where he investigates matters relating to the sacred shrines of Musalmans and Hindus; on Fridays he visits the Hall of Prayer to take the name of God.

20. *Conclusion.*—*Hinduwan* or Hindu sovereignty ended at Delhi with Pithor, and Musalman usages commenced from the time of Rungaddin, who became Padshah in the era of Sakaditya 843. Here ends the narrative of the country of *Nâko.*[55]

CHAPTER II

TIMURLANE BECOMES EMPEROR OF DELHI.

21. *Timurlane's early life as a shepherd.*—After the death of the Daigati Nawab, his grandson Timurlanga became afflicted with extreme poverty.[58] His mother earned her bread by spinning cotton yarn for others, and Timur tended the goats of a local blacksmith ; thus did the mother and her son live somehow on what they earned by their own labour. Timur took the goats to the field every day ; at noon his mother gave him in the field his breakfast consisting of one-quarter seer of bread, the same amount of *bhang* and the same amount of water.

22. *Timur blessed by a prophetic faquir.*—One day a faqir of the Lohalangar[59] [iron-chained] order went on shouting at the place where Timur's goats were grazing, to the following effect : " The person who will give me bread, *bhang*[60] and water, each measuring one-quarter of a seer, will be appointed by me Padshah of Delhi." Timur's mother was then proceeding to give her son his noontide repast. Timur, on hearing the cries of the faquir, went to give him the bread, *bhang* and water. The mother dissuaded her son from doing so, saying : " You will suffer from hunger. Do not part with your bread to the faquir." Timur disobeyed his mother's bidding and gave his breakfast to the faquir, who ate it and became extremely pleased.

The faquir then said to Timur : " Lie flat on the ground with your face downward." Timur obeyed, and the faquir inflicted seven strokes on Timur's body with the iron chain that girdled his person, saying, "I confer on you the Padshahship of Delhi for seven generations." Saying this, the faquir vanished. Timur became afflicted with pain from the strokes of the iron chain that he received from the faquir, and his mother said: "I forbade you, and you disobeyed my words. Now, you are throbbing with pain from the blows of the mad faquir." Then the mother and son went home.

23. *Timur's master dreams the site of hidden treasures.*—Some time later, Timur's master the blacksmith said one day to Timur: "I have no man to-day to heat the furnace. So you should work with me in the forge to-day." The furnace was heated and the smith, after hammering iron for some hours, became exhausted with fatigue and fell asleep peacefully with his mouth wide open. Then an insect as big as a black bee with the colours of gold, silver and diamond, issued out of the smith's mouth and flew into the house. Timur saw the insect and chased it. The insect, after flying over to the ruins of the fort of Khattam Shâh Padshah, entered again into the mouth of the smith. Timur returned to the smithy and began to blow the bellows. The smith awoke from his sleep and said: "I have dreamt a dream. I wandered over the rampart of Khattam Shah Padshah and saw gold coins strewn all over the fort." Timur then said, "You have seen something in your extreme fatigue. Besides, a day-dream is always false, and never true."

24. *A miracle of Timurabad.*—At night Timur with his mother excavated a part of the old fort and

came upon piles of gold mohurs strewn all over the place. The mother and son extracted a basket of coins and deposited them in their house.

Timur saw a dream that very night in which a faquir said to him: "Exhibit the gold mohurs to the people and you will be Emperor of Delhi." Then Timur during the self-same night took with him baskets of mohurs and scattered them in the thoroughfares of the town. The next morning the people became astonished at the sight of the gold mohurs strewn all over the bazaars. A wâqâyânavis in the service of the Padshah of Delhi lived at Timurâbâd, and he reported the matter to Jâlâl Hussain,[61] Emperor of Delhi, in the following words: "There have been elephant-like piles of gold mohurs at Timurâbâd last night." On receiving this news the Padshah became astonished.

25. *Timur occupies the throne of Delhi.*—Timur then maintained a large number of elephants, horses, cannon and sepoys and became the master of the fort of Khattam Shah Padshah. The Padshah of Delhi heard this news and despatched a Nawab to capture Timur and take him to Delhi. The Nawab proceeded to Timurâbâd. fought with Timur, but being repulsed he returned to Delhi. Timur pursued him as far as Delhi with 80,000 soldiers and camp-followers.

Then the Lohalangar faquir, who had partaken of the bread, *bhang* and water from the hands of Timur, went to Delhi. There was a man named Sharif Muhammad, and he was the preceptor of the Delhi Padshah. The Lohalangar faquir said to him:—"You say you are the preceptor of the Padshah. I will play a practical joke upon the Padshah, save him if you can." The preceptor of the Padshah said: "Wherein lies your power? Better save your own life and remain silent." Then the Lohalangar faquir struck three blows on the earth with his iron chain, and instantaneously the Padshah with the Raja of Peshowâ flew up into the air, and dropped down again on the earth. Then the imperial preceptor paid his homage and reverence to the Lohalangar faquir and departed from the place. The Lohalangar faquir went to unknown quarters after placing Timur on the throne of Delhi.

Timur thus became the Emperor of Delhi. After his death he was succeeded by his son [descendant] Shâh Bâbar who was succeeded by his son Shah Humayun who was succeeded by his son Shah Akbar, who was succeeded by his son Shah Jahangir.

CHAPTER III

Humayun's flight and restoration.

26. *The boast of Humayun Padshah.*—Salutation to Sree-Krishna. Humayun Padshah of Delhi used to say frequently while sitting at the durbar: "I do not know of any man likely to thwart my sword" Dariâ Dâdullâ Kâzi could not stand this repeated bragging of the Emperor, and he said: "Why do you vaunt in a manner irritating to the Almighty Khodâ? Now you say there is no man to thwart your sword; such a man will come out whose strength you will not be able to oppose, and for whom you will have to flee leaving

the throne of Delhi. He will become the Padshah of Delhi. Thus it has been enscrolled in the scriptures." The Kazi said as above.

27. *The future rival of the Emperor.*—The Padshah was seized with apprehension and he said to the Kâzi: "Would you be able to show me the Nawab's slave who, you say, will measure my strength in future?" The Kâzi replied: "I cannot undertake to show him in the ordinary fashion, saying, "Here is the man." I shall be able to show him after having identified him with the marks specified in the scriptures."

The Padshah said: "I am prepared to act as you recommend: please state your suggestions."

The Kâzi replied—"Please arrange the necessary provisions for holding a banquet and I will show you the man there."

At the instance of the Kâzi the Padshah collected food provisions and invited his nobles. He made the Kâzi sit near him, and ordered the guests to partake of tne cheer which consisted of bread and *sak*[62].

One Sher Khan, a trustworthy sepoy serving under a pânch-hazari Nawab, brought out a knife with which he cut his bread and ate. The Kazi pointed him out, saying,—

"O Padshah-Hazarat, this is the man who will baffle the prowess of your sword." The Padshah beckoned his confidants near him and said, "Now, mark this attendant of the Nawab: you shall have to recognise him hereafter."

28. *Attempts to capture Sher Khan.*—Four days after this feast the Padshah despatched a messenger to

the Nawab asking the latter to see His Majesty the following morning, in the company of his sepoy Sher Khan. Having received this command of the Padshah the Nawab summoned the sepoy to his presence and said—"The other day you cut and ate your bread before the Padshah; for this I have been commanded to take you with me. You are a servant in our family for the last three generations; how can I inflict upon me the sin of causing your death by making you over to the Emperor? Do as you think proper. For your sake, I am prepared to face whatever the Padshah may be inclined to do." Having said so he caused the flight of the sepoy.

The Nawab proceeded to the presence of the Padshah on the next day. The Padshah asked the Nawab whether he had brought with him the sepoy Sher Khan, to which the Nawab replied, "O Padshah-Hazarat, I have despatched him to the interior and I have sent for him yesterday on the receipt of the Padshah's command. I will present him before His Majesty when he comes back."

The Padshah then said: "I have not summoned him with any evil intention. It is for his good that I want him in my presence. So please bring him quickly." The Nawab acceded to the request, saying that in obedience to the command of the Padshah he would deliver his servant within eight or ten days. The Nawab has himself imparted secret counsel to the slave and caused his flight; will he now capture and deliver him to the Padshah? The Nawab simply made a false statement before the Emperor, and tried to gain time so that the slave might flee further still. On the expiry of ten or twelve days, the Padshah asked the Nawab : " How is this that you have not yet brought Sher Khan sepoy to me?" To this the Nawab replied : " I sent messengers to the perganah to which he had gone. He could not be found there, and I searched for him in other places too. There is none who can give any clue regarding his whereabouts. He might have heard of the Padshah's summons, and have consequently fled to some unknown place."

The Padshah then said to the Nawab : " If Sher Khan cannot be produced, you will be looked upon as Sher Khan, and you will not be spared. Despatch a larger force to the place whither he has gone, and find him out. Get accurate information about his movements and report the same to me. In case Sher Khan is not found, remember that your days are numbered." The Nawab deputed men to search for Sher Khan at the instance of the Padshah.

29. *Sher Khan, a fugitive in Sewa.*—After some time, the messengers sent in quest of Sher Khan came back and reported to the Nawab that the sepoy had taken shelter in Sewâ and avowed that the information was correct.[63] The Nawab reported to the Padshah : " The men who went to search for Sher Khan sepoy have returned, and they have informed me that they have positively known that he has sought refuge in Sewâ." The Padshah said to the Nawab : " All this is your trickery." The Nawab was dismissed and imprisoned.

The Padshah summoned to his presence his Kazi, Dariâ Dâdullâ, and said,—" Sher Khan sepoy, of whom you once said that he would oppose me in strength, has now been living in Sewâ; I have received authentic report of this fact." The Kâzi replied: "I have said I found in the scriptures. That is all I have to say. What shall I say more?"

30. *Sher Khan defeated by the Padshah.*—The Padshah despatched a panch-hazari Nawab with forces to seize the person of Sher Khan and bring him to the Emperor's presence. On the arrival of the Nawab, Sher Khan, with the help of an army, encountered the imperial troops. A terrible battle ensued between the two armies. Sher Khan won, and the imperial commander of five thousand perished in the battle. Half the soldiers were also killed, and the other half somehow preserved their lives. Sher Khan marshalled his forces and marched against Delhi with the object of invading it. On receiving the intelligence, the Padshah came forward to oppose the invaders. The advanced troops of the Emperor fought with the troops of Sher Khan, who, being unable to hold his stand, returned once more to his place of refuge. He again collected his forces and marched against Delhi where he encountered the imperial army in a deadly battle. A large number of men were killed on both sides. Sher Khan, being unable to resist, retreated from the battle-field.

31. *Sher Khan instructed in correct methods of warfare.* Sher Khan deserted his comrades and fled alone. Losing all hope of victory, he took shelter in the house of an old woman of the city. Sher Khan said to the old woman: "Here is the money, go to the bazaar and buy for me a dish of rice of a quality which is generally taken

by well-to-do people." The old woman did not know that her guest was no other than Sher Khan. She went to the bazaar with the money and purchased a platter of rice which was placed before Sher Khan. Sher Khan was extremely hungry; and why should we blame him if he lifted the morsel from the middle of the pile of rice? The old woman said, "Sher Khan falls upon the centre of the troops of the Delhi Emperor; and being unable to stand, he finally retreats from the field. If he rounds up his enemies commencing from one side only, the Padshah of Delhi will be surely defeated. If rice is eaten from one side, the quantity gradually diminishes and one's hunger is also appeased." Sher Khan remembered this timely hint of his hostess, and commenced his operations by rounding up the enemy from the confines, and halted at his camp facing the Narmadâ.[84]

32. *Sher Khan's victory over the imperial troops.*—The Padshah marched with an army against the rebel, and there were numerous engagements between the two forces. For full one year there was no decisive victory or defeat on either side. A band of jugglers used to display their feats in the camp of Humayun Padshah as well as in that of Sher Khan. Sher Khan said to the jugglers: "I will reward you a huge sum of money if you can find out and inform me at what particular moment, out of the eight divisions or *prahars* of day and night, the army of Humayun Padshah remain in an unguarded condition." At the instance of Sher Khan, the jugglers went to the camp of Humayun Padshah and inquired into the camp-life of the soldiers and came to know that they remain watchful throughout the eight

prahars and that at the fourth *danda* of the early morning, nearly ten-sixteenth of the men remain unguarded; only one-sixteenth remain vigilant. This fact was communicated to Sher Khan by the jugglers.

Sher Khan took with him a hundred and forty soldiers selected from the pick of his army; and having crossed the Narmadâ at night fell upon the Emperor's troops in the early part of the morning. The soldiers of the Padshah, being unguarded at the moment, dispersed in whatever direction they could. The fugitives were killed wherever they could be met.

Humayun took refuge with the Padshah of Rum, and Sher Khan sat on the throne of Delhi with the name Sher Shah.[65] The Nawabs and Omrâos of the older regime were neither dismissed nor killed, but they were retained in their former offices. Humayun Padshah fled alone, leaving his wife, son and dependants at Delhi.

33. *Sher Shah retains the rank of Humayun's consort.*—Sher Shah once said to the Begum and Prince Akbar, "You should consider Humayun to be the real ruler of Delhi, Humayun is my father and you are my mother, and Akbar is my brother.[66] You should eat and dress as you used to do before, and I shall not reduce your supplies." A water-jug was lying somewhere there, and Sher Shah said to Humayun's consort, "Please pass on the jug this side, as I want to drink water." The Begum handed over the pot and Sher Shah drank water therefrom.

34. *Sher Shah's magnanimity.*—While sitting at court Sher Shah said to his Uzir and his Dewan, "By the grace of God I have become the Padshah of Delhi: nothing

can be higher in the destiny of a mortal, and for me there is nothing else to be achieved. I drank water from the pot given to me by the Begum of Humayun Padshah: I have made the exalted consort of the Emperor of Delhi do service to me, and this I regard as the meridian of my good fortune." The Uzir, the Dewan and the assemblage at the durbar praised Sher Shah, saying: "God has blessed you with good fortune on account of this noble intelligence of yours. Your preservation of the family of Humayun in their former dignity and style will perpetuate your fame as long as Delhi exists."

35. *Humayun's indignities at the Persian court.*— Humayun Padshah stood at the gate of the Sultan of Rum and sent the following message: "Humayun, the Padshah of Dehli, is waiting at your door."

The Padshah of Rum said: "Why should the Padshah of Delhi come to me? It must be false. Let him say positively who he is."

Humayun replied: "I am really the Humayun of Delhi. The reason for which I have deserted my country and taken shelter here will be communicated to you in detail."

The king of Rum did not first admit Humayun to his durbar, but allowed him separate quarters and supplied provisions for food with the remark, "Let him stay there for this day. He will be given audience at the court some time later." Humayun refused to take the food supplied to him by the Rum Padshah as it was unworthy of the ex-Emperor: this was partaken of by his retainers. Humayun said to the noble deputed by the Sultan to attend on him: "Bring me the food taken by the Padshah, and I will pay what it may cost," and handed over a gold mohur to the latter. The food was brought accordingly.

The courtyard facing the audience-hall of the Padshah of Rum was covered with mud, and Humayun saw the mud when he was conducted to the court through that way. A servant ran up and rubbed Humayun's feet with oil. The Padshah of Rum observed that after Humayun had crossed the courtyard the servant wiped off the mud from the Emperor's feet.

Humayun stood in front of the Padshah of Rum; and seeing that no seat was offered to his lord, a servant laid a shield on the floor and covered it with a cloth and Humayun Padshah took the seat thus prepared for him.[67]

36. *The Sultan of Persia denounces Humayun.*—After some time the Padshah of Rum addressed Humayun: "O Humayun, Padshah of Delhi, how many attendants like this had you at Delhi?"

Humayun said: "By your blessings, I had a large number of followers like this."

The Padshah of Rum then said: "Why did you flee from Delhi, fortunate as you were in the enjoyment of the services of faithful servants like this one?[68] You have been the rulers of Delhi for three generations, you had such blessings and opportunities, still you could not hold your stand, and had to flee for life. At least a hundred thousand men would have been found who would have willingly sacrificed their lives for you if you had only asked them to do so. During your Padshahate you must have regarded the gratification of your desires and pleasures as of supreme importance, without investigating into the weal and woe of you subjects. The minds of the people therefore became disaffected towards you on the slightest provocation. This disgrace of yours will last as long as Delhi exists, and your name will be an object of ridicule among the Musalmans. You are a man to be severely condemned. You are lifeless, what is the harm if severe strictures are passed upon you?"

Humayun Padshah made the following reply: "Of all the hated persons in the world, I am the one who merits the severest reprobation. My disgrace has spread over the whole earth. By coming to the deliverance of this reprehensible one you will earn eternal fame to last as long as Delhi exists. With what words shall I contrive to please you? Whatever you say of yourself fully maintaining your prestige and fame will be effected."

37. *Humayun invades Delhi with Persian troops.*—The Padshah of Rum offered Humayun a seat worth one lakh of rupees. The Padshah handed over from his throne a martial robe, and all the necessary articles of food, as well as a good place for residence, with the following words: "That you have taken refuge with me in solicitation of my help, you have nothing to say, everything rests with me now." He gave to Humayun Sawars and Nawabs to the extent of three lakhs, making up a total of seven lakhs of soldiers with musketeers, shieldsmen and others, saying: "Go now and occupy Delhi."

Humayun returned with this army and attacked Delhi.

38. *Humayun again defeated by Sher Shah.*—Being unable to oppose Sher Shah in strength, Humayun fled a second time to Rum. The Padshah of Rum said to Humayun : " Formerly you said that you would be able to reoccupy Delhi with an army of three lakhs of soldiers only; now, you have not been able to retake it even with seven lakhs of soldiers." Having said so to Humayun, the Padshah inflicted appropriate punishments upon his Mansabdars, Nawabs and soldiers who were found delinquent.

The Padshah supplied to Humayun a fresh army of twelve lakhs strong, including six lakhs of horse, manned this time by veteran Nawabs. With this vast army Humayun was sent back to Delhi. The Padshah addressed his men as follows, " If that ordinary individual , a fit object of our compassion and favour, wins victory over two Padshahs, the discredit will ring through ages. Knowing this, act in a manner which will enable you to occupy Delhi." With these words he granted leave to all with appropriate presents and gifts.

This army in full force attacked Delhi. A series of battles were waged with Sher Shah. First came the battle with big guns, then the battle with ponies and riders, and then of the shieldsmen ; but Sher Shah could not be vanquished in any way. Sher Shah conferred with his men and said,—" All right, I will deal in a manner which will prevent the soldiers of the Rum Padshah from coming here again." Saying so, he selected seven hundred horsemen with him, and with swords in both hands he made a sudden attack upon the enemy in the early part of the morning, and massacred a large number of horses and men. The rest of the imperial army took to their heels and fled to Rum. Instead of going to Rum, Humayun Padshah retired to the interior on this occasion.

39. *Humayun's restoration to the throne.*—Sher Shah sent a man with a letter containing the following message to Humayun: "You need not wander about from place to place, leaving your wife and son, and afflicting your body with pain. You are my father, and I am your son. I would invite you to come back to Delhi, and I will retire to Agra. The empire will be divided into two parts, one of which will go to you and the other to me. I will take a solemn vow in accordance with the injunctions laid down in the scriptures. If you agree to this proposal, you should come immediately to Delhi."

On receiving this invitation Humayun came to Delhi. Sher Shah entered into a sacred covenant by which he divided the empire into two parts, and Humayun ruled at Delhi and Sher Shah at Agra. This is how the Padshahship of Delhi was partitioned into two portions. Sher Shah and his descendants ruled at Delhi for three generations, covering a period of 20 years, 6 months and 10 days. Here ends the story.

CHAPTER IV

Raja Man Singha subjugates Bengal

40. *The Mogul Empire on the accession of Jahangir.*—Salutation to Sree-Krishna. On the death of Humayun

his son Shah Akbar became the Padshah. On Akbar's demise his son Jahangir became the Padshah. Akbar had two Wazirs, Nazahat Khan and Mâtamad Khan. On the accession of Jahangir to the Badshahate, Nazahat Khan Wazir was removed from office, and Sayid Khan appointed in his place. The Padshah conducted the affairs of the state with Mâtamad Khan and the newly appointed Wazir.

Jahangir Padshah one day asked his two Wazirs, "Let me know the names of the countries with their Rajas and Padshahs who paid homage to Emperor Akbar but have refrained from doing so during my reign." The two Wazirs consulted the records and said,—"You have lost sovereignty over the following chiefs and territories,—Muhammad Murad Khan Padshah of Hussain-âbdâl, Shâhdul Padshah of Piran, Raja Bitholdas of Bund, Mohan-Madhur Singha of Rameswar-Bandar; Achinta Zemindar of Jaleswar-Bandar; Kiledar Khan, Nawab of Benares Sarkari; Hussain Khan Padshah of Gaur in Bengal, and the kingdom of Bengal with their Rajas and Zemindars." The Emperor commanded that Subhas with forces be despatched against the refractory rulers with the object of subjugating them.

The Wazir said, "We have only two tanks of coins, one of gold mohurs and the other of silver, accumulated during the period from the reign of Timurlanga to Akbar Padshah. The gold and silver mohurs of the two tanks should now be extracted, with which alone you will be able to conduct the wars in all quarters simultaneously by maintaining a large army of sepoys and officers. Akbar Padshah was very prodigal in expenses. We have searched in the treasury and have found there only seven crores of rupees, besides one more crore representing your own earning. With these eight crores of rupees it will be difficult to carry on the campaign in all the theatres of war at the same time."

Jahangir Padshah then replied, "It will bring disgrace to my father if the money from the tanks be raised and spent. People will say Akbar Padshah was bankrupt as his son had to carry on his Padshahship with the help of ancestral wealth. This report will gladden the hearts of our enemies."

41. *Proposal for the invasion of Gaur.*—The Wazir then said, "Let the campaign against foreign enemies be postponed for the present; specially because the Rajas and Padshahs of those territories live at a considerable distance from us. At present there is Hussain Shah Padshah of Gaur, a highly refractory chief. Kiledar Khan Nawab of Baranasi and the Zemindars and Rajas are also of a hostile disposition. They are not very far from Delhi. After their subjugation you should take up the subjugation of Hussain-âbdâl, Piran-Maluk and others. Bengal is an extensive territory where you will acquire a vast amount of wealth and property, with which you will be able to subdue other countries. Besides, in a dish of rice, one can eat up the whole pile without burning his fingers if he commences from the four corners. If, in a hurry he thrusts his hand right into the very middle of the platter, he will only scald his fingers and his tongue. There is Mândhâtâ, Raja of Amber, a commander of 8,000, whom

you have deputed against the countries of the Sultans, which he has accordingly invaded and subdued by this time. Summon him back, and despatch him to the war against Hussain Shah, who has impregnable forts and garrisons. None but Mândhâtâ will be able to subjugate him."

42. *Man Singha starts on his expedition.*—The Emperor agreed to the proposal of the two Wazirs, summoned Mândhâtâ from his campaign, honoured and rewarded him with rich presents, and despatched him to the Gaur war. Mândhâtâ first visited his own principality of Amber where he collected the Rajputs to whom he said, "My kinsmen who are deputed to the wars under the orders of the Padshah do not get any time to build up their strongholds; and it transpires, that for doing so, they will have to wait for a period of time intervening the planting of a mango sapling and the enjoyment of its fruits. He is afraid lest, in a period of recess, I construct my forts and assume independence. I am despatched to all the wars, and I do not get any time to rest; my soldiers are harassed and they curse me."

Then Raja Mândhâtâ, marched to Bengal, at the head of an army consisting of 70,000 imperial soldiers, 22 Omrâos of senior and junior ranks, his own contingency of 20,000 Rajput warriors, as well as his brothers and nephews. He paid his respects to the image of Kesavrâi Gosâin at Mathurâ where he arranged for the construction of a temple; he also ordered the erection of a brick-house at Brindâban for the shelter of the monkeys. He performed Srâddha at Gayâ, after which he reached Benares.

43. *Subjugation of Benares.*—Mândhâtâ despatched

two Rajput envoys to Kiledar Khan of Benares with the following message, "You have eaten the salt of Emperor Akbar, but you have turned your face against his son Jahangir Padsahah, a monarch of great prowess and valour. You will not know any peace in your life here and hereafter. If you desire your welfare, come and offer your submission to me, and I will protect you in the hands of the Padshah. If not, remember you are but the husk of corn before my army."

On the receipt of this letter Kiledar Khan thought within himself. "It will be disastrous if I court the friendship of Mândhâtâ, the Padshah will surely kill me. And if I flee I will not be able to escape. Mândhâtâ has come with an army befitting a Padshah. Under these circumstances, death in fighting is preferable." He did not send any reply: on the other hand the two messengers were turned out with blows and the letter torn to pieces.

The two messengers cried out, "The Musalmans dare to turn us out with blows! We shall prove the mettle of Rajputs." During the scuffle the Ukils killed a number of nobles and also rushed towards the Nawab with a view to kill him; but they were inflicted with spear wounds of which they died. On receiving report of this tragedy, Mândhâtâ became furiously incensed, and despatched Thâkur Amar Singha, Thâkur Kesor Singh, Thâkur Rahirâman and five Nawabs. They marched towards the fort, and their troops surrounded it on all sides.

Kiledar Khan then collected seven thousand sepoys with whose help he waged a furious battle with the invaders. The Nawabs said to the three Thakurs, "Ask Mândhâtâ to send us some muskets like those of

Kiledar Khan, we have too many big guns. We shall gain victory if we fight with small guns." The three Thâkurs replied—" We have a numerous army, and it may be possible to achieve victory with the help of muskets. But such a fighting will be uncustomary and unjust. Fighting with elephants and horses will be advisable."

A battle then ensued between the two forces. The Nawab lost a large number of his soldiers. Thâkur Kesor Singh fought with Nawab Kiledar Khan on horseback for a considerable time. Kesor Singh killed the Nawab by piercing him with a spear. His two sons were killed by gun-shots. The children and dependants as well as the belongings of the Nawab were despatched to Delhi. The remnant of his forces surrendered to Mândhâtâ who enlisted them in his army. The general after creating confidence in the hearts of the people of Benares, appointed a Nawab as Subha of the place, after which he marched against Hussain Khan.

44. *The fortifications of Gaur.*—Mândhâtâ then reached the territory of Sobhâchând Thakur, situated on the east of Muger. Mândhâtâ had married the daughter of the Raja of Jaintapur which had been renamed by the Bangals as Adamâbâd. As a mark of this relationship Raja Barish-sâl came with precious presents and submitted to Mândhâtâ. Mândhâtâ honoured the Raja with presents and said, " As commanded by the Emperor, I have come to subugate Gaur. How can I successfully attack its forts? What is the number of strongholds in Gaur? How impregnable are the forts? What is the strength of the army?" Raja Barish-sâl replied,—" One will be amazed at the splendour of the soldiers

and their arms and weapons. The forts are made of stone and brick and are extremely insurmountable. There are three passages leading to the fortifications ; one runs along the entrance of the fort, this is one path leading to the first fort ; there is another on the left by the route through Sikarpur ; there is a third way on the right through Purâ-Perganâh which will lead you to another fort. The stronghold of Hussain Shah can be reached after crossing these three fortfications. There is a Zemindar at Dacca named Ise Khan Masandali. He is a very influential potentate and poses as the Padshah of Bengal. I can also arrange his submission to you."

Raja Mândhâtâ then despatched Nawab Pardal Khân with eight thousand sepoys and camp-followers by the Sikarpur route. Nawab Ayâz Beg and Uzbeg proceeded by the route through Purâ-Perganâh, in the company of twelve thousand sepoys, and Thakur Bitholdas and the son of Raja Barish-sâl. The general Raja Mândhâtâ with Raja Barish-sâl marched by the middle route with all his army.

45. *Message to Ise Khan Masandali.*—Then letters were despatched to the Zemindar Ise Khan Masandali[69] by the followers of Raja Barish-sâl's son, one from Raja Mândhâtâ through the retainers of Ayâz Beg, another from Raja Barish-sâl himself through Thakur Bitholdas. The message ran as follows : "We have come to fight against Hussain Shah Padshah ; and you should come and join us."

Raja Barish-sâl wrote, "As there has been long friendship between yourself and me, I have spoken well of you to Raja Mândhâtâ. The Raja is a great warrior, and has subdued many countries. You should come and be friends with us, otherwise you will be subjected to misery in future."

46. *Ise Khan's reply.*—Ise-Khan then sent an Ukil with a reply, as well as precious gifts. " I a ma Zemindar, and hence unconcerned with wars. For the present please accept my friendship conveyed through this note. On Raja Mândhâtâ's arrival at Dacca, I will offer my submission in person." He wrote to Barishthasâl, " If I meet the Raja personally now, I shall also be commanded to take up arms, which is a bad thing for the future. We are Zemindars, and war-complications are not safe for us."

Mândhâtâ permitted the messengers of Ise Khan Masandali to depart after having bestowed on them rich presents, and asked them to send with Ayâz Beg and Bitholdas men who were acquainted with the routes and interiors. The request was accordingly communicated to Ise Khan Masandali by his messengers. He despatched large quantities of rice, pulse, mûg for Ayâz Beg and Bitholdas, as well as a man who was versed in the knowledge of the routes and defiles.

47. *Man Singha's ultimatum to Hussain Shah.*—Proceeding by the central route Raja Mândhâtâ sent a Wakil to Hussain Shah of Gaur with the following message, " Your forefathers were on friendly terms with the Emperors of Delhi[70]. Now, what pride has prompted you to turn your back against the Emperor Jahangir? Specially I am Mândhâtâ, Raja of Amber. I have borne in my armpit dozens of Padshahs like yourself; I have caused the death of many, while others have been released through me. So you should come

and offer your submission to me. Our family has never been known to have harmed anybody: still if any one persists in being unfriendly I shall certainly destroy and exterminate him."

Hussain Shah despatched the following reply, "Jahangir is the Padshah of Delhi, and so am I of Gaur. There was friendly interchange of embassies before. He had discontinued sending men, and so have I. Mândhâtâ is only an Omrâo; why should I, a Padshah, pay my homage to him? What touch of genius has led him to pen such a letter? If he has come for war, let him come." The letter of Mândhâtâ was torn to pieces and his envoy expelled. On this Raja Mândhâtâ rushed to the attack of the advance fortifications; by mere display of valour he caused the soldiers of the garrison to flee back to Hussain Shah.

48. *First encounters.*—There were battles at the forts situated on the way through Purâ-Perganah by which Ayâz Beg and Bitholdas had marched. There were severe massacres at these encounters, and many soldiers of the garrisons of Gaur were killed. Then the soldiers of Ayâz Beg and Bitholdas riding on Tâzi and Sujarnis ponies scaled the forts and took possession of them. The remnant of the garrisons made good their escape and joined Hussain Shah Padshah. The soldiers at the forts situated on the Sikarpur route, through which Nawab Pardal Khan had marched, strenuously opposed the attack of the imperialists for three days, after which they also took to their heels. Pardal Khan encamped on the northern side, well prepared to face the attack of the enemy; Ayâz Beg

and Bitholdas halted on the east, while Raja Mândhâta stood in readiness on the western side. The artillery were posted as follows : rows of cannon on the front, then of muskets, and *chandravans* and *rai-babs*, then the sepoys and spearmen, by which they encompassed the enemy on all sides. Hussain Shah in person stood in front of the forces of Raja Mândhâtâ ; while his son Jalal Hussain was posted in front of the army of Pardal Khan ; and his nephew Paris Muhammad against Ayâz Beg and Bitholdas. Sporadic encounters, lasting for two or four days, continued for six months.

49. *Hussain Shah seeks the support of Bengal chiefs.*—Hussain Shah Padshah sent the following message to Ise Khan Masandali, to the Zemindar of Sala, to the Raja of Jharkhanda, to the Raja of Morung on the north, to the Raja of Cooch-Behar and Raja Raghunâth : "From ancient times Gaur and Delhi have been ruled by separate Padshahs. It is unjust on the part of Jahangir Padshah to despatch Mândhâtâ. The imperialists have besieged Gaur for six months in order to occupy it, blocking the passage of our traders and retainers, for which my subjects are in great distress for food. So I want to attack the intruders by issuing out of our garrisons. You should all support me in the project. We shall fight from the front, and you should march by the three routes and kill the imperialists, with the object of repulsing and driving away Mândhâtâ. Otherwise, having attacked me to-day he will proceed to attack you the next day."

To this Ise Khan Masandali replied, "I am a Zemindar to whom wars are not proper. Whoever may wield the sovereign power I am his subject. It is befitting for you Padshahs to engage in mutual conflicts." The Raja of Jharkhanda and other Rajas deputed messengers to say, "All right, we shall fight from the rear."

50. *Victory of Raja Man Singha.*—On the receipt of these assurances, the forces of Hussain Shah came out of the fortifications on the three sides and fell upon the imsperialists. A furious contest ensued. Hussain Shah lost a large number of his soldiers who were killed by the cannon-shots of Mândhâtâ. War-elephants armed with huge iron clubs rushed at the soldiers and destroyed many of them. Soldiers were also killed with *chandravans* and *dabas*. Then ensued a terrible fight on horseback attended by heavy massacres and losses on both sides. Neither did the imperialists nor did the troops of Hussain Shah prefer to retreat from the fight. Raghunâth Raja, the Cooch-Behar Raja and others who promised to fight from behind did not turn up, saying, "Mândhâtâ is a great Raja. It will be disastrous to us if we fight with him and thereby assume the designation of rebels."

In the evening engagement Hussain Shah fought mounting on an elephant. Thakur Chandravâl, uncle of Mândhâtâ, who was riding on a Sujarnis pony, whipped his steed and spurred him on. The horse following the hint lifted its two legs and placed them on the forehead of the elephant. Thakur Chandravâl then struck Hussain Shah with his spear, and threw him down, and thus perished the Padshah of Gaur. Thakur Dipsing riding on horseback severed the head of the elephant, which died. The garrisons on the north were also defeated. His son perished in the battle. The army on the eastern route were vanquished. The nephew of Hussain Shah fled. Raja Mândhâtâ won victory in the battle.

Hussain Shah's wives and children fled. After collecting the belongings of Hussain Shah, Mândhâtâ made an inventory of the articles seized, and after sealing them properly, he submitted his waqâyâ to Delhi. He then retired to Dacca. Ise Khan Masandali came and submitted his homage to Mândhâtâ. Raja Raghunâth, and the Raja of Cooch-Behar as well as other chiefs paid tributes to the Padshah and established friendly terms with Mândhâtâ, who renamed Dacca as *Jahangirnagar*, and appointed Ise Khan Masandali as Zemindar, to whom he made suitable presents. Mândhâtâ then returned to Delhi.

51. *The recital of Markandeya-Chandi.*—On his way Mândhâtâ saw Brahmans reading the *Chandi* on the bank of the Ganges.

The Raja enquired,—" What is this book that you are reading ? "

Brahmans—" It is *Chandi*, a portion of the *Markandeya Purana.*"

Mândhâtâ,—"What is the result of the recital of this book ? "

Brahmans,—" The man who hears the recital of three rounds of *Chandi* goes to Kailâsa or heaven. If it is recited more, the result is unmentionable."

Mândhâtâ—" Then please, recite three rounds of the book in my name."

Saying thus, the Raja offered to the priests a reward of one thousand rupees. During his march, the Rajas who resided near about interviewed Mândhâtâ with presents for himself and the Padshah. Mândhâtâ also offered presents to them, and assured them of his protection and aid.

52. *Man Singha's eulogy of Hussain Shah.*—After subduing Bengal and the territories around it, Raja Mândhâtâ proceeded to Delhi and paid his respects to Emperior Jahangir who bestowed on him high honours and costly presents. He was retained in his former mansab of the rank of a commander of eight thousand, and was given a cash reward of three lakhs of rupees for eating *pan* and *tambul.*

The Padshah then said to Mândhâta, "From your experiences of military operations in diverse localities, tell me of the magnitude of Hussain Shah's heroism as a warrior."

To this Mândhâtâ replied, "Hussain Shah is the greatest of all the soldiers I have encountered in my military engagements in different places. His courage is indomitable, and he fights without caring for his life. He has been killed only through the prowess of the Emperor. He is peerless in heroism."

CHAPTER V

JAHANGIR'S CONQUEST OF SECUNDERABAD

53. *A short sketch of Secunderabad.*—Salutation to Sree-Krishna. On the death of Humayun, Shah Akbar

became the Padshah. On the death of Akbar his son Jahangir assumed the title of Padshah. The Emperor Jahangir after ascending the throne went out on tour to visit places being accompanied by 500,000 soldiers. After some time he marched towards the Deccan. Some *bairagis* or itinerant mendicants wno had travelled in various places said to the Emperor, " There was a king named Sekendar Padshah. He constructed a city and a bazaar named Secunderabad with beautiful stones of diverse colours by engaging lapidarists. That place is fit for the Emperor. The kingdom is now ruled by a monarch named Nasir Muhammad Padshah. He does not pay tribute to anybody, and with regard to the peace and prosperity of his kingdom he is unrivalled."

54. *Jahangir's expedition to Secunderabad.*—On hearing this from the bairâgis the Emperor Jahangir marched towards Secunderabad, and from a distance of three days' journey he despatched a courier to Nasir Muhammad with a letter to the following effect: " The city of Secunderabad which has been built by Sekender Padshah is fit for us, and not for you. So please move to some other quarter. I will establish a camp at Secunderabad. If soft words cannot move you, you will be afflicted with distress when I invade and occupy your territory."

On receiving this letter Nasir Muhammad Padshah sent the following reply, " Jahangir Padshah has become mad. Such a letter should be addressed to bondsmen and slaves. He is a sovereign, and I am also a sovereign. He thinks that I will desert this place out of fear; such an idea should never find quarter in his heart."

55. *The imperialists cross impassable dikes.*—The reply seriously infuriated the Emperor and he proceeded towards the capital of Nasir Muhammad, and came upon a huge ditch which was as wide as a river. It was impossible to cross the ditch there being no place to moor the boats. Being amazed at the sight of the ditch, the Emperor said to some of his swift horsemen, "Let the horses first attempt to cross the moat being fitted with howdah-like seats, and they will be followed by Potla, Suluf, and Batel boats carrying soldiers who will attack the hostile fort." In obedience to the command of the Emperor, horses harnessed with seats were made to swim over the ditch. Crocodiles and sea-horses had been let loose in the ditch, and they seized and devoured many of the horses and soldiers of the Emperor, and dragged down others beneath the waters. The Padshah seeing their sad plight asked the Wazir of the reason of the disappearance of the soldiers under water, to which the minister replied that they were eaten up by the sea-monsters roaming about in the ditch.

The Padshah enquired of the means by which the dike could be crossed, and Sabre Khan Uzir replied, "There are two huge cannon at Delhi, named *Killa-shikist* and *Koch-shekan*. Let us fetch them from Delhi, and place the guns on the sides of the ditch on a mound constructed at a higher level than the hostile fort. If we fire the two guns towards the rampart of Nasir Muhammad by loading them with stone-balls, his fort will be destroyed, his soldiers killed, and on hearing the roar of the guns the crocodiles and sea-monsters will disperse; then our men will be able to cross the ditch safely."

In accordance with the suggestion of the Wazir, the two big guns were brought from Delhi and mounted on a mound higher than the elevation of the hostile fort. They were loaded with stone-balls and splinters of bricks and potteries, and then fired. The men and soldiers of the enemy's camp were blown off. The guns roared with a terrific blast which rent the earth into chasms, broke down the trees and produced waves on the waters. Many of the alligators and sea-horses perished, while the rest dipped below the waters. The soldiers of Jahangir Padshah now crossed the ditch without any difficulty, and attacked and occupied the fort.

56. *Jahangir establishes a court at Secunderabad.*— Then King Nasir Muhammad retreated with the remnant of his army to another fort, and remained in preparedness for a contest. Jahangir after occupying the first fort marched against the next, in the precincts of which he secretly laid powder mines and covered them with grass. During the darkness of the night Nasir Muhammad issued out of his fort with an army intending to inflict a surprise attack on the Emperor's camp. Jahangir also came out and set fire to the mines. The soldiers of Nasir Muhammad were burnt to death. Being victorious in war the Emperor captured the fort of Nasir Muhammad and occupied the throne of Secunderabad. He then gave suitable presents to all

the nobles there, including the revenue officials, such as Chaudhuris and Pâtwaris, and firmly established his suzerainty at Secunderabad. The Emperor also appointed a Court there with Sher Khan Bahadur Amir-ul-Omrâo, a commander of seven thousand, at the head of the following Nawabs: Hasan Khan, Dasil Khan, Sarif Khan, Latif Khan, Yusuf Khan Sipar-salâh. He also established a garrison there with eight thousand soldiers, having the usual quota of Ek-hazaris, Do-hazaris and Tin-hazaris. The total strength of the imperial detachment left at Secunderabad, including the seven thousand soldiers of Amir-ul-Omrâo Sher Khan Bahadur came up to 15,000. The Emperor then returned to his capital Delhi.

CHAPTER VI

Conquest of Secunderabad by Siliman Padshah.

57. *Description of Secunderabad.*—Salutation to Sree-Krishna. There was a vast wilderness in the midst of the sea covered with dense forests. Sekendar Padshah who was formerly in the country of Irân, went and settled there, from which he earned an income of rupees forty lakhs and fifty thousand. He named that country Secunderabad. After living in that place for some time Sekendar Padshah came back to his throne at Irân, leaving Muhammad Galib Khan Nawab, a commander of 9,000, in charge of Secunderabad measured 220 *kos* in length, and 103 in breadth. The town was built with stone and brick

and renamed Hirânagar or the city of diamonds. It was situated at a distance of three months' journey from Delhi. In the shops were sold pearls, corals, rubies, emeralds and other precious articles. Aquatic horses came out of the sea in winter to bask on the sands. Men used to capture and tame them. They used to be called *Dariai-ghoras* or sea-horses, and their price ranged from rupees 1,000 to rupees 1,500 each. The pigs of that country were of the size of horses, their hoofs and feet being like those of horses. All the inhabitants there are Musalmans, there being no Hindusthani person there. People lived on maize and eggs of China ducks. There was no paddy or rice. It could be had only when some merchants from this part placed it on the market; its price used to be rupees three or four per seer.

58. *Siliman Padshah intends to conquer Secunderabad.*—There was a port named Faranga, where lived Siliman Padshah. One day the Padshah said to his Wazir: "Secunderabad is a beautiful place, fit for the residence of a Padshah. There is a Nawab there named Muhammad Galib. It is reported that Sakendar Padshah is now dead. So I intend to attack and occupy Secunderabad. What means do you suggest?"

The Wazir replied: "That country can be conquered only by the most dexterous expedients. It was formerly a forest in the midst of the sea, full 220 *kos* in length and 103 *kos* in breadth. Sekendar Padshah had brought men from all quarters and settled them there. It has an army of 60,000 soldiers, who use Turki, Tâzi, Sujarnis, Arbi and Dariâi ponies. The kingdom is surrounded on all sides by sea-water. Its three sides can be traversed by boat in one-and-a-half *prahar* and ten *dandas*. We have the sea on one side, where we have expert soldiers trained in the art of fighting by boats, such as Batel [Patil], Suluf [Salb] and other kinds of war-boats. The country has four forts on the east, west, north and south, all made of bricks and stones. It has, besides, a rampart of trees, which have been planted close to each other, so that they have now assumed the shape of a compact wall, the trunks touching one another. There is another rampart of thorny bamboos whose trunks have also become compact. There is besides an encompassing ditch in the shape of a circle studded with floating batteries. There is also the wall of the sea. In the heart of the kingdom is situated the capital of the Padshah, which has walls and forts made of stone and brick. Big cannon resembling the trunks of plantain trees have been mounted all round the wall at intervals of twenty-five cubits. Hence the place is very impregnable and dangerous. It can be conquered only by the employment of diplomacy and tact. The kingdom is so invincible that no one has been able to conquer it. You will not also succeed in occupying it unless you take recourse to diplomatic stratagems."

59. *Siliman Padshah's plan to conquer Secunderabad.*—Siliman Padshah convened a meeting of his counsellors and said, "I want to invade and conquer Secunderabad. Do confer, and let me know the means by which we shall be able to achieve success." The ministers assembled came to the following conclusion after a

prolonged deliberation: "Secunderabad can never be conquered by open warfare. Let five hundred of our most clever and trustworthy soldiers proceed to Secunderabad and live there in the service of the Nawab. They should study the strength and position of the soldiers, and forts and other military resources of the place. Let some of our merchants proceed there with ships loaded with merchandise, and let them live there, being engaged in peaceful commercial pursuits. Let a damsel in disguise be palmed off to the Nawab as the grand-daughter of the Padshah, with instructions to kill the Nawab somehow or other. Then fight, and occupy his territory."

60. *Siliman Padshah's diplomatic proposal.*—After hearing this device suggested by the Wazir and other ministers, Siliman Padshah despatched the following message to Muhammad Galib Khan, Nawab of Secunderabad:—

"We live in the country known as Farang, and Muhammad Galib Khan lives at Secunderabad, almost in our neighbourhood. We are designated as Padshahs and he as Nawab, this is the only difference between us. On the other hand he has a larger assortment of war-materials and weapons. I have no influential friend and ally. If the Nawab has no objection I wish to establish friendly relations with him. This has been necessitated by the report that the Pathans are contemplating to invade his territories as well as mine. I will stand by him when his kingdom is overrun by the enemy, and he will do so when my kingdom confronts such an unfortunate plight."

The messengers of Siliman Padshah proceeded to Secunderabad and handed over the letter to the Nawab who became highly delighted, and honoured the ambassadors with rich presents. The Nawab presented his daughter named Gul-Makhmal to the son of Siliman Padshah with a dowry of precious robes and articles.

61. *Nawab Galib Khan's reply.*—He sent her with his envoys who also carried the following message to Siliman Padshah :—

" I am extermely delighted to receive your message. You have written about the establishment of cordial relations between the two states. This desire has been cherished by me for a long time. I wish the friendship which existed before between Saiyid Padshah and Arbal Khan Padshah should now be re-established between you and me. You are far from the truth when you assert that there is no difference between a Nawab and a Padshah. A horse is thin and slender in body, yet it flits in war witn the speed of hurricanes ; the Telengi bullock is of enormous bulk and handsome features, but can it stand comparison to a horse ? The horse is a horse and the ox is an ox. How do you expect that you and I will be each other's peer ? "

Siliman Padshah became extremely delighted on the receipt of this reply accompanied by the gift of the Nawab's daughter. She was admitted and kept with due honour and dignity. The Padshah in his turn sent with his messengers one Lolin, very handsome and ingenious in all things, who was palmed off as the Padshah's niece intended for the Nawab, who believed her to be really a beautiful and clever scholar and married her.

62. *Farangi spies at Secunderabad.*—The Padshah then deputed five hundred soldiers to live in disguise. They went to the advance fort of Secunderabad, and informed the inmates that they had come to see the Nawab with the intention of employment in his territory as underlings. The soldiers living at the forts informed the Nawab accordingly who invited the supplicants to his presence. The soldiers were all young men, and properly trained in the wielding of arms and weapons. As they looked smart and handsome, the Nawab employed them as servants on good pay. They soon won the confidence of their master.

After this the Padshah sent five ships loaded with valuable merchandise for carrying on trade. The captain of the boats presented precious articles to the Nawab and earned his estimation, who then permitted the merchants to trade in his dominions. The Padshah also prepared a fleet of Jalia, Batel and Suluf boats and equipped them with arms of war. The Jalia boats were harnessed with quilts of straw looking like deer-skins; they were then stuffed with fish-scales and attached to the sides of the boats, leaving sufficient space for the oarsmen to ply the vessels. The Batel boats were constructed to accommodate elephants and horses.

63. *Murder of Nawab Galib Khan.*—Then Lolin, who was presented to the Nawab, spread a sheet of poison-cloth on the body of the Nawab at the time of sleep. The Nawab died. The miscreant then escaped early next morning and took shelter in the ships of the

merchants. The news was communicated to Siliman Padshah, who came post-haste in boats attended by soldiers. The soldiers of the advance fort came to inform the Nawab, but they found that the Nawab had already breathed his last. The brothers and sons of the Nawab, hearing the report, asked the informants not to allow the invaders to proceed.

64. *Siliman Padshah occupies Secunderabad.*—There was hard fighting between the forces of the Nawab and of the Padshah. First, there was an engagement on boats. The soldiers of the Nawab hurled arrows and gun-shots, but they produced no effect as they were small, and struck only the quilts stuffed with the scales of fish. The oarsmen pursued the Nawab's boats and came near them. Many soldiers of the Nawab perished by the arrows and bullets of the Padshah. The Nawab's army saw that arrows and bullets could not retard the advance of the enemy; and this time they met the latter with long spears as the enemy approached the precincts of the fort. There was severe fighting attended by heavy casualties on both sides, but neither of the belligerent forces turned their face.

When Siliman Padshah discovered that the fort could not be captured though he had fought in so many ways, he deputed some reliable emissaries to instruct his own soldiers and the merchants of the ships and boats as follows: "This is the opportune moment, and they should act in whatever way they think proper." On this, the five hundred Farangi sepoys who had accepted service under the Nawab, acting in concert with the men of the boats, set fire to all the places, including the bazaar and the fort, and cut down the enemy on horseback. They created a confusion inside the fort, where also they massacred a large number of the Nawab's men. The soldiers posted at the fort fled of their own accord.

Then the Padshah, winning a victory in the naval fight, got on land and conquered all the forts. The kinsmen of the Nawab all perished in the battle. Siliman established his court at Secunderabad and lived there, protecting the subjects. From that time till now [say 1682 A.D.] Secunderabad has continued to be the territory of Siliman Padshah. Some time afterwards his son was placed in charge of the Faranga country.

65. *Muhammad Ali, the narrator.*—From this territory of Siliman Padshah, Delhi is situated at a distance of three months' journey. Muhammad Ali is a Mogul of that place.[71] He is a very great scholar,[72] and knows all the *loghats* or languages, Arabic and Persian. He taught the sons of Mansur Khan, and for this he received an honorarium of full rupees one hundred per month. The above incidents have been taken from his mouth.

CHAPTER VII

Jai Singha's subjugation of Eastern India.

66.—*A slave sits on the throne of Delhi.*—Salutation to Sree-Krishna. Jahangir Padshah of Delhi had four sons, Shah Jâhân, Shah Alâgzâhâ, Sultan Khuram and Muhammad Jâhân. Shah Jâhân became the Padshah of Delhi by killing two of his brothers by a stratagem. Muhammad Jâhân fled in the guise of a faquir, and on the death of the Turki Padshah in an island, he married the widowed queen and became Padshah of that kingdom. Turki ponies breed in the kingdom of the Turki Padshah.

Shah Jâhân sat on the throne of Delhi. Once a slave of Nawab Sââdullâ Khan, named Muhammad Sayid, visited the Padshah's court as an attendant of the Nawab. The slave possessed marks of a future Padshah, which were noticed by the Emperor, who said to the Nawab, "Give me your slave Muhammad Sayid, and I will give you two slaves in return." To this the Nawab replied, "I am a slave of Your Majesty; what objection can a slave have?"

The Nawab returned to his residence with the slave to whom he said, "The Padshah wants you as you are endowed with the marks of a sovereign. He will kill you. Make good your escape by some means or other." The slave said, "If I flee, the Emperor may cause you some harm." The Nawab replied. "Whatever may befall me, you should save yourself anyhow." The slave fled accordingly and took shelter with Shah Bhramarâ, literally the prince of vagrants.

Shah Bhramarâ said, "Who are you? Why have you come here?" The slave replied, "Shah Jahân intends to put me to death as I have the marks of a sovereign. So I have fled and sought your protection."

The faquir said, "I will give you three crores of rupees. Go and become a Padshah." The slave, with the help of this money, raised and maintained an army, and encountered Shah Jahân Padshah in a terrible contest. Shah Jahân, being defeated, escaped to Rum and took shelter with the Padshah of that kingdon.

When Muhammad Sayid Golam ascended the throne, Shah Bhramarâ conferred on him the name of Shah Muhammad. The faquir said that the new monarch had only three years more to live and not an hour more. Having heard this prophecy of the faquir, the usurper wrote to Shah Jahân Padshah at Rum, " Come back and become Padshah. I am renouncing the throne." The Padshah of Rum gave to Shah Jahân a number of soldiers and attendants who re-installed him on the throne. The slave of the Nawab, after renouncing the throne, said with prayers and apologies, " I am a slave of your slave. I fled in fear of you, and became eventually the Padshah. The enjoyment of a Padshahship is not meant for me; the Padshahship of your kingdom befits you alone." Shah Jahân Padshah came back to Delhi. The slave of the Nawab died, and the Emperor appointed his son a commander of 5,000.

67. *Shah Jahan's visit to Jai Singha's capital Amber.*— Seeing the influence and power of Raja Jai Singha, the Emperor Shah Jahân thought within himself, " How shall I kill Jai Singha? If I can get rid of him the kingdom of Amber will fall into my hands, and my sovereignty will also be free from danger. Otherwise he may do me mischief some day. So let me visit his state and examine its strength and resources."

Thus thinking, the Emperor said to the Raja one day at Am-Khas, " Well, let me confer on you the honour of a visit to your state."

The Raja replied, " Grant me leave for a week."

The Padshah said, " Yes, all right, you may go."

The Raja then proceeded to his capital and conferred with his ministers and relatives, saying, " The Padshah, intending to invade and occupy our kingdom, is coming to examine its resources on the pretext of conferring a favour."

The Rajput counsellors replied. " Let the Padshah come, we shall seize his person and imprison him. and all the Rajput chiefs united will appoint you Padshah instead."

Jai Singha said. " It was never done by our family. Though the Padshah may do us wrong, being misguided, we should never act in a hostile manner as proposed. We have never been unfaithful to the Padshahs of Delhi."

The Raja then made arrangements for numerous varieties of food for the Emperor, and erected a raised platform for the Padshah, befitting the Emperor's position and dignity. The Raja then informed the Emperor of his readiness to receive him, and Shah Jâhân went to Amber as promised before.

Raja Jai Singha posted at regular intervals along the routes extending over a distance of eight *prahars'* journey, lengthwise and breadthwise as far as the eyes could see, soldiers attired in uniforms and ornaments of gold and silver and equipped with the five weapons, spears, swords and shields, jamdar, guns and arrows and bows, as well as horses and elephants harnessed with saddles and ornaments of gold and silver. The roofs and walls of the houses situated in the city and the market-place were covered with trappings of gold and silver, giving the appearance of continuous relays of ants. Along the route, at the interval of a distance of one *danda*, were established outposts with elephants, horses and sepoys and the Raja commanded that at every such station soldiers should be posted on the advent of the Emperor, as he in his travels was accompanied only by a limited number of soldiers.

On the approach of the Padshah, men were placed at the chowkis or stations. The Emperor was dismayed at the sight of the splendour and pomp of arms and weapons, of elephants. horses and sepoys.

On reaching Amber the Padshah turned back and saw that men were being posted at the chowkis or outposts. Wherever he turned his eyes he saw only spears and weapons.[73] The Emperor was seized with fear and said to the Wazir, "The Rajputs have by a stratagem managed to capture me, and there is no remedy. Besides they have placed soldiers at the chowkis." The Raja received the Padshah with great hospitality, and pleased him with the presents of precious articles. The Emperor returned, having pleased all the nobles of the Raja by making gifts of numerous presents.

68. *Jai Singha deputed to Eastern India.*—During the confusion that followed the flight of Shah Jahân Padshah, and the occupation of the throne of Delhi by the Nawab's bondsman, there was anarchy in Bengal. The Raja of Orissa occupied the imperial fort by ousting therefrom the Mogul Nawab. The fort of Rajmahal was attacked and captured by Raja Chandrabhâl. The Raja of Morung seized the fort and established his independence at

Morung. Cooch-Behar also asserted its independence, and the Rajas of Dacca, Chittagong, Sylhet, Gauhati and Arrakan committed ravages in the country and ruled in their own names. On receiving reports of the above, Shah Jahân said to Jai Singha, "Bengal has always been subdued by your family. So you should proceed there."

The Raja said, "All right, I will go. Please issue orders for supplying me nine Nawabs, five of our Rajput Rajas, and a few cannon." The Raja was given what he wanted, and despatched to Bengal.

69. *Cooch-Behar's contribution to Nao-roza expenses.*— Jai Singha halted at Patna, and sent messengers to the rulers of the nine principalities, Dacca, etc., with letters to the following effect, "Have you heard of the might of the Emperor Shah Jahân? Have you also heard the rattling of my invincible sword as well as that of Mândhâtâ? If you have, then come promptly and become friends with us, or otherwise be prepared for war."

On receiving this message the Raja of Cooch-Behar brought valuable presents to the Emperor and Jai Singha, and Nawab Galir Beg was despatched to settle the boundaries of Bengal and Cooch-Behar.

The river Ghâghât was fixed as the boundary between the two territories. Rangpur became the thana of Cooch-Behar on this side of the river, and the imperial outpost was established at Tâjhât on the other bank and placed in charge of Nawab Galir Beg. An ambassador of Cooch-Behar was to remain at Dacca, and it was stipulated that he should hand over to the Nawab of

Dacca one lakh of rupees as *selami* for presentation to the Padshah during the Nao-rozâ festival.

70. *Nao-roza festivities.*—What is Nao-rozâ? The Padshah amuses himself for nine days, from the seventh day of the white moon to the full moon day in the month of Kartick. The wives of the Nawabs, and Mansabdars, the begums of the merchant-princes, as as well as of other commercial magnates, are to go to the inner apartments of the Padshah's palace. In the interior, a place is nicely constructed with marble stones. There are tanks, each of which is covered on all its four sides with flowers of all hues and colours, crimson, yellow, white and black, including the lotus and the lily, and on the water float ducks, herons, water-crows, chakravakas or ruddy sheldrakes, all made artificially of the eight metals. The birds are tied to strings by which their movements are regulated. Crackers, rockets, squibs, and scintillators, all made of explosives, are placed in a gala fashion on the site near about the water. Rose-water, *attar* and *argaza* waters are sprinkled on the decorated floor. The ladies attractively decorate the stalls where they display their articles for sale. Gorgeous white canopies are pitched at intervals. Mainas, parrots, bulbuls, shrikes, magpies, swallow-tails, all tamed at home, pour forth their melodious strain. The stall-owners and shopkeepers as well as the wives of the merchant-princes, all dressed in their finest apparel and ornaments, display their wares consisting of diamonds, pearls, topazes, rubies, coral beads and other articles of gold and silver. The ladies of the Padsah's Begum-mahal and other ladies of the palace, as well as the

wives of the Nawabs and Mansabdars in their gorgeous dresses and ornaments purchase articles offered for sale. The Emperor accompanied by music flowing from rubab, tambourines, syrangis, flutes, timbals, brazen pipes, setaras, violins, trumpets, and other instruments proceeds to the place where the wives of the nobles and merchants are selling their articles. The Emperor indulges in mirthful laughter and jokes when he higgles about the price of the articles he intends to purchase. The articles are to be purchased at the price demanded by the amiable sellers. No man is admitted into the place; of men only the Padshah has access. In this way the sales and purchases continue for nine days. The Padshah spends nine lakhs of rupees during the Nao-rozâ. The stipulation with Cooch-Behar was to the effect that it would contribute a sum of rupees one lakh every year towards the expenses of the Nao-rozâ. Masim Khan of Bengal came and offered his submission of his own accord.

71. *Subjugation of Morung.*—The Raja of Morung and other chieftains prepared themselves for war. Raja Jai Singha, being indignant, deputed Nawab Kilis Khan with seven thousand soldiers against Morung. The war with the Raja of Morung continued for three months. The Raja could not stand in the fight and he offered his submission. Hawks and kuhis are found in Morung in abundance. The Raja presented to the Padshah ten kuhis, ten hawks and ten murchulis or peacocks' tails; Raja Jai Singha was also given five specimens of each of the above birds as well as other precious articles. Nawab Kilis Khan remained in charge of the fort of Morung.

72. *Subjugation of Nepal.*—The Raja of Nepal surrendered voluntarily. Copper is found in abundance in his territories. The Raja presented to the Padshah ten big caldrons of copper, each capable of holding rice for one hundred men, and one hundred small pitchers; to Jai Singha were given four caldrons and forty small pitchers and other articles. With this the Raja offered his submission.

73. *Subjugation of other territories.*—Nawab Adam Khan was placed in charge of Jahangirnagar, while Nawab Jâhid Beg and Nawab Uzbeg remained at the Châtgâon thânâ. Hostilities ensued with the Maghs. The insurgents were defeated, and some Maghs with their wives and children were removed to Dacca and made to settle there. There is still a place at Dacca called Maghar-bazaar. Chilim Khan was sent to the thânâ at Sylhet, who occupied the place, and captured some Firinghis who were subsequently taken to Dacca, which has got a section still known as Firinghee-bazaar. Raja Naranarayan of Cooch-Behar was at that time the monarch of Kamrupa[74]. He continued to live in friendly terms with Raja Jai Singha.

Raja Jai Singha remained at Patna for some time. Having subdued all the Rajas of the place, he left Nawabs in charge of the various thânâs, after which he proceeded to bathe in the Ganges. Chandrabhâl, the Raja of Rajmahal, came and offered his submission of his own accord, and Jai Singha pardoned him after extracting from him one lakh of rupees. He then distributed large charities in adoration to the Ganges, and constructed a tower at the Mâna-Mardana bathing ghat with stone and brick.

74. *Subjugation of Orissa.*—Jai Singha despatched Jabardust Khan against Oreshâ or Orissa. He failed to capture the fortress, though the hostilities continued for a length of time. In connection with this affair, and with the object of paying a visit to Jagannath, Jai Singha proceeded to Orissa, Raja Subal Singha of the line of Raja Indradyumna, was the king of Orissa. On Jai Singha's reaching Orissa Subal Singha died, as fate would have it, in his bed while asleep. His son Siva Singha succeeded his father. Raja Jai Singha deputed a Wakil to Siva Singha with the message: "A princess of your family was married to our house some time ago. You are my nephew according to the relationship thus established. Both the families have been enjoying mutual friendship and affection to a very great extent. I have come here under the orders of the very-powerful sovereign Shah Jahân Padshah. After subduing Bengal I have come to see Jagannath. So you should arrange for my adoration of the Thakur or image and thus afford an opportunity of knowing each other. If not, be prepared for war. You have done wrong by attacking the imperial thânâs, which has made the Padshah highly indignant towards you."

Having heard this from the Wakil, Siva Singha thought within himself, "My father is dead and my reign has not been properly consolidated. Besides, there exists an old relationship between the family of Jai Singha and ours. Jai Singha is a veteran warrior and he has subdued the whole of Bengal. I do not think I shall be able to successfully oppose him in strength. Under these circumstances submission will be the better course." Thus thinking, Siva Singha marched with his troops to welcome Jai Singha from a distance. He also offered hospitality to the soldiers and followers. Jai Singha worshipped at the shrine of Jagannath. He presented to the image a diamond of the value of one lakh of rupees, a cloth valued at one thousand rupees for fastening on to the standard, and an annual grant of twenty maunds of ghee for burning lamps; he also arranged for the payment of a monthly salary to the man entrusted with the charge of lighting the lamps daily.

75. *The title of Mirza-raja conferred on Jai Singha.*—After establishing friendly terms with the Raja of Orissa, Jai Singha appointed Jabardust Khan Subha of that place. He then halted at Rajmahal from where he submitted a despatch to the Padshah stating all the particulars about Bengal, and the names of the Nawabs posted at the various thânâs. The articles presented by the Rajas were also sent to the Emperor. The Padshah became extremely delighted, and sent some presents to Jai Singha and conferred on him the title of Mirzâ-râjâ. Similarly, presents and titles were also conferred on the other Rajas, Nawabs and Mansabdars. The Padshah wrote to Jai Singha, "The Rajas and Zemindars of Bengal and Orissa are rebellious in their disposition. You should remain at Patna until the thânâs are well consolidated or until I summon you to my presence."

76. *Jai Singha deputed against Kashmir.*—Jai Singha had a *bag* or estate at Patna yielding an income of one lakh of rupees per year, where he constructed a magnificent residence. He also repaired the entrances of the

fort of Muger, and established a market-place named Jai-Singha-pur.

After this the province of Kashmir became rebellious. Jai Singha was summoned from Patna and despatched against Kashmir. These are the details of the events.

CHAPTER VIII

SHAH JAHAN'S INTERVIEW WITH PRITHIVI SHAH

77. *Shah Jahan's longing to see his peer.*—Sitting at the Roz-dewân, Shah Jahân once said to his Wazir, " The Almighty God has blessed me with the Padshahship of Delhi, and has bestowed on me all the things necessary for the pleasure and enjoyment of a mortal. He has not withdrawn from me any favour. Yet my heart longs for seeing a man who is as great as I am, or is greater than myself. The men whom I see around me are all inferior to me in position and power. So you should make an attempt to find out my peer." Being thus commanded by the Emperor, the Wazir, Asaf Khân Khân-Khânâ Sipah-sâlâr said, " With regard to the enquiry made by the Padshah-Hazarat, I am not in a position to give a reply at once. Give me time to investigate into past accounts, and I will place the information in time at the feet of the Emperor."

78. *Search for two equal sovereigns.*—Saying so, the Wazir consulted the records deposited in the archives of

the Padshah, the Wazir and the Kâzi, and gathered the following facts and communicated them to the Emperor. "From the time of the Hindu King Judhisthira to Bahram Shah Padshah, which covered a period of 2954 years, there were 58 sovereigns on the throne of Delhi. During this period we come across synchronous sovereigns of equal strength and position. From the time of the Hindu King Samudrapâl to Pithor Raja, covering a period of 1122 years, 1 month and 28 days, there were 62 sovereigns. From the reign of the first Musalman Padshah to that of Jahangir, during the period of 769 years, 4 months and 15 days, there were 51 sovereigns. The total number of Rajas and Padhshas thus comes up to 113, covering a total period of 1,891 years, 6 months and 13 days. During this period we do not meet any two contemporary Rajas or Padshahs of equal strength and power.

79. *Raja Prithivi Shah of Kandor.*—With regard to the enquiries whether there is any great monarch whose kingdom is conterminous to that of the Padshah of Delhi, the Wazir consulted the ancient records and ascertained the following facts, "The kingdom of Prithivi Shah[75], son of Chandra Raja of Kandor, to the south of Delhi, is contiguous to the kingdom of the Mogul Padshah. His men are more warlike than those of the Delhi Padshah; they are also of a superior *dil* or heart. The rulers of his family eat the powdered grains of burnt pearls. The distance between Delhi and the junction of the two states represents a journey of 35 days, and that between the capital of Prithivi Shah to the same boundary can be covered by a journey of 37 days; and

it is very convenient to go there as there are villages and rivers on the way."

The Wazir submitted the above details to the Padshah in response to the enquiry lodged by His Majesty some time before.

80 *Shah Jahan desires to see Prithivi Shah.*—The Padshah then said to the Wazir, " Arrange to despatch an intelligent Wakil of ours to visit the court of Prithivi Shah Raja with costly presents. Let him say to the Raja, " Shah Jahân Padshah desires to have an interview with you. If you also participate in the same desire then send men to fit up a place at the junction of the two territories." The messenger of Shah Jahân communicated to Prithivi Raja the intention of the Padshah.

Prithivi Shah then replied, " Shah Jahân Padshah of Delhi has expressed his desire to see me; similarly, I also cherish the desire of seeing him." Having said so he deputed a clever Wakil to Shah Jahân Padshah with the following message, " When we see each other I will address him as ' Shah Jahân Padshah, my younger brother,' and he, in his turn should address me as ' Prithivi Shah, my elder brother.' If he agrees to this proposal, his men as well as mine will come and prepare a place on the boundaries of the two kingdoms. Both of us shall be accompanied by a numerous train. A clever man should be entrusted with the task of preparing the venue of our interview so that there may not be any hitch on the occasion."

81. *Meeting of the Padshah and the Raja.*—The two Wakils informed Shah Jahân Padshah. The Padshah

said, "I bind myself to the proposal of Prithivi Shah Raja. I will address him as my elder brother. Asaf Khan Wazir will proceed to prepare the camping ground. The Raja will also send a competent man for the same purpose." Thus saying he despatched a Wakil with precious presents who communicated to Prithivi Shah what Shah Jahân had said. The Raja deputed an efficient Pâtra or noble to prepare the place.

The Pâtra and the Wazir proceeded to the junction of the two territories. A camp was constructed for Prithivi Shah at a distance of one prahar's journey from the boundary, the Wazir also prepared a place for Shah Jahân at the same distance. There was a distance of two prahars on the east as well as on the west. The hollows and pools were filled up. A ditch was excavated at the boundary which resembled a half-moon. On the actual site of meeting between the Raja and the Padshah ditches were constructed at a distance of twenty cubits.

Prithivi Shah and Shah Jahân moved in the month of Agrahâyan and saw each other in Phâlgun. Shah Jahân had marched facing the south, and Prithivi Shah facing the north. Thus coming from both sides the two sovereigns met at the point where the ditch was the narrowest.

82. *Exchange of royal greetings.*—On seeing Shah Jahân, Prithivi Shah said, "I have received the highest pleasure possible for a mortal body."

On seeing Prithivi Shah, Shah Jahân said. "I have been blessed with the sight of a great man and the desire of the human body has been fulfilled."

Prithivi Shah replied, "Does my younger brother Shah Jahân Padshah of Delhi enjoy happiness of heart in all ways ?"

Shah Jahân made the reply, "O my elder brother Prithivi Shah, Khodâ, the great God, has made me Padshah of Delhi ; can anything be more gratifying to the heart than this, except the limitations springing from my birth and race ?

Prithivi Shah said, "You have said well by acknowledging that nothing is more glorious than the Padshahship of Delhi. You should not remember at all the limitations of your birth."

Shah Jahân said. "By seeing and talking with you all the uncleanliness of my heart has been removed."

Prithivi Shah said, "The discrepancy which existed before between my eyes and ears has now disappeared after having a sight of the Padshah of Delhi attended by his army."

Shah Jahân said, "My eyes have been blessed with a great fortune by seeing Prihtvi Shah with his men."

83.* *Duel between two Rajput warriors.*—By seeing each other the two sovereigns feasted their eyes to the fill, and their joy knew no abatement.

Just at that moment a Rajput Raja of Prithivi Shah rushed forward with shield and sword, and he was faced by another Rajput prince of the camp of Shah Jahân. The two warriors then stated their cause to their respective lords, "A Raja and a Padshah are here. We have cherished the desire of attaining paradise by dying in a face-to-face combat. Our pious resolve can be accomplished only if the two sovereigns be pleased to accord the necessary permission." The two monarchs then permitted them, saying; "May your cherished wish be fulfilled." On obtaining the permission solicited the two warriors, armed with shield and sword, rushed to the presence of the sovereigns and their followers. Uttering the name Nârâyana they at the same time inflicted blows on each other with their swords, and the bodies of each fell simultaneously severed into two equal pieces. A piece of fleece-white cloud descended from heaven and covered the lifeless remains of the combatants. After a while the cloud disappeared; and nothing else was visible; but the sound of tinkling bells could only be heard. The people assembled uttered shouts of praise and glory.

84. *Exchange of presents between the sovereigns.*—Prithivi Shah presented to Shah Jahan 1,500 horses in all, including four Irâqi, eight Arbi and twelve Sujarnis ponies. He also presented precious cloths, and pearls and diamonds, as well as other articles worthy of a monarch, amounting to six crores of rupees, besides five crores presented to the Padshah's train.

The Padshah presented to Prithivi Shah four hundred elephants and five hundred horses, and other precious articles amounting to a total of five crores of rupees, in addition to another four crores presented to the members of the Raja's retinue. The two sovereigns then took leave of each other after offering assurances of mutual friendship.

The Pâtra gave to the Wazir, horses including one Irâqi pony, and two Arbi, and articles to the value of one crore and a half of rupees. The Wazir gave to the Pâtra, eighty elephants and articles of the value of one and a half crores of rupees. The other people in the retinue of the two sovereigns also exchanged presents.

The Pâtra and the Wazir were praised by all for controlling the functions without any hitch or misunderstanding though the soldiers and retainers of the two camps were as large as the sea. Here is finished what was said by Gakulpuri.

CHAPTER IX

Sultan Suuja's Expedition to Kandahar

85. *Proposals to conquer Kandahar.*—Salutation to Sree-Rama and Sree-Krishna. On the death of Jahangir Padshah, his son Shah Jahan became Padshah, and sat on the *takt* or throne in an auspicious moment. The events which took place during the first eight years of his reign are recorded in other books; only the events which took place after the lapse of eight years of his reign will be found in this book.

One day, sitting in his court at Dewâni-âm surrounded by his ministers and counsellors, Shah Jahan Padshah put the following question to his Wazir relating to the strength of the Padshah of Khândâr or Kândahâr, "How powerful is that Padshah? What is the strength of his army? How invincible is his fortress?" The Wazir replied. "The fortress of the Padshah of Khândâr is highly impregnable, his soldiers innumerable, and the splendour of his elephants and horses unlimited. But who can be greater than Your Majesty? You can easily attack and conquer the country."

86. *Prince Shuja's expedition against Kandahar.*—According to the decision of the court, one Galiz Khan, an Omrâo commanding 7,000, was despatched as Subha to Khândâr with Muhammad Khan and Zalandar Khan. Galiz Khan proceeded to the spot, and witnessing the impregnable character of the fortress sent a written communication to the Emperor.

The Padshah deputed his son Shah Shuja to Khândâr at the head of an army of 20,000 sepoys commanded by ten haft-hazari, chai-hazari and panch-hazari Omrâos, including Raja Jai Singha. The prince received instructions as follows, —" If Shah Safi, the Padshah of Khândâr, takes the battle against you personally, then you should proceed to the battle yourself.[76] But if he sends another man in his place, you should not go. In the latter case you should despatch Galiz Khan with soldiers, and halt yourself at the thana of Kabul."

With these instructions Shuja was given leave to depart; he was also presented with rich gifts. The following command was issued to the Nawabs in charge of the imperial thanas in the neighbourhood of Khândâr, " You should send to the fort of Khândâr rice, pulse, radish, ghee, sugar and other necessaries to feed the soldiers to enable them to engage themselves in war."

Thus Shah Shuja, the son of the Emperor, went accordingly to Khândâr in the company of a large army. The prince was preceded by an Omrâo at a distance of one prahar's journey while another followed up in the rear at the same distance, while one Nawab accompanied him on the right and another on the left. In this array did the Padshahzada march to Khândâr. When the prince was within a distance of three days' journey, the commander in charge of the advance line of fortifications sent a written report to Shah Safi Padshah about the approach of Prince Shuja.

87. *Shah Safi prepares for war.*—Shah Safi wrote back to the commander of the fort, "You should remain in readiness with soldiers, arms and munitions, and despatch six thousand troops and fall upon the invaders." The commander remained ready for action with his soldiers as instructed by Shah Safi, and deputed six thousand soldiers to attack the imperialists. The soldiers thus despatched were dismayed at the sight of the magnificence of Shuja's army, and came back without any action. The commander of the fort of Khândâr sent information to Shah Safi on the war-array of Prince Shuja, on which Shah Safi thundered at Shah Jahan Padshah. He summoned his counsellors and said, "If Shah Jahan, the Delhi Padshah, had taken the field in person, I would have gone to the battle myself. It will be unbecoming on my part to fight with his son." Thus saying, he despatched to the fort skilful warriors, sirdars, elephants, horses, arms, munitions and other war materials. The two armies stood ready for action near the four fortresses of Khândâr.

88. *The imperialists occupy Kandahar fort.*—From his spies Prince Shuja received intelligence of the resolution of Shah Safi not to take the field in person, and acting according to the instructions of his father, the prince

made presents to Galiz Khan and appointed him commander-in-chief of the whole army, and gave him assurance of reinforcement when necessary. The prince remained at the fort of Kabul, ready for action. There was severe fighting between the two armies lasting for one day and one night and two *prahars*. The imperial troops could not in any way capture the fort. The Khândâr army fought from within the fort, for which they did not sustain heavy casualties on their side, whereas Galiz Khan lost as many as 20,000 soldiers.

Galiz Khan then adopted a novel device. He excavated a big tank at a distance of one prahar's journey from the fort. A tunnel was dug up connecting the tank with the dike encircling the fort. The moat-water was thus drawn through the tunnel towards the tank, resulting in the drying up of the moat, and the filling up of the tank.

Galiz Khan then said to his soldiers, "I will pay at the rate of rupees ten to an old man, eight to a boy, and five to a young man. The ditch should be filled up by each of you throwing one basketful of earth." Being thus commanded, the soldiers threw earth into the ditch and filled it up. Galiz Khan spent twenty lakhs of rupees in carrying out this measure.

Then Khosar Khan, commander of the Khândâr fort, seeing that the moat had been filled up with earth, adopted a counter-device in his turn. He sewed up big cases of rhinoceros skin, stuffed them with powder, placed them in a row on the ditch and then set fire to them. The fire burnt up the ditch which resumed its previous shape. The earth thrown in by the imperial-lists was blown off to unknown quarters. Being unsuccessful in capturing the fort by any means Galiz Khan reported the matter to the Padshah of Delhi. On the receipt of this intelligence the Padshah expressed his admiration for Galiz Khan saying :—" The method adopted by Galiz Khan was excellent ; but the one adopted by Khosar Khan was superior of the two. Praised be the counsellor ! Praised be the commander ! " The Padshah thus showered heaps of praises upon Khosar Khan.

The Emperor advised Galiz Khan to capture the fort by whatever contrivance he might adopt under the circumstances. Galiz Khan then adopted a fresh method : the moat was filled up once more by throwing in plantain trees and the bodies of elephants, horses, camels and buffaloes killed specially for that purpose. Seeing this Khosar Khan as before, stuffed skin bags with powder and set fire to them. What effect could the fire produce on objects which were so damp ? The fire only touched the surface and merely scalded them. With this trick Galiz Khan conquered the fort. After the reduction of the fort, the commander attacked the Padshahi fort, where he fought for a long time without any success. At length an underground passage was dug up as far as the fort, and it was filled with loads of powder. On setting fire to the mines the fort was burnt down ; and earth, elephants, horses, soldiers were all blown up. The imperial troops advanced along the path thus cleared and captured the fortress. Seeing the fall of the two advanced forts, the commander offered his submission to Galiz Khan, who rewarded him with presents. The contest was now transferred to another Padshahi fort. Being unable to capture the same, Galiz Khan excavated a ditch which could be crossed by soldiers on horseback. The imperial troops marched along the ditch and reached the precincts of the fort. The soldiers on horseback stormed the fort and occupied it after an engagement. The booty obtained at the four forts, consisting of elephants, horses, men, cows and other articles were sent to the Padshah at Delhi. Having received the intelligence of victory Shah Jahan despatched rewards of mansabs and presents.

On thc receipt of the presents from the Padshah, Galiz Khan placed four Nawabs in charge of the four forts of Khândâr, and proceeded to meet Shah Shuja. The Prince honoured Galiz Khan with numerous presents and appointed him Subha of Khândâr. He then returned to the presence of the Padshah at Delhi. This is how the fort of Kândahâr was reduced.

CHAPTER X

LETTERS OF THE REIGNS OF JAHANGIR AND SHAH JAHAN

89. *Jahangir's letter to his rebellious son Khurram.*— Emperor Jahangir wrote the following letter to his son Sultan Khurram, afterwards Shah Jahan, when he, having quarrelled with his brothers Parvez and Khusru, wandered about raising the standard of revolt against the authority of his father and Emperor :—

" Sultan Khurram, the captivator of the mind,

like an idol of the eyes, son of an Emperor who is the receptacle of good luck and who always treads on the spiritual path, you should note carefully, being anxious for the favour and blessing of the Emperor as a token of his affection. Let shame be heaped upon that son who, deviating from the reverence shown by all good sons, stood aloof from the attitude of submission, by assuming hostility and declaring a revolt in the capital against his Emperor and father. Has any son in this family attempted war against his father in the past? If our son, endowed with luck and wealth, desire to wield his sword and conquer new territories, it is well and good, and who can object to such a course? All right, he should now return to our presence and, accompanied by the Omrâos, who are our well-wishers and benefactors, he should undertake a war expedition against the Padshas of Irâk and Abbâs. They have dishonoured your father's coins, and your duty lies in dishonouring their coins in return. On the other hand, is it proper on the part of dutiful sons to fight against their fathers for the sceptre, the umbrella and the throne? Still more, the acquisition of the umbrella and the châmar does not rest with oneself. They are enjoyed by him alone upon whom God confers them. If the prince comes to the presence of the Emperor with a scarf round his neck and explains his condition, he may be again an object of our affectionate glance. What more can be written? One seeking his welfare will not long remain carefree."

90 *Sultan Khurram's reply.*—Sultan Khurram sent Emperor Jahangir the following reply to the above

letter; when the Emperor's letter reached the hands of Khurram he kissed and lifted it to his eyes and head; and while reading the same he bowed down at every letter, after which he penned the following note with due submission :—

" He who is the pillar of the most excellent empire will, out of the abundance of his own love and affection, make my prayer fruitful. There is no one except Your Majesty to forgive the transgressions of my ignorant self, however unpardonable they might be. I have been a victim of shame and repentance since I took up an offensive and disloyal attitude towards you. Your feet alone can offer salvation to this sinful one. You have spoken of my displaying feelings of hostility and disaffection against my father and Emperor. It is very astonishing that such an idea which was foreign to my heart has been attributed to me, ill-fated as I am. As long as the Padshah enjoys bliss and happiness, nothing untoward and improper will spring from me. Did Sulaiman Paygambar suffer imprisonment at the hands of the ants in days of yore? So, what power have I to quarrel with the Emperor? As to the imputation that I am anxious for the throne, I want to say that I pray, may the Emperor remain effulgent over my head by illuminating the umbrella and the throne as long as the moon and the sun exist, so that I may remain without any anxiety under the shadow of his umbrella-like feet. The Padshah may be pleased, as a token of his own magnanimity, to forgive whatever offence I might have committed. I have ventured to entertain such hopes at the two feet of the Emperor.

"You have said that a thing is enjoyed by one upon whom God confers it. To this I would say that if God has conferred the emperorship on Parvez, I have also been provided with my blood-drinking sword. Parvez has obtained the Padshahship from the Emperor, while I have been subjected to false scandal and disgrace. If my sword, like a blood-sucking tiger, becomes appeased after tasting the blood of Khusru, then I shall not entertain any apprehension regarding Parvez. When Parvez has intended my ruin, it is not proper that I should remain inactive and careless. So I have come away being afraid of insult and humiliation. If in course of time it becomes necessary, I will certainly renounce my hostility; if, on the other hand, hostility is intended, I will take it up without delay. Competent persons, after having served me, are offering their services at the two feet of the Padshah. Is all this proper? As long as I do not become Padshah, I am at least under his authority and power.

"I have been asked to take up arms against Irâk and Abbâs. If under the command of the Emperor, I, a Pâdshâhzâdâ, wield the sword in a battle-field, I will not dread even mighty Padshahs. If all the duties and operations were entrusted to me at that time, the fort of Kândahâr would not have fallen into the hands of the Padshah of Abbâs from within a distance of eleven cubits. When the Deccanites rebelled, Parvez was in his mother's womb. I have subdued them twice by wielding my sword with extreme hardship and at the imminent risk of my life. How I captured the fort of Kankarâ, and how I converted to Islam the formidable enemies living in the recesses of hills and forests which had never before been subjugated by any one, is still talked of in Hindusthan aud is also known at the two feet of the Padshah-Hazarat. If it is desired, the fort of Kândahâr resembling a mountain of rocky stones, will be destroyed immediately on my arrival. As long as I have the sword of Jahangir Padshah in my hands, I will not seek anybody's aid for the key to open the door of my prosperity."

This is what the prince wrote in explanation of his intention after which he sounded a note of humiliation:—

"Wandering on the whirlpool of life I have not been able to attain success in my enterprises, whether at the beginning or at the end. People living under my shelter have been protected and maintained in the past, while others have fled for their lives eluding the search of their pursuers. I am the most abominable slave of His Majesty; it is surprising that the Padshah has been affected by the revolt of such a negligible person. Just as the most powerful and princely falcons, which are a dread to all the birds, are captured in the net of the cruel hunter, I, a slave, wherever I may be, am in the sheath of Your Majesty. Regarding his desire to reinstate me in his special favour I beg to say that as I have been deprived of the opportunity of personally offering my obeisance to the Padshah, I only pray that the Emperor may show me a great favour by desisting from pursuing my footsteps. What more punishment is necessary for me? This has proved sufficient:

what shall I write more? I pray that the Padshah will not take any umbrage against this mad one."

91 *Shah Jahan's letter to the Adil Shahi Sultan.*— During the reign of Emperor Jahangir the Adil Shahi Sultans of the Deccan used to send annual presents and Wakils with letters to the Mogul court. As they ceased to do so subsequently Shah Jahan Padshah despatched the following letter to the Adil Shahi ruler :—

"Glory to the Almighty God, the fulfiller of all prayers, supplications and desires, Who as a token of His extensive powers, has placed me in the exalted office of an Emperor, out of a drop of water as it were. It is extremely improper that the rulers of the dominions of Bijapur, Golconda and Bhâgnagar, situated on the sea, have been circulating *gaj-mohurs* or independent coins in their realms, and looking upon one another as Padshahs like the bird Hud-hud. They should even now pay heed to my command. They should circulate Shah Jahani gajmohurs if they desire to save their necks; otherwise I will let loose all the swift-footed and powerful kites of the world, the exterminators of the royal falcons, skilled in the extraction of skins and flesh with their sharp and pointed talons and beaks. They should carefully give ear to the warning. They should not remain inactive like the hare, deer and *randra* (?) For this we have sent Muddhamatta [Muhammad] Khan accustomed to bring us glory, the chief among the Omrâos, intelligent and efficient in action, who is near us in our confidential deliberations and, the disgracer of our enemies. If you seek your welfare, you should carry out our wishes to the best of your ability. What shall I write more? May your heart be gratified."[77]

92. *Reply of the Adil Shahi Sultan.*—The Adil Shahi Padshah sent the following reply to the Emperor Shah Jahan:—

" The only receptacle of adoration and praise is the fear-scaring feet of the Almighty God. All promises pertaining to one's duties should be made to Him alone, Who looks upon as dust all those who install themselves on the pinnacle of the mountain of pride. On hearing and reading your message, unapproved by the wise and indicative of your self-esteem, laughter has been caused here in all quarters.

" Besides you have cited the instance of the kite and the Hud-hud. The story is as blatant as the sun and the moon. In the beginning of creation the bird Hud-hud was endowed with a variegated covering, and it was also made the lord of all with a crown on its head. This supremacy of the bird has prevailed automatically for many long ages. Though Mehtar Paygambar (God) conferred sovereignty on the kite for a couple of days, yet during the continuance of the order and rank fixed by the Ordainer of all things, can the kite, raised to eminence only recently, ever strike the Hud-hud with its claws? In these circumstances, how can a new order of things supersede time-worn ordinances? Yes, the hare sleeps peacefully but it subsequently inflicts upon the pursuer considerable strain and disappointment. Hence, to those who have the welfare of their subjects always in their mind, the attempt . . . . (Here the letter ends abruptly).

CHAPTER XI

AURANGZEB'S ACCESSION TO THE THRONE

93. *Dara deplores his delayed prospects of sovereignty.*—Salutation to Sree-Krishna. Emperor Shah Jahan had four sons; the eldest was Dara Shah with mansab 20,000, sawar 20,000; Shah Shuja with mansab 15,000, sawar 15,000, Aurangzeb with mansab 12,000, Sawar 9,000, and Murad Buksh.

Emperor Shah Jahan had his future calculated by astrologers to whom he said, "How many years shall I live more?" The pandits consulted their books and reported that he would live for ten years more. Dara Shah said, "O father, I have heard the astrologers saying that you will live for ten years more. I am now fifty years old. O father, if you live for another ten years I shall be sixty years old. Of what use is the Padshahship of Delhi to a sexagenarian? If my father has compassion upon me he should abdicate the throne for ten years and make me Padshah."

94. *Shah Jahan divides his empire.*—Emperor Shah Jahan then placed Shah Shuja at Rajmahal in charge of the twelve divisions of Bengal; Aurangzeb at Aurangabad; Murad Buksh at Kabul. He further instructed his three sons as follows: "I have conferred the emperorship on Dara now when I am in good condition. Nobody should object to this arrangement as long

as I live. You should act as you like under my orders."

He said to Dara,—"You should not accept the imperial revenues due from the three places." With these instructions he despatched his three sons to their respective charges. He placed Dara on the throne and himself saluted his Emperor-son. Shah Jahan lived inside the fort of Delhi having constructed his quarters properly. He said to Dara, "Pay me every month the sum of rupees one lakh and twenty thousand. The amount should be paid to me on the appearance of the new moon."

95 *Self-immolation of Mumtaz Mahal.*—The principal begum of Shah Jahan, the mother of the four Padshahzadas said one day to her husband, "I am not accompanying you to your newly built quarters. I have now come to considerable age. Through your favour I have enjoyed all the pleasures which can fall to the lot of a mortal. Four tiger-cubs have been born of me. They will not abide by the arrangement you have made, and they will die by the hands of one another. What is the good of my being burnt in the fire of affliction and sorrow? I will die with the name of God on my lips."

Saying thus the begum prepared herself for death; and uttering the name of Khodâ she put an end to her life by swallowing poison.

96 *Sultan Dara Shukah imprisoned.*—Six months after this Shah Shuja attacked Delhi with an army of 1,00,000 sawars, but his forces were defeated, and he fled back to Rajmahal being unable to take his stand.

Aurangzeb said to Murad Buksh, "I have already made up my mind to become a faquir, and I will not bid for the Padshahship now. If the Almighty God allows I will make you Padshah instead. I have been a faquir before and I will remain as a faquir. Put me in some corner, and I shall live in the religion of a faquir."

To this Murad Buksh said, "You are my elder brother. Keep me in any fashion you like, and I will abide by your counsel." Having said so Murad Buksh marched to Delhi by the western road. Dara came out of Delhi and encountered the forces of his brothers at a distance of two days' journey from the capital, and waged a severe fight with the army of Aurangzeb. There were heavy losses on both sides. Murad Buksh reached Delhi by the southern gates. Being attacked on both sides Dara could not resist the combined forces of his brothers and fled. He was captured and enchained in golden fetters. Murad Buksh was placed on the throne and made Padshah. Aurangzeb in concert with Murad Buksh informed Shah Jahan, "We two desire to pay our respects to our father." Shah Jahan replied, "My words have not at all been honoured; so you need not salute me now. You may salute me afterwards if you preserve the life of Dara."

97. *Friendship between Aurangzeb and Murad Buksh.*—Aurangzeb and Murad Buksh used to take their dinners together. Aurangzeb dined occasionally at the residence of Murad Buksh ; so did Murad Buksh at Aurangzeb's. Noticing the undivided friendship of the two brothers the people also ceased to look upon them as two different individuals.

On one occasion Aurangzeb invited Murad Buksh to dine with him. Cakes of numerous varieties were prepared, as well as delicious jellies. On the arrival of Murad Buksh, Aurangzeb said, "O Padshah, take some cakes, and rest here for a while, we shall have our dinner when it is ready." Murad Buksh said, "All right, I shall rest after partaking of the cakes." When he slept, he was seized with intoxication, and could not regain his senses by any means.

Aurangzeb then posted his men in order, and said, "The Padshah is sleeping, you should not make any noise at all." Having cast his glance he saw that the new Padshah had lost his consciousness, due to severe intoxication. He was then chained with golden fetters.

98. *Sultans Dara and Murad murdered.*—Aurangzeb then placed Dara and Murad Buksh on the back of an elephant and displayed them to the people by beating drums. As the people might be provoked to sympathetic action after they had known that the two brothers were living, Aurangzeb decided to put an end to their lives. Aurangzeb brought a dish of gold and with a knife beheaded his two brothers, Dara and Murad. With their blood imprinted on his forehead, Aurangzeb sat on the throne and became the Padshah.

99. *Mir Jumla's expedition against Sultan Shuja.*—Then the Emperor despatched Mir Jumla to Bengal with his son Muazzam and 1,00,000 horse, elephants, cannon and all necessary war materials. The general was presented with a sirpâo and received the following mandate of the Padshah, "Direct your efforts to the extermination of Shuja. I also appoint you Subha at

Dacca. Shaista Khan Uzir is my maternal uncle whom you should see on your way." Mir Jumla agreed to pay a visit to Shaista Khan at the instance of the Emperor, whom he had requested to issue orders to Shaista Khan to grant an interview to the general at any time and dismiss him very quickly. The Emperor agreed to ask his uncle not to detain Mir Jumla very long in the interview.

100. *Mir Jumla insulted by Shaista Khan.*—Mir Jumla then retired to his own residence and conferred with his confidants saying, "I have no mind to go to Shaista Khan. At the same time I cannot but go, as the Emperor has commanded me to see his uncle. How can I see Shaista Khan?"

Mir Jumla's friends gave the following advice: "We have heard that Shaista Khan remains engaged in cleansing his teeth up to the fourth danda of the day. If you go to him at that time he will certainly bid you farewell from the door." In obedience to the command, of the Emperor, Mir Jumla stood one morning at the door of Shaista Khan and said to the janitor at the door, "Please ask a servant to tell Shaista Khan that Mir Jumla is at the door, and wants leave at once." The door-keeper asked a servant to tell the Nawab that Mir Jumla was waiting at the door and that he wanted leave at once. The servant did not communicate the message to the Nawab, but reported falsely that Mir Jumla was asked by Shaista Khan to wait for some time at the door as he was then engaged in brushing his teeth. Mir Jumla said, "It is surprising that such a shirker is attached to a durbar like this,

Well, door-keeper, please send for another servant to carry the message." The door-keeper asked another servant, who told the Nawab that Mir Jumla was at the door and that he wanted leave at once, and Shaista Khan said,—" Mir Jumla knows all these things. How is this that he has come to see me at this ungodly hour? However, call him in."

Mir Jumla paid his greetings to Shaista Khan, but the latter did not give up rubbing his teeth, nor did he leave his seat, and neither did he place his hand on the breast. Shaista Khan said to Mir Jumla, "I repeat what the Padshah has taught you. You may think that you have been deputed to subdue Shuja because there is no other Nawab at Delhi. You have no bread in this land: the Padshah, out of compassion, is providing your descendants with bread. Try to perpetuate this bread. If the mission with which you have been deputed be crowned with success then only people will know that you are a trusted man. People do not know you now, whether you are honest or wicked." Saying so, Shaista Khan bade farewell to Mir Jumla, and despatched to Mir Jumla's quarters horses, swords and robes as presents to the general; but they were worthy of a commander of 5,000. Mir Jumla went home and said,— "The prestige which I managed to acquire during these seventy years of my life has all been burnt to ashes at the hands of Shaista Khan."

101. *Sultan Muazzam's marriage to Fatima.*—Mir Jumla and Prince Muazzam then attacked Shah Shuja, and had a series of daily engagements with the latter.

Shuja seizing an opportunity sent a messenger to Sultan Muazzam with the following proposal,—" My daughter Fatima is a captivating maiden, and Muazzam should come and marry her." That was a fraternal war, and Prince Muazzam hearing of a beautiful maiden and himself being of an amorous disposition could not resist the temptation. He visited Shuja in the company of 10,000 horses. On the arrival of Sultan Muazzam, Shuja thought he had practically won a victory. Shuja married his daughter to his nephew Muazzam and kept him there.

102. *Mir Jumla's warning to Prince Muazzam.*—Aurangzeb received the intelligence of Sultan Muazzam's marriage to Fatima and the prince's stay in Shuja's residence. The Emperor wrote a letter to Mir Jumla : " Alas ! The war against Shuja has been well completed indeed ! Mir Jumla has not even been able to keep my son ! If he thinks he is unable to do anything, let him say so. and I will despatch another Nawab with forces."

To this Mir Jumla sent the following reply,—" I will bring the war against Shuja to a victorious termination, and I would ask the Padshah not to entertain any doubt or apprehension. As regards the blame he has pinned on me for the desertion of Sultan Muazzam, I would like to inform the Emperor that if I, Mir Jumla, only shake the sleeves of my cloak dozens of such Padshahzadas will come out."

Mir Jumla despatched a man to Prince Muazzam with the following message : " Do you think that Shuja will ever occupy the throne by ousting the

Emperor Aurangzeb? If not, act in a manner that will ensure your safety and well-being in future. You said you would join me in the war from the south. The words of a great man are never violated. Act properly; then only you will remain in peace and happiness." The prince read this letter and acted accordingly.

103. *Flight of Prince Shuja.*—On a following day, while proceeding to war, Shuja speared Rashid Khan the senior from behind. Rashid Khan turned back and said, "At whose instance have you done this, O Shuja? Now I realise that you have been bereft of all hopes, and Aurangzeb has become Padshah without any obstruction." Having said so Rashid Khan breathed his last.

On another occasion, Shuja proceeded to the battle-field riding on an elephant. There ensued a terrible contest with heavy bloodshed. Rashid Khan's son who was holding the marchula, or fly-whisk made of peacock's tail, said— "O Padshah, everything will be thrown to the winds if you are fired at from a distance. So you should dismount from the elephant and ride on a horse." There was severe fighting as soon as Shuja became a sawar after alighting from his elephant. Shuja was defeated. Having heard of the prince's defeat his soldiers deserted their ranks and joined the forces of Mir Jumla. Shuja boarded a boat and escaped to the country of the Mags.

Having received this intelligence Aurangshah presented a *sirpao* to Mir Jumla and conferred on him the title of Majum Khan. The Emperor commanded the general to remain as Subha of Dacca with an army of 40,000 horse and to despatch Sultan Muazzam with the rest of the troops to Delhi.

104. *Mir Jumla's invasion of Assam.*—Majum Khan wrote to the Padshah, "As to my appointment as Subha of Dacca, I will remain at that place only after I have subjugated Cooch-Behar which has become disloyal as well as Assam which has wrested back Kamrup.[78] I solicit the orders of the Padshah." Sultan Muazzam having reached Delhi was despatched to Gwalior and placed at its environs.

The Padshah commanded Majum Khan, to leave his son Muhsud-ami Khan[79] (Muhammad Amin Khan) at Dacca and subjugate the two provinces by conducting the expedition in person. The Padshah on receiving the intelligence of Majum Khan's entrance into the country of Gauhati after the subjugation of Cooch-Behar conferred on him the title of Khan-Khana. Having heard of Mir Jumla's march through Assam, Aurangzeb said to Shaista Khan, "The Khan-Khana has marched to Assam without my orders." Shaista Khan replied, "He has no bread in this land. He has thus acted to provide for his children and descendants."

105. *Death of Mir Jumla.*—Having reached Pându on his way back from Assam, the general was honoured with the title of Khan-Khana Siphar-Sâlâh Sira-mauli. When he reached Bouroitolâ he died. Dilâl Khan with the remnant of the army proceeded to the presence of the Padshah, having taken Muhsud-ami from Dacca.[80] They took with them the elephants

and princess which were brought from Assam, and paid their respects to the Emperor. The Padshah said to Dilâl Khan, "Well Dilâl, you have come, but where did you leave the Khan-Khana?" The Padshah put this question twice; he wiped away the tears from his eyes and said to Muhsud-ami, "I bestow on you all the property which belonged to your father as well as the rank of a panch-hazari. You should remain with me. I appoint Shaista Khan Subha of Dacca." Then turning to Dilâl Khan the Emperor said, "Well, Dilâl Khan, you have come back after undergoing severe hardships. Go and remain as Subha at Aurangabad." He was also honoured with the present of a *sirpao*. Here is finished this episode.

CHAPTER XII

MIR JUMLA'S CAREER FROM GOLCONDA TO GARHGAON

106. *Attempt to capture Mir Jumla.*—Salutation to Sree-Krishna. Hasan Muhammad Khan, the Padshah of Golconda, had no son though he was far advanced in years.[81] He adopted the son of a Nawab who was his wife's elder brother. The old Padshah said, "People would have obeyed if you had been my son, but they will hesitate to do so as you are the son of a Nawab. So you should bring the people under your obedience during my life-time." All the Nawabs and officers accepted the adopted son as their future king. Mir Jumla Dewân, the son of Mirza Hazru, happened to

be the only dissentient.[82] So attempts were made to seize the person of Mir Jumla.

107. *Mir Jumla aids Aurangzeb.*—Having heard this, Mir Jumla, accompanied by 400 elephants, horses and troops fled with the object of going to Delhi. Aurangzeb was then living at Aurangabad ; he detained Mir Jumla at his court. In the meantime Shah Jahan had abdicated the Padshahship and conferred it on his eldest son Dara, which gave rise to enmity among the four brothers. Shah Shuja was at Dacca and Murad Buksh at Kabul. Aurangzeb said to Mir Jumla, " Let us proceed to attack Dara at Delhi." To this Mir Jumla replied,— " I have come from Golconda with my allegiance mentally offered to the Emperor of Delhi, and I will not lift my sword against His Majesty . I will proceed to any other quarter you order me to go." With these words Mir Jumla gave to Aurangzeb 100,000 gold coins, saying. " You may spend this amount and attack Dara." Besides, Mir Jumla bore all the expenses of Aurangzeb's campaigns which amounted to eighteen crores of rupees.

Aurangzeb vanquished Dara and Murad Buksh, and staying at Delhi he summoned Mir Jumla to his presence. On his arrival the Emperor said, " You should proceed to attack Shah Shuja who is at Dacca. I send my eldest son Sultan Muazzam to accompany you, besides 100,000 cavalry. You should also take with you elephants and cannon, and all necessary materials for war."

108. *Mir Jumla's humiliation at the hands of Shaista Khan.*—The Padshah honoured Mir Jumla with numerous presents and gave him leave to depart, saying, " The

general should on his way see Shaista Khan Wazir who is my maternal uncle." To this Mir Jumla replied, "Yes, I will see him, as commanded by the Emperor. But he should ask Shaista Khan to grant me an interview at any time I choose to go, and give me leave quickly." The Emperor promised to ask his maternal uncle to dismiss Mir Jumla after a short interview.

Mir Jumla retired to his residence and conferred with his trusted friends, saying, "I have no mind to go to Shaista Khan. At the same time I cannot but go, as I have received commands from the Emperor. But I have also procured the Padshah's orders that Shaista Khan should grant me an interview at any time I go, and dismiss me quickly from his presence. I solicit your counsel on this subject."

His friends discussed the matter jointly and said, "Shaista Khan remains engaged in cleansing his teeth up to the fourth danda of the day. If you go to see him at this time he may give you leave to go by simply admitting you to his presence."

Accordingly Mir Jumla waited at the door of Shaista Khan early in the morinng. He beckoned the *duwardar* or door-keeper and asked him to summon an attendant and send the information to Shaista Khan. The servant did not inform the Nawab, but he said, as coming from the Nawab, "Mir Jumla should wait for a while at the door. I am engaged in *datwan* or brushing of my teeth." Mir Jumla said, "It is curious that such a servant is permitted to reside in such a durbar; well, duwârdar, you should beckon another personal attendant of the Nawab to give him the information." The janitor called an attendant and sent information a second time.

The servant informed Shaista Khan accordingly, who said,—" Mir Jumla knows all these things. But how is this, that he has come at this unseasonable hour? However, call him in," Mir Jumla offered his *muzura* or greetings to the Nawab, but the latter did not give up rubbing his teeth, nor did he leave his seat, and neither did he place his hand on his breast.

Shaista Khan said to Mir Jumla, " I repeat the instructions delivered to you by the Emperor at the time of despatching you to fight with Shah Shuja. Do not think that you have been deputed by the Padshah of Delhi to subdue Shuja because there is no other Nawab in this country. You have no *ruti* or bread in this land; the Padshah, out of compassion, is providing your descendants with bread. Act in a manner by which you may perpetuate your bread or position. If you can accomplish the mission with which you have been deputed by the Padshah, then only people will know your merits. They do not know you now whether you are honest or wicked."

With these words the general was given leave to depart. The horses, swords, and robes which were sent to Mir Jumla's residence as presents were worthy of a Nawab commanding only 5,000. Mir Jumla went to his quarters and said,—" The prestige which I have acquired during these seventy years of my life has all been burnt to ashes to-day at the hands of Shaista Khan."

After Mir Jumla's defeat of Shah Shuja, the Padshah conferred on him the title of Majum Khan; he was honoured with the distinction of Khan-Khana when he reached Gauhati after the conquest of Cooch Behar; he was further decorated with the title of Khan-Khânâ Siphar-Sâlâh Sira-mauli when he entered Garhgaon.

CHAPTER XIII

RAJA RAM SINGHA'S DEPUTATION TO ASSAM

109. *Troops under Nawabs despatched against Sewa.*—Salutation to Sree-Krishna. After Aurangzeb had ascended the throne by slaying his three brothers Dara Shah, Shah Shuja and Murad Buksh, he asked his Uzir Amânat Kahn, "Please tell me which of the kingdoms once held in fee by my ancestors have now refrained from accepting our allegiance." The Uzir consulted the official records, and Subhas were despatched to those states which had not till then bowed their head of submission to the Moguls. Kandarpa Singha, the Raja of Sewa,[83] was found incorrigible, for whose subjugation Nawab Sulatifat Khan, a commander of 6,000, was despatched with five other Nawabs, five Rajas as well as all necessary provisions for war. Sulatifat Khan fought for three long years, but could not achieve any success. The Emperor being displeased recalled Sulatifat Khan from the field, and sent Bahadur Khan as Subha to conduct the war.[84] Bahadur Khan in his turn became friendly with Kandarpa Singha, the Sewâ-raja, and remained there for two years and a half. He was also withdrawn from the war, and Nawab

Shâmser Khan Bâruhâni was despatched instead, but he died during his stay at Sewâ after some time.

110. *Ram Singha appointed commander of the Sewa expedition.*—Aurangzeb became indignant at the repeated failure of the Sewâ expedition, and he said to Raja Ram Singha, "Mândhâtâ was your grandfather. The reputation of his valour has spread to all the quarters. Your father Jai Singha was also a great warrior, and he has been honoured with the title of Mirzâ Raja. And so the fame of your family's heroism has been known in all countries. You are fortunate to be born in such a family, and so I ask you to proceed to the Sewâ war. The Nawabs who were sent before could not do anything to Sewa."

Being thus commanded by the Emperor, Ram Singha submitted as follows :—

"Yes, I will proceed to the Sewâ war. But you should withdraw from the field the army of the Nawabs, as I want to fight singly with my Rajputs of Amber. In the latter case we shall share the same honour or blame in the event of our victory or defeat. If we fight jointly, your Nawabs will get all the credit if there be a victory. Besides, the Nawabs who were sent before to the Sewâ campaign will try to do me harm, knowing that I have been sent in supersession of them. It must be admitted that the Nawabs have not proved themselves a match for Sewâ, which has led Sewâ to look upon them as imbecile. Thus my association with the Nawabs will lead to the diminution of the prestige connected with my name. So the imperial forces manned by the Nawabs should no longer remain in the field. I shall fight with my own men."

111. *Ram Singha's ultimatum to Kandarpa Singha.*—As suggested by Ram Singha, the Emperor ordered back all the Nawabs previously despatched to the Sewâ campaign. Ram Singha was made Mansabdar with the rank of a commander of 6,000. He was provided with elephants and horses, and was offered suitable presents. Ram Singha was then sent to the Sewâ war, and the general took leave of the Emperor. Ram Singha first went to Amber where he halted for a week. He took with him a body of his chieftains and the following Thâkurs,—Amar Singha, Dip Singha, Madan Singha, Ugrasen Rao, Dâmodar Singha, Krishna Singha, Suk Singha, Râgharâi and Anandarâi, and forty more Thâkurs attached to the Rajas who were Ram Singha's brothers and nephews. He also took with him 80,000 Rajput sepoys as well as numerous gunners, beldars, dafadars, labourers and shieldsmen. The total strength of his army was 300,000 and with them he proceeded to the Sewâ campaign.

On reaching the jurisdiction of Sewa, Ram Singha despatched messengers to the Sewa Raja with a letter to the following effect: "I am the grandson of Maharaja Mândhâtâ, and the son of Mirza Raja Jai Singha, and my name is Ram Singha. You must have heard the sound of our family's swords. There exists also a long-standing friendship between your family and mine. Our family has never shown its back in any war. You are also familiar with the prowess of the Emperor Aurangzeb. The Nawabs who were sent before against you failed in their mission ; so some of them have been executed and others expelled. The Emperor wanted to send his son Sultan Muhammad, but I dissuaded him from coming, and I have come myself on account of the long friendsip subsisting between us. So come, and let us meet at a convenient place : if on the other hand you want war, be prepared for the same, and do not delay."

112. *Ram Singha's victory over Sewa.*—Kandarpa Singha, the Raja of Sewâ, received the imperial ambassadors, and sent the following reply to Ram Singha's message : "The arguments which you have set forth in your letter are true and wholesome. But if I enter into any friendly terms with you, people will laugh at and upbraid us both saying that we have become friends being unable to oppose each other in strength. So war seems to me the better course."

Then there ensued a terrible contest between the two parties. The soldiers of Ram Singha were great experts in spear-fighting. They were insensible to pain even when they received wounds from weapons on account of their bodies being saturated with opium of which they were habitual consumers. They preferred death to retreat from battle. On the other hand, the soldiers of Sewâ took to their heels when they had to face a very hard contest. So in the war a large number of the soldiers of Sewâ fled from the battle-field or were killed. Seizing an opportunity during the thick of the fight, the Bheel soldiers of Ram Singha surrounded the Raja of Sewâ. Ram Singha gained a decisive victory in the war.

The Sewâ Raja then enquired what Ram Singha was going to do with him, whether he would be taken to the presence of the Padhshah or be let off. Ram Singha said, "This is out of the question now, as you did not act before according to our advice. You will be taken to the presence of the Emperor. But I will intercede on your behalf with the Padshah so that no harm may be done to you. You shall place your head below and I will place mine on top of yours."

Ram Singha wrote a detailed despatch on the war and sent it to the Emperor, who asked Ram Singha to escort the Sewâ Raja to the court after having left Jumsher Khan in charge of the army. Ram Singha accordingly appeared before the Padshah with the Sewa Raja. Ram Singha was honoured with rich presents.

113. *Sewa Raja before Aurangzeb.*—The Emperor asked the Sewâ Raja, "You are the great chief of Sewâ, and of a very long standing too. Your ancestors had served mine. You have now become unfaithful to us. May I know the reason? Are you defying me on the strength of any secret alliance you have formed with any other power? Or do you think I am impotent in my authority?"

Thus replied Kandarpa Singha, the Raja of Sewâ: "My forefathers never served your forefathers in person. They only sent articles and supplies through their envoys according to time-honoured customs. On ascending the throne you have insisted on the payment of tribute, and you have introduced the system of obligatory personal service. This is why we have ceased to be under your vassalage."[85]

The Emperor said: "You did not serve before, nor did you pay any tribute. We have now seized your person. Wherein now is your honour gone? I can now kill you, or do whatever I like with you. So consent to accept our allegiance, and live in peace and plenty by paying us tribute. Otherwise you will be killed, being trodden on by elephants."

The Sewâ Raja hurled the following retort, "I cannot do what we never did before nor can I accept your suggestion even on pain of death." The Emperor, being indignant, ordered the Raja to be put under the feet of elephants. But Raja Ram Singha implored the Emperor on behalf of the Raja of Sewa, and asked the Padshah not to kill the Raja, who was accordingly imprisoned, being chained with shackles of gold.

114. *Kandarpa Singha's escape from prison.*—After staying in prison for some time, Kandarpa Singha said to Ram Singha, "You brought me here with assurance of safety. I cannot understand why I am now detained in prison, and I do not know what else is in store for me. All this is due to you. I have in my life subdued many people." Ram Singha earnestly entreated the Emperor to release the Raja but in vain, and Ram Singha became sorely grieved at heart.

A son was then born to Ram Singha, who was named Keshore Das. On that occasion Ram Singha used to send out articles of food and ornaments, loaded in huge boxes of copper, brass and silver, to the Rajas and Nawabs. He cut asunder the chains of the Sewa Raja, put him in a box and sent him back to his kingdom and it was not detected at any of the imperial gates and outposts.

115. *Ram Singha's first offence.*—The Emperor ascribed the escapa of the Raja to Ram Singha and accused the latter, saying: "What have you done with the Raja of Sewâ?"

To this Ram Singha replied, "I implored you so earnestly on his behalf and, as you were not willing to let him off, he has made his escape."

The Padshah replied, "It is you who allowed him to escape"; to which Ram Singha said, "If you think I have been instrumental in the escape of the Sewa Rajâ, he is under my thumb, and there should be no fear on that score."

The Padshah did not say anything, but remained silent, cogitating within himself.

116. *The Sikh Guru Teg Bahadur escapes from captivity.*—Then there was a saint of the faith of Guru Nânak, and he became the guru of a large number of Brahmans and Kshattriyas. He would not take the name of Ram or Krishna, nor of any god or goddess. On meeting a disciple of his own faith he would simply say, "Om, ai, Guru; Om, ai, Guru," and nothing else. The Brahman Bhattacharyas or priests and the Kâzis of the Musalmans reported to the Padshah, "This man does not belong to any particular school or faith; he goes about ravaging the country." The Emperor asked the guru to appear before him, but he did not come. On the other hand he defied the authority of the Padshah, and roamed about plundering and destroying the country, attended by thirty thousand Nânak-panthi sepoys. The

Padshah became indignant, and he deputed Alo Khân Pathân who captured the guru. The Padshah ordered the guru to be executed, who for fear of his life sought the protection of Ram Singha, who became a surety for the Sikh leader. But the aforesaid Nânak-panthi guru also made his escape.[86]

117. *Ram Singha's second offence.*—The Padshah accused Ram Singha, saying: "How is this that you have allowed the guru to flee, though you yourself stood a surety for him?"

To this Ram Singha replied, "What is he? Only a Raja or a Nawab is worthy of your vengeance. He is only a mendicant faquir. To accuse me for his escape will cause people to laugh when they hear of it."

Hearing the explanation offered by Ram Singha with regard to the escape of the Sikh guru, the Padshah said to himself, "This Ram Singha has begun to commit one misdeed after another. Remembering the services rendered to the state by his father and grandfather, I cannot say anything to him. Besides, any punishment inflicted on Ram Singha may lead to a concerted action on the part of the Rajas against me, and I shall be alienated from them all." Thus thinking, the Padshah did not propose to do anything to Ram Singha.

118. *Dangers of Assam wars.*—And it came to pass that the Swarga-Maharaja of Assam attacked the fort of Gauhati and captured the Nawab Sayid Piroz Khan. On receiving this intelligence the Padshah said to Ram Singha, "Raja Jai Singha, son of Raja Mândhâtâ, fought in the Bengal war and subdued that province. Now, you proceed to the war with Assam."

The reason for which the Padshah said thus to Ram Singha was this :—Not a single Nawab who had been deputed to the Assam wars could ever come back safely ; some died of themselves, while others were killed in the battle ; the waters of Assam are poisonous, its air unhealthy and its hills are covered with dense forests ; and the Emperor wanted that Ram Singha should die in Assam. Devising this plan, the Padshah deputed Ram Singha to Assam.

119. *Ram Singha deputed to the war against Assam.*— The Raja took with him the Rajput Bheels of his own State, Rashid Khan Nawab and others, and took leave of the Emperor. The Padshah appointed two of his own men as Dewâns to accompany Ram Singha in his expedition, Mirza Saiyid Saf, the Dewân of the Perganas, and Mir Raji, the Dewân of the laskars and sepoys. The emperor also deputed Bahlol Khan, the Daroga of seven hundred Iasols, and Sultan Ali, the Daroga of three hundred Ahudis. Mir Gazar Beg Hazi was appointed wâqâyânavis of the expedition and the Emperor said to him, " Ram Singha is an untrustworthy man. He may enter into a collusion with the Swarga-Maharaja. You should send regular reports to me regarding his movements, and the success or ill-fate of the expedition."

The Raja halted on the way with his detachment. The Nawabs who were commissioned to accompany the Raja joined him subsequently with their quota of supplies. There was a garden at Patna founded by Ram Singha's father Jai Singha. The Raja stopped there for a week awaiting the arrival of the remaining portion of his army.

120. *Ram Singha warmly received by Shaista Khan.*—From Patna, Ram Singha proceeded towards Jahangirnagar in order to have an interview with Amir-ul-Omrâo Shaista Khan who was the sworn friend of the Raja's father Jai Singha. On account of this old friendship Ram Singha came to Dhaka. On hearing of the approach of the Raja, Shaista Khan welcomed him with great cordiality and splendour. The son of Aburnamir Khan and the two Dewâns, Raja Nandalal and Rai Muraridhar, escorted the Raja with elephants and horses, marching to the notes of the five musical instruments. The path lying on the march was splashed with water by a host of chikâbardars, and the roofs of the houses in the bazaars through which the Raja passed were covered with golden and silvery cloths. The court-chamber of Shaista Khan was also draped with costly carpets up to the ceiling. There were placed six hundred incense-pots fuming with the vapour of burnt aloe. In every room tassels of pearls and corals were suspended from the overhanging canopies.

The Raja approached the Nawab and, addressing him as uncle or *chacha*, saluted the latter by touching his feet. Shaista Khan clasped Ram Singha to his bosom by twining him by the neck, and kissed the Raja's head. The Nawab presented to Ram Singha precious elephants and horses, and a sword named Khanjar whose price amounted to 25,000 rupees.

Nawab Shaista Khan then imparted the following instructions to Ram Singha: "Act in a way that you may remain in the good graces of the Emperor. Aurangzeb Padshah is a shrewd diplomat. Shujanagar

[Hazo in Assam] is an unhealthy place; its hills are covered with forests, and poisonous waters flow in its streams during the two months Baisak and Jaistha. The air that blows is also infected with poison. For this reason our men die there in numbers, and you should live very carefully. Do not drink any water but that of the Lauhitya or Brahmaputra. Do not admit the women of that place into your mahal; they are wicked and treacherous."[87] The Nawab further advised, "Please write to me when you fall short of food-stuff, war provisions or money; I will send them to you, looking upon you as one of mine."

Ram Singha became extremely delighted with the reception given to him, and said to the Nawab, "The advice which you have given to me is generally imparted by a father to his son." The Raja then took leave of the Nawab whose sons saluted Ram Singha by touching his feet, and escorted him to a considerable distance. Ram Singh then arrived with his army at Shujanagar.

CHAPTER XIV

AN ACCOUNT OF THE NAWABS OF DACCA

121. *During the reigns of Jahangir and Shah Jahan.*—Salutation to Sree-Krishna. Here follows an account of the Nawabs who ruled at Dhaka. Raja Mandhata, father of Raja Jai Singha who was the father of Raja Ram Singha, subdued Gaur at the instance of Jahangir Padshah, after which he proceeded to Dhaka and changed

its name to Jahangirnagar. He remained there for some time, after which he went to the presence of the Padshah at Delhi, leaving Mus-haf Khan, a commander of 4,000 in charge of Dacca.

Having heard that Mus-haf Khan, a junior Omrao was placed in charge of Jahangirnagar, Emperor Jahangir asked the Wazir Mahmad Khan, "A junior Nawab like Mus-haf Khan is not fit to hold charge of Jahangirnagar. Bengal is a country so large that it deserves administration by a Padshah. The Rajas and Zemindars of that country are great trouble-makers. So, you should arrange to send a commander of 6,000 to that place." One Burham Khan, a Dargahi and a commander of 6,000, who was the son of the nurse who had brought up the Emperor's son, was despatched as governor. The son of a nurse is called Kokâ. This Burham Khan Kokâ came and stayed at Jahangirnagar. After this Jahnagir died, and was succeeded by Shah Jahan, who deputed Nawab Islam Khan. The latter was subsequently removed and Azam Khan appointed instead. When Shuja came to Rajmahal, Azam Khan's daughter became the chief begum of the prince. Azam Khan remained at Jahangirnagar.

122. *Shaista Khan's commercial enterprises.*—On Aurangzeb's acccession to the throne, Nawab Shaista Khan came to Jahangirnagar with his five sons, two sons-in-law, Nawab Nurulla Khan, Muhammad Maqim, Zohag Beg, and other Mansabdars. He lived there for some years.

Shaista Khan used to import by ship salt, supari or betel-nuts and other articles, and sold them in Bengal on profitable terms. Besides, he accumulated seventeen crores of rupees by procuring two or three tolas of gold for one gold mohur. He also sold salt and supari to the merchants and traders in the city of Dacca. The latter were thus debarred from making purchases and sales on their own account.

Manowar Khan,[88] son of Masim Khan, Zemindar of Bengal, was despatched to the Padshah at Delhi as a prisoner chained in iron shackles with the charge that the administration of Bengal could not be carried on smoothly owing to his obstructive acts. The merchants and traders complained to the Padshah at Delhi regarding Shaista Khan's acts of injustice. Manowar Khan added to the allegations by saying, "O Padshah-Hazrat, Shaista Khan has contrived to be as great as you are. He has become the Padshah of Bengal."

The Emperor became indignant and sent Manowar Khan as a prisoner to Gwalior, saying, "However wealthy and prosperous Shaista Khan may be, he is still a subject of mine. He ventures to place Shaista Khan on the same level with me!" This incensed the Emperor, for which he sent Manowar Khan to Gwalior, which is a place where rebels are detained in custody.

The Padshah asked the Wazir as to the advisability of recalling Shaista Khan from Jahangirnagar. The Wazir, Amanat Khan, said, "It is not desirable that Shaista Khan should be withdrawn by levelling charges against him, as he is a benefactor of yours. You should call him back in a friendly way." The Emperor wrote accordingly to Shaista Khan, "I am now old and so are you. Our days should be spent in devotion to God.

Besides, you are a man of intelligence, and I desire to be absent from Delhi in order to subdue a few more Padshahs as I have a mind to die in the battle-field, leaving my eldest son Sultan Muhammad and yourself in charge of the affairs here. You should come back with all your relations." Having received this *farman* or command Shaista Khan came back with his whole family.

One Fede Khan Kokâ, son of Aurangzeb's nurse, and a commander of 6,000, came to Jahangirnagar in place of Shaista Khan.

123. *Sultan Azamtara at Dacca.*—Sultan Azamtara, son of Aurangzeb, received report from men that Bengal was an excellent place for hunting fish and deer; it also produced musk, agar and other precious articles. He said to his father that he wanted to go to Bengal, adding that Sultan Shuja had ruled there before. Prince Azamtara, accordingly, came to Bengal in place of Fede Khan Kokâ. He destroyed the quarters of Shaista Khan and erected his own residence at the same site. There was an extensive marsh over which a river had flowed before. It was filled up with bamboos and woods which were purchased at a cost of 80,000 rupees; a market-place was constructed there with bricks and stones for the convenience of shopkeepers and tradeswomen. There were emporiums of salt worth 152,000 rupees at several places on the bank of the Bangsah river, which Shaista Khan could not transport. They were left in charge of one of his Mansabdar Khans who happened to be near. The Kotwâl reported to the Emperor's son about this salt, "I want to deposit the salt at the sarkar or royal store-house. The place will

be cleared as the salt depots have occupied a large area of land. We shall then get ample space for establishing markets and shops."

To this Azamtara replied, "Shaista Khan is a subject of ours. It will look odd if we appropriate his goods, and people will condemn this action of ours. To transact business with his commodity by sale or distribution befits a mean person. So, you should destroy the depots and pour down the salt into the river." The Kotwâl demolished the stores and threw the salt into the Bangsha river, and erected markets and shops in the place.

124. *Sultan Azamtara, a hunter.*—The Padshahzada appointed Mir Maulla his Dewân and handed over the duties of the state to the Dewan and the Hazurnavis, Malukchand, and passed his days in hunting on horseback. Besides, he confiscated the household belongings of one Muhammad Maqin, a Mansabdar in command of 700, on the pretext of an offence, and degraded him to the position of a Mansabdar of 200. In this way he lived at Dacca for one year.

125. *Mansur Khan at Gauhati.*—The Barphukan[89] of Gauhati sent the following message to Mansur Khan and Baduli Phukan, "I am ready to surrender the fort [of Gauhati]. Let Mansur Khan come." This message was communicated to the Padshahzada, who summoned Mansur Khan overnight to his presence, and asked him to go to Gauhati.

Mansur Khan replied, "I, an old subject of yours, intend to die on the battle-field. I am prepared to go to Gauhati if you send me there in the same rank and magnificence in which had proceeded Mirza Jâhina, Majum Khan and Raja Ram Singha. Or if you send me alone, I am prepared to go in that manner. What objection could I have?" The Padshahzada promised to confer on him the rank and precedence formerly allotted to Ram Singha and asked him to go. Shahji and other mansabdars were despatched in the company of Mansur Khan who now came to Gauhati and took possession of the garrison which had already been evacuated by the Barphukan.

126. *Prince Azamtara's misrule in Bengal.*—Prince Azamtara had once gone out a-hunting. Alone he pursued a deer on horseback. He wended his steps homeward singly, being unattended by his followers, after bagging several deer and other animals. He had on his head an aigrette worth one lakh of rupees which fell somewhere in the jungle and was lost. On meeting the prince the Dewan asked him where he had left the jewel. Azamtara felt his head and, not finding the jewel there, returned home. The prince sent for the Zemindar in whose jurisdiction the jewel was lost, and asked him to recover it. The Zemindar sought for it without any success. The prince extorted from the Zemindar one lakh of rupees as the price of the aigrette. One of the retainers of the Zemindar came upon the jewel and fled with it to Guzrat. On receiving this news, the Zemindar pursued the absconder and ultimately succeeded in recovering the gem from him. The jewel was returned by the Zemindar to the Padshahazada, who retained the jewel, but did not return the money.

Thus did Azamtara rule in Bengal. He neglected the duties entrusted to him by the Emperor ; he simply roamed about hunting on horseback. The loss of a jewel is highly inauspicious and objectionable. The wâqâyânavis wrote a detailed account of the incident to the Emperor at Delhi ; and Aurangzeb being furiously annoyed recalled Prince Azamtara from Jahangirnagar. The prince had offered to the newswriter a pony, with saddlery and harness worth one thousand rupees, requesting him not to communicate anything to the Emperor that would place the Prince in bad odour with his father; but the wâqâyanavis replied, "I can never be untrue to the salt of the Padshah;" and he sent his report to Delhi.

127. *Shaista Khan again at Dacca.*—Shaista Khan was once informed by his Khezmatgar that Azamtara had thrown into the river all the salt that was stocked in the Nawab's emporium at Dacca, estimated at a value of 152,000 rupees. The Khezmatgar asked the Nawab to report the matter to the Emperor, at which Shaista Khan said, "Is the loss so significant that I should inform the Emperor about it ? If I do so, it will not be safe for my children in future, as Azamtara may some day become the Padshah."

Shaista Khan then sought the mediation of the chief begum and the Wazir, and he himself said to the Padshah, "I am now far advanced in years, and cannot even remain erect before His Majesty. Besides, I have constructed a tomb at Dacca with care for burying my remains. So I want to pass the few days of my life at Dacca." Shaista Khan, accordingly came back to Dacca in place of Sultan Azamtara.

CHAPTER XV

Schedule of distances from the Mogul Capital

128. *Distances from Delhi to other important places.*—Salutation to Sree-Krishna. Here follows a statement of the distances from Delhi to other places having thanas[90] :—

To Rasatpur ..	3 days,	0 prahars and	4 dandas.
„ Agara ..	2 „	3 „	0 „
„ Gulbah ..	0 „	0 „	5 „
„ Ahmedabad ..	2 „	2 „	0 „
„ Malpur ..	11 „	0 „	0 „
„ Itast ..	1 „	3 „	0 „
„ Hariduwar ..	2 „	3 „	0 „
„ Gharath ..	10 „	0 „	0 „
„ Kanauj ..	5 „	2 „	5 „
„ Hasana-Abdal ..	11 „	0 „	0 „
„ Karnat ..	1 „	2 „	4 „
„ Bahrambad from Karnat, 1 day.			
„ Garirdwar from Bahramabad, 1 day 1 prahar.			
„ Kashmir from Delhi, 12 days, 2 prahars.			
„ Khayerabad or Naukhas, 7 days 1 prahar.			
„ Hayedarabad, ..	23 days	0 prahars,	6 dandas.
„ Lakhirabad-thana in Samarkand	28 „	0 „	0 „
„ Rohtap ..	6 „	3 „	0 „
„ Mathura ..	8 „	1 „	0 „
„ Bijaypur ..	22 „	1 „	4 „
„ Khangraka-Bilar-bandar ..	23 „	0 „	0 „
„ Dhameli ..	8 „	1 „	0 „

,, Marahat	..	7	days	3	phrahars,	0	dandas.
,, Tajgaru	..	8	,,	1	,,	0	,,
,, Muhmedabad	..	15	,,	1	,,	0	,,
,, Sitabpur	..	2	,,	1	,,	0	,,
,, Ajmer	..	5	,,	0	,,	2	,,
,, Gujrat	..	16	,,	0	,,	2	,,
,, Illahabad	..	8	,,	2	,,	..	
,, Nurnagar	..	2	,,	3	,,	..	
,, Surat-bandar	..	19	,,	2	,,	0	,,
,, Khidrabad	..	3	,,	2	,,	4	,,
,, Laganpur	..	8	,,	1	,,	2	,,
,, Ahal-nagar	..	3	,,	0	,,	6	,,
,, Ilampur	..		..		..	7	,,
,, Lahore	..	6		2	..	4	,,
,, Lahore (South City).	..	3	,,	1	,,	4	,,

129. *Distances from Agra to other important places.*—

From Agara to Rabija	..	1	day	1	prahar	4	dandas.
Do Gogarnagar	..	1	,,	0	,,	0	,,
Do Ajmer	..	5	,,	1	,,	0	,,
Do Raitap	..	0	,,	2	,,	4	,,
Do Saratpur-Sikeli	..	0	days	2	prahars	0	dandas
Do Islampur	..	1	,,	2	,,	0	,,
Do Muhammadabad	..	2	,,	..		..	
Do Ujjalpur	..	7	,,	3	,,	4	,
Do Amber	..	10	,,	0	,,	10	,,
,, Delhi to ,,	..	13	,,	0	,,	6	,,
,, Agara to Prayag	..	6	,,	0	,,	0	,,
Do Patna	..	2	,,	2	,,	0	,,
Do Burhanpur	..	9	,,	2	,,	0	,,
Do Gwalior	..	2	,,	0	,,	0	,,

130. Distances *between other places*.—

From Gwalior to Paradiksha ..	3 days	3 prahars	0 dandas.
„ Paradiksha to Barbara	2 „	2 „	0 „
„ Barbara to Burhanpur ...	2 „	2 „	0 „
„ Kanauj to Itast ...	1 „	1 „	0 „
„ Itast to Nadiya-tatu ...	1 „	0 „	0 „
„ Nadiya-tatu to Lahore ...	1 „	0 „	4 „
„ Aurangabad to Hasana Abdal ..	2 „	0 „	10 „
„ „ Kabirband-mahda	6 „	2 „	2 „
„ „ Gulasabad ..	4 „	0 „	0 „
„ „ Baraksal ...	28 „	0 „	0 „
„ „ Subidpur ...	2 „	2 „	0 „
„ Kashmir to Bharatipur ...	4 „	0 „	0 „

CHAPTER XVI

ALLIES OF SAWAI JAI SINGHA OF AMBER

131. *Rajas and Zemindars who helped Jai Singh II.*— (There is a leaf missing here, which would have given us a few more names of Rajas and Zemindars. The page begins by saying, " 500 horses and 500 camels," which must be the equipment of some Raja mentioned in the missing leaf.—*Translator*).

1. *Raja Raorup Sing* lived at Patnagram at a distance of 9 days' journey, with 2,000 soldiers, 2 elephants, 250 horses and 300 camels.

2. *Raja Gopal Sing* lived at Karauligram at a distance of 20 days' journey, with 2,000 soldiers, 20 elephants, 300 horses and 2,000 camels.

3. *Raja Rao-Kusal Sing* lived at Zilagram at a distance of 12 days' journey, with 5,000 soldiers, 5 elephants, 250 horses and 200 camels.

4. *Raja Dip Sing* lived at Bhararigram at a distance of 4 days' journey, with 2,000 soldiers, 1 elephant, 200 horses and 300 camels.

5. *Nawab Wajit Khan* lived at Gosawaligram at a distance of 10 days' journey, with 5,000 soldiers, 5 elephants, 400 horses and 500 camels.

6. *Raja Gad Sing* lived at Jauligram at a distance of 8 days' journey, with 2,000 soldiers, 1 elephant, 500 horses and 250 camels.

7. *Raja Krishna Sing* lived at Kutagram at a distance of 15 days journey, with 2,000 soldiers, 2 elephants, 100 horses and 200 camels.

8. *Raja Jalum Sing* lived at Rajgargram at a distance of one month's journey, with 2 elephants, 500 horses and 250 camels.

9. *Raja Bud Sing* lived at Budigram at a distance of one month's journey, with 10,000 soldiers, 40 elephants, 200 horses and 1,000 camels.

10. *Raja Indar Sing* lived at Chaupargram at a distance of 9 days' journey, with 1,500 soldiers, 1 elephant, 200 horses and 210 camels.

11. *Raja Bhawar Sing* lived at Pehelegram at a distance of 20 days' journey, with 2000 soldiers, 2 elephants, 300 horses and 210 camels.

12. *Raja Badan Sing* lived at Diggram at a distance

of 25 days' journey, with 12,000 soldiers, 40 elephants, 1,000 horses and 10,000 camels.

13. *Raja Suryyamal Sing* lived at Pratapgarh-gram at a distance of 25 days' journey, with 14,000 soldiers, 60 elephants, 2,000 horses and 250 camels.

14. *Raja Pratap Sing* lived at Bharathpurgram at a distance of 25 days' journey, with 5,000 soldiers, 15 elephants, 1,000 horses and 500 camels.

15. *Raja Prataprai* lived at Unaragram at a distance of 9 days' journey with 5,000 soldiers, 2 elephants, 500 horses and 300 camels.

16. *Raja Syam Sing* lived at Bachuagram at a distance of 3 days' journey, with 15,000 soldiers, 5 elephants, 500 horses and 1,000 camels.

17. *Raja Bakat Sing* lived at Ekbarpurgram at a distance of 4 days' journey, with 2,000 soldiers, 2 elephants 200 horses, and 500 camels.

18. *Raja Bano Sing* lived at Bichangram at a distance of 2 days' journey, with 5,000 soldiers, 2 elephants, 1,000 horses and 2,000 camels.

19. *Raja Pratap Sing* lived at Babaligram at a distance of 4 days' journey, with 2,000 soldiers, 1 elephant, 1,000 horses and 500 camels.

20. *Raja Lal Sing* lived at Antaragram at a distance of 5 days' journey, with 1,000 soldiers, 2 elephants, 1,000 horses and 800 camels.

21. *Raja Jut Sing* lived at Barialgram at a distance of 6 days' journey, with 3,000 soldiers, 2 elephants, 1,000 horses and 500 camels.

22. *Raja Simram Sing* lived at Atergram at a distance of 1 month's journey, with 12,000 soldiers, 40 elephants, 1,000 horses and 250 camels.

23. *Raja Syam Sing* lived at Majpurgram at a distance of 7 days' journey, with 2,000 soldiers, 1 elephant, 500 horses and 200 camels.

24. *Raja Krit Sing* lived at Kambangram at a distance of 20 days' journey, with 12,000 soldiers, 20 elephants, 1,000 horses and 1,500 camels.

25. *Raja Baloram Sing* lived at Bangargram at a distance of 1 month's journey, with 1,500 soldiers, 20 elephants, 1,000 horses and 1,000 camels.

26. *Raja Bahadur Sing* lived at Ghâchieagram at a distance of 15 days' journey, with 5,000 soldiers, 15 elephants, 1,000 horses and 1,400 camels.

27. *Rao Guzarmal* lived at Rewâligram at a distance of 20 days' journey, with 11,000 soldiers, 20 elephants, 500 horses and 2,000 camels.

28. *Rao Brindaban Sing* lived at Manoharpurgram at a distance of 2 days' journey, with 12,000 soldiers, 10 elephants, 1,000 horses and 1,500 camels.

29. *Raja Kisor Sing* lived at Marâchgram at a distance of 2 days' journey, with 15,000 soldiers, 49 elephants, 2,000 horses and 6,000 camels.

30. *Raja Eklakha* lived at Jarpurgram at a distance of 9 days' journey, with 7,000 soldiers, 5 elephants, 1,000 horses and 600 camels.

31. *Raja Mirzabeg* lived at Narnau at a distance

of 3 days' journey, with 12,000 soldiers, 5 elephants, 1,000 horses and 1,000 camels.

32. *Raja Jadu Sing* lived at Terogram at a distance of 10 days' journey, with 12,000 soldiers, 5 elephants, 500 horses and 1,500 camels.

33. *Rao Pheriram* lived at Chatasgram at a distance of 2 days' journey, with 5,000 soldiers, 5 elephants, 500 horses and 1,000 camels.

34. *Raja Malabar* lived at Ramporagram at a distance of 2 month's journey, with 80,000 soldiers, 80 elephants, 500 horses and 8,000 camels.

The above Rajas gave their support to Sewai Jai Singha.

CHAPTER XVII

Desultory History of Ancient Assam

132. *Legendary kings of Kamarupa.*—Salutation to Sree-Krishna. Kâmapristha extends from the Dui-muni-sila to the Mânas river including the river Sonkosh in Kâmapristha. The territory lying between the Bar-Sonkosh to the two extremities of Morung is known as Ratnapristha, while Bhadrapristha extends from the Kalang river to the Kailas river flowing in Kariabâri. The region between the Dekkaravâhini and the Dui-muni-sila is known as Saumârpristha. Mairanga Dânava, son of Brahmâ, was the first ruler of these four pristhas. Mairanga Dânava's son was Hatakâsur, Hataka's son Sambarâsur, Sambarâ's son Raktâsur. Then ruled

Narakâsur of a different dynasty; he was succeeded by his son Bhagadatta whose son was Dharmapâl, his son Karmapâl, his son Prithvipâl, his son Suvâhu. The last ruled in an impolitic and unjust way at which Kâmâkhyâ became angry and drove him to Kailas.

133. *Raja Dharmapal.*—One Dharmapâl, a Khetri, came from Gauda and became King of Kâmarupa. He erected his palace on the Godanda-parvat, and imported Brâhmans, Kâyasthâs and Kalitâs from the following six places, Gauda, Kanauj, Mandartalâ, Jabai-sâhân, Tirhut and Bârakâ. With the above people he established a council of Pandits and continued to govern the country.

134. *Kendu-kalai Bapu.*—One Kendu-kalâi Bâpu used to offer worship to Kâmâkhyâ by singing devotional songs, at which the goddess became pleased and danced in utter nudity. Hearing this, the Râja begged the Brahman to show him the dance of Kâmâkhyâ. The Brâhman promised to show him the dance and directed him to peep through a chink-hole. Kendu-kalâi with other devotees clapped their hands and sang songs, and the goddess danced as usual. But, having caught a glimpse of the Râja through the hole, she was seized with shame, and fell flat on the ground, with her face downward, bereft of her habiliments. She became wroth and cursed the king, saying that any member of his family having a sight of her would perish instantaneously; she also cursed Kendu-kalâi, saying his line would be extinct.

135. *Pratap Singha and Chandraprabha.*—Dharmapâl's son was Raktapâl, his son Soma Pâl, his son Pratâp Singha, who erected his capital at Kanyakâgrâm. He

subjugated the Bhuyâns of Upper Assam, and became a great king by bringing them under his suzerainty. His son was Arimatta. One day Pratâp Singh bathed in the Brahmaputra with his wife. At night Brahmaputra caused him to see a dream to the effect that the king should deliver his consort Chandraprabhâ to the river, threatening to destroy his kingdom by bringing in a deluge over his villages and towns in the event of non-compliance. The nobles and ministers advised the king to renounce his affection for his consort, as it was for a wife of his that the country was on the verge of destruction. The king delivered the queen to the Brahmaputra, having put on her her complete set of ornaments. After some time the Brahmaputra threw her on the bank at Amarâjuri near Nilâchal. A Brâhman took the queen to his house and maintained her as his own daughter.

136. *Arimatta commits patricide.*—Some time later, the queen gave birth to a son. A serpent covered the new-born baby with its hood like an umbrella. The Brâhman who had given shelter to the queen saw a dream prophesying that her son would become king of Kâmarupa. The prince's face and head looked like those of an *ari* fish, for which he was named Arimatta.

After becoming king, Arimatta subdued the people around him and fought against his father Pratâp Singha who was then reigning in Upper Assam, without knowing that his antagonist was his own father. Pratâp Singha fell in the battle. On his return Arimatta communicated the intelligence of Pratâp Singha's death to his mother, who, having received the news, began to wail and narrated to her son the old story of the Brahmaputra.

The son replied. "It was unjust on his part to deliver you to the Brahmaputra, and for this sin he has died unknown at my hands." Chandraprabhâ followed her husband on the funeral pyre, and Arimatta performed the expiation ceremony for killing his father unawares, as well as the funeral obsequies of Pratap Singha. He then became king of Kâmarupa.

137. *Construction of the rampart Vaidyar-garh.*—Then he began to construct a rampart, having employed each of his subjects for one prahar by rotation. During the construction of the fort, poisonous insects and snakes used to kill the workers. A *vaidya* or physician exercised his virtues and said, "The snakes and insects will cease to kill men if they utter the name *vaidya*." At this the body of workers shouted *Vaidya*, *Vaidya*, and thus escaped from death. So the rampart became known as Vaidyar-garh. Six scores of tanks were excavated within the walls of the fort.

138. *Phingua's conquest of Kamarupa.*—One Phinguâ Raja of the family of the kings of Kamatâ, having subdued the territories commencing from Bihâr, threw up stockades at several places in Dakhinkul. He erected a fort in the village Sonkurihâ within the jurisdiction of Barbhâg, and waged a severe battle with Arimatta Râja at Vaidyar-garh. Being unable to defeat Arimatta, Phinguâ negotiated with Arimatta's wife Raktamalâ who said, "He should fight when I send information after having rubbed my husband's bow-strings with *khar* [an alkaline substance]. Victory will then be achieved."

This was done, and then ensued the battle. The arrow would not shoot itself from the bow-string on account of the latter's oily character. Phinguâ won the day. Arimatta dived into the river and disappeared. Phinguâ then fetched Arimatta's wife Raktamalâ and killed her, saying: "She has betrayed her own husband and how can we expect her to be faithful to us?" Arimatta's son, Raktasingha, ascended the throne after having killed Phinguâ. The new king carried on a liaison with a Brâhman woman, and consequently lost his kingdom on the curse of the Brâhman who was thus wronged.

139. *Revival of the Bara-Bhuyans' supremacy.*—The Bâra-Bhuyâns then asserted their supremacy. They subdued the house of the Swarga-Mahârâjâ and the Sandikâis, and erected a fortress at Hâthisâl in Karaibâri. They also subjugated Ghila-Bijaypur and constructed roads and tanks in the vicinity of the Karatoyâ-Ganga, After this, one Masalanda Gâzi of Bengal ruled here for some years.[91] Then came Husain Shâh Padshah's son Sultan Gayâsuddin who died at Garurachal. The Bhuyâns attained suzerain power once again.

CHAPTER XVIII

Rival Koch Princes at the Mogul Court

140. *Raghudev establishes his headquarters at Ghila.*—Prince Chilârâi or Sukladhwaja, brother of Mahârâjâ Naranârâyan of Cooch-Bihâr, died leaving a son named Raghudevanârayan. Naranârâyan shifted his capital as the Râja of Morung threatened an invasion of Bihâr. Raghudev was with his uncle. Chilârâi had the following

Barâs and Buruks or officers—Kabindra Pâtra, Yudhisthir Bhandâr Kâyastha, Sri-râi Laskar, Kaipur Giri, Sonâbar, Rupâbar, Sardâr Kabirâj, Gopâl Châulia, Gadâi Barkâyastha, Gadâdhar Châulia, Purandar Laskar, as well as others. They now said to Raghudev Pâtkowar or the heir-apparent: "If you remain like this, you will always be subservient to the king. Mahârâja Biswa Singha at the time of his death had bestowed Bihâr upto the Bar-Sonkosh river upon Naranârâyan, and the eastern portion of his kingdom upon Chilârâi Dewân. We now propose to make you a Râja at Ghilâ so that you may become an independent monarch. Get possession, by some means, of your father's elephants, horses and other provisions, and then come out on the pretext of a travelling excursion."

Raghudev accordingly said to the Râja: "If Your Majesty permits I intend to go out on a travelling expedition."

The king replied,—"I love you more than a son, so I have appointed you my heir-apparent. Do as you like."

Raghudev said: "I want to take with me the officers, elephants, horses and provisions belonging to my father."

The king replied: "All that is mine is also yours. Take with you whatever you choose."

The prince took with him his father's accoutrements and property, and after travelling for some time crossed the Sonkosh river, and, seeing that snakes were being eaten up by frogs he established his headquarters at Ghilâ. Naranârâyan continued to remain at Bihâr.

In the meantime a son was born to Râja Naranârâyan, and he was named Lakhshminârâyan.

Raghudev then deputed two Barâs to Naranârâyan with the following message: "The Mahârâja has now been blessed with a son. Nothing untoward will happen during the life-time of the Mahârâja; but after his demise things may not go so smoothly with his son. Two tigers cannot live in the same den. If the king approves of my leaving Bihâr for good, he should appoint me king over the territory belonging to my father, according to the partition of the kingdom made by my grandfather. Then we shall all remain in peace and happiness." The king became pleased with this proposal, and said: "My nephew has thought well. It is an excellent proposal." The king offered the royal sceptre, umbrella and throne to Raghudev and made him Râja with his headquarters at Ghilâ. There was no man so handsome and virtuous as Mahârâja Raghudevanârâyan, and he ruled for thirty-two years.

141. *Hostility between Raghudev and Lakshminarayan.*— As Maharâja Naranârâyan demanded tribute from Raghudev, there was a war between the two, but it occurred only once. After the death of Naranârâyan, Raghudev fought with his son Lakshminârâyan. Raja Raghudev was defeated, and he returned to his territory, leaving behind his royal umbrella at Bihâr. Laksminârâyan detained this insignia of royalty as a souvenir of his victory over Raghudev. The defeated prince now conferred with his men, Sil Khân, Fateh Khân, the king's son-in-law Purandar Laskar, Nitâi Chandra Nâzir, Thakur Panchânanda, Kabindra Pâtra, Gadâdhar

Baruâ and other Barâs and Buruks, as a result of which he made preparations for invading Bihâr. Hearing this, Lakshminârâyan marched towards Ghilâ. Raghudev came out victorious; and Lakshminârâyan took to his heels after being repulsed. Raghudev Râja did not lose any of his Barâs and Buruks.

Raghudevanârâyan had the following sons,—Parikshit, Indranârâyan, Jadurâi, Bhawa Singha, Mukundadev, Balinârâyan, Mân Singha, Mahindra Singha, Gohâin Magal, Gohâin Râichanda, Sundarnârâyan, Gohâin Maidân, Gohâin Mehnarâyan, Madhunârâyan, Brishaketu, Anantanârâyan, Pratâpnârâyan and Bijoy Singha.

Mahârāja Raghudevanārâyan breathed his last on a full moon day in the month of Agrahâyan.

142. *Balinarayan's death.*—At the instigation of Parikshit, a Mech murdered Indranârâyan by twisting his neck. Parikshit then ascended the throne. Hearing of this disturbance, Lakshminârâyan entered Ghilâ by the gate of Kâmâkhyâ-guri. There followed a terrible battle, wherein Balinârâyan, brother of Lakshminârâyan, was transfixed by a spear at dusk by Parikshitnârâyan's *dhali* or shieldsman Rupâbar through ignorance, being taken for some unknown sardâr. When Rupâbar came to know that it was no other than Balinârâyan he unsheathed his sword and laid it before the prince, saying: "You are the brother of the king, and I, a *paik* or subject of yours, have wounded you. So you should cut me down with your own hand, by which my sin will be expiated." To this Balinârâyan replied: "What shall I gain by killing you? Besides, it will not be easy to save my life. You are permitted to commit

even an act of unrighteousness if commanded to do so by the person whose salt you eat. More especially, you have slain me through ignorance, and so you are exempted from all guilt." Saying this, Balinârâyan breathed his last. Parikshit then removed the body of Balinârâyan and cremated it with *agar chandan* according to the custom of the country. His bones were sent to Bihâr. Twelve Kârzis including Pâra Kârzi were captured in that battle[92].

143. *Parikshit and the Karzis of Cooch-Bihar.*—Parikshit's elephant named Mahindra-singha demolished the camp of Lakshminârâyan. Parikshit also captured two elephants belonging to Lakshiminârâyan, who fled with his *mahadoi* or queen-consort. A Pathan of the camp of Parikshit intended to capture Lakshminârâyan, but he was dissuaded by his master from doing so, who said: "My aunt is with the fugitives. I shall be reprimanded by people if I capture him at this stage." Lakshminârâyan, being thus defeated, returned to Bihâr.

The captive Kârzis bowed down to Parikshit. But Pâra Kârzi refused to do so. Parikshit said to Pâra Kârzi: "All other Kârzis have paid their obeisance to me. But you have not done so. What is the reason?" To this Pâra Kârzi replied,—"With this head I have bowed down to Mahârâja Lakshminârâyan, and I cannot bow down to you." The Râja became indignant, and ten stripes were inflicted on the Kârzi daily. Still he did not pay his obeisance.

Lakshminârâyan then sent his *Katakis* or messengers to Parikshit, asking for the release of the Kârzis.

Parikshit demanded in turn his father's umbrella left behind at Bihâr. Lakshminârâyan returned the umbrella, and Parikshit made presents to the Kârzis and gave them leave to depart. Pâra Kârzi now bowed down to Parikshit, who said. "You did not bow down before. Why have you done so now?" The Kârzi replied: "To me you are the same as Mahârâja Lakshminârâyan. If I had bowed to you before, you would have attributed it to my fear for my life." The Kârzis then departed for their country.

144. *Mukarram Khan's expedition against Parikshit.*—Parikshit used to conduct a pillaging expedition to Bihâr every year. Being unable to tolerate these oppressions, Lakshminârâyan presented his daughter, and offered his allegiance to the Padshah, with the complaint that he could not peacefully govern his kingdom on account of Parikshit.[93] The Padshah despatched Nawâb Mukarram Khân and twenty-two Omrâos with Lakshminârâyan, charging them to bring Parikshit as prisoner without taking his life. During Mukarram Khân's march, the Râja of Susanga, Raghunâth Rai, also complained to him regarding Parikshit's frequent depredations.[94] Mukarram Khân gave assurance to the Râja, who placed a contingent of his army under the command of the Nawâb. Lakshminârâyan also handed over his army and officers to Mukarram Khân and proceeded in advance to Bihâr, fearing that the city would be pillaged during his absence, as it was then empty.

145. *War between Parikshit and Mukarram Khan.*—Mukarram Khân encamped at Dhubri. Parikshit des-

patched Fâteh Khân of Phulaguri at the head of his troops and officers. There ensued a terrible battle with Mukarram Khân, in which the Phulaguriâ Fâteh Khân was captured. One Paramananda Doloi, who was on a war-elephant, died in the engagement. The elephant demolished a large number of camps, but it was subsequently captured. Fighting on land remaining indecisive there ensued a naval engagement. Purandar Laskar had a hard fight with Kuber Khân of the Bangâls. Kuber Khân perished in the fight, and Purandar destroyed a large number of the hostile camp. Then followed a battle with the son of Kuber Khân. Purandar fell in the battle. After the death of Purandar the Râja spent some time in negotiating through Wakils, after which he retreated from the fight, crossed the Manâh, and halted at a stockade erected at Solâ. The Bangâls also pursued the fugitive, and halted on the other side of the river.

146. *Parikshit and Lakshminarayan before the Padshah.*— The nobles and ministers of Parikshit held a conference among themselves, at which they came to the following decision ;—" If the Râja surrenders to the Bangâls, he will be carried off as a prisoner. There will be no more a king in this land ; we shall then establish cordial terms with the Bangâls, and govern the country as independent chiefs." With this intent they said to the Râja : " Save your Râj by offering submission, as we fear we shall not be able to oppose the Bangâls in strength."

Wakils were despatched to Mukarram Khân with the message : " I promise to deliver to the Padshah an annual tribute consisting of 2 maunds of âgar or lignum aloes, 100 elephants, 200 tângon ghorâs or ponies, 500 *thungas* and *kamalis* or blankets, musks, and 400 yak-tails.[95] I will give half of the above presents to Mukarram Khân. I hope he will retire from the place."

To this Mukarram Khân replied: "It is not proper that I should do *haram* or injustice to the salt of the Padshah, and so I will not retire from here. All right, let the Râja himself come. There will be peace and concord if the Râja bows down to the Padshah. I also promise solemnly that, if anything untoward is likely to happen to the king, I will put forward my life first, irrespective of what may befall the Râja afterwards. The Padshah simply wants to see the Râja, having heard his name for a long time."

Then Parikshit, accompanied by his nobles and ministers, offered his submission to Mukarram Khân, who received the Râja with great honour, presented to him clothes and ornaments, and took him to the Padshah. On this side, Nawab Sayid Bâbâkar or Abu Baqr, remained at Hazo. Mukarram Khân took with him Lakshminârâyan also, who offered his allegiance to the Emperor.

The Padshah said to Lakshminârâyan and Parikshit: "You should both carry on your kingship being friends with each other. And Parikshit, Lakshminârâyan is your *chacha* or uncle; bow down to him by touching his feet." To this Parikshit replied: "What you have said is just and proper. An infuriated lion kills elephants as he chooses and eats them. Sometimes he desists from slaughter at the intercession of the female ones. The great ocean attains increase or decrease at the stipulated period. But men and animals are not subjected to increase or decrease through us. You are in that position too. There exists a feeling of animosity between himself and me. I will never lower my head to him, not even at the cost of my life." The Padshah being indignant seized Parikshit and detained him.

147. *The Cooch-Bihar princes leave the Mogul court.*—The Padshah gave leave to Lakshminârayan and said: "You should ask me for things which are not available in your kingdom." The Râja replied: "I have all things in my country, except *purud*, *kali* and *tarowal* or sword, and Irâqi ponies." He was given leave to depart after being presented with horses and swords.

Mukarram Khân, interceding on behalf of Parikshit, procured his leave as well. The Padshah requested the Râja to ask for articles not found in his territory. Parikshit said; "Everything is found in my kingdom. I would request the Padshah to give me a picture of His Majesty, so that I may always salute it." The Padshah replied: "We do not give our pictures to anybody and everybody. I give one to you on the understanding that you will refrain from any hostility to our family. If, on the contrary, you become unfriendly to us, you will be destroyed." The Râja took leave and departed with due humility.

148. *Parikshit sent again to Delhi.*—Having heard of Parikshit's departure from the presence of the Padshah, the Burâs and Baruks of Kâmarupa wrote to Islâm Khân, Nawâb of Dacca, that they would flee from

the kingdom if Parikshit returned. The Nawâb also received intimation to that effect from the imperial court. When Parikshit reached Dacca, the Nawâb said: "I hear Parikshit has brought a picture of the Padshah. When he comes to see me he should leave behind the picture as in the event of the picture being brought to the court, I shall have to leave my seat and bow down to it." Parikshit did not pay heed to this advice, and he went to the presence of the Nawâb with the picture, seeing which the Nawâb advanced from his seat and saluted it. The Nawâb flew into a rage, and wrote to the Padshah, and sent also the letter of the Barâs and Buruks of Kâmarupa in which Parikshit was described as a *haramzada*. The Nawâb also reported about Parikshit's harassing of the Râjas and Zemindars living in the neighbourhood of his territories, adding, "These are the misdeeds of Parikshit. The Padshah has released a tiger of the woods after having captured him once. When he returns to the forest, the country is not to subsist." The Padshah wrote to the Nawâb asking him to send Parikshit again to His Majesty's presence. The Nawâb accordingly sent Parikshit to Delhi.

149. *Parikshit dies at Tribeni.*—The Râja reached the pilgrimage of Tribeni, where he asked the Brâhmans as to the resultant merits of a visit to that sacred place. The Brâhmans replied, "Whatever desire a man cherishes here before death is attained. No sin accrues from suicide if committed in this place by him." Having heard this the Râja said: "No one gets an opportunity of visiting the pilgrimage, and how long

does one's life exist?" With this vow he distributed charities and renounced his body.

Kabi-sekhar, son of Kabindra Pâtra, Srirâm Laskar and other companions of the Râja then went to the presence of the Padshah. The office of *Kanungui* of the vilâyat Cooch Hajo was conferred on Kabi-sekhar. The Nawâb gave leave to the other companions of the Râja some of whom were appointed as Chaudhuris, some as Pâtwaris, and others as Laskars.

CHAPTER XIX

KOCH HAZO UNDER THE MOGULS

150. *Koch Raja Dharmanarayan.*—Sayyid Bâbâkar pursued [the Assamese] from Hazo to Sâmdharâ. The soldiers of the Swarga-Mahârâja captured him at the latter place. Mirza Bâqi then came to Hâzo and stayed there for some time. He was turned out from the place, and Bahram Beg remained at Hazo. The latter was also removed, and Nawâb 'Abdullah Islâm remained at Hâzo. Then Momâi-tâmuli, an officer of the Swarga-Mahârâja proceeded with Râja Dharmanârâyan, and captured 'Abdullah Islâm, who was sent to Garagrâm. The Dhekeri territory or Western Assam was given to Râja Dharmanârâyan.

151. *Ibrahim Karori organises the perganas.*—The Baruâs and Buruks headed by Kabi-sekhar had taken leave of the Padshah and returned to their own country. They were accompanied by Sheikh Ibrâhim Karori who came to re-organise the administration of the country.

During the Râja's reign there were only *gaons* or villages, and no perganas. Sheikh Ibrâhim introduced the perganâ system. The whole area was designated Villayat Cooch Hazo,[96] which was divided into four sarkars,—Sarkar Kamrup, Sarkar Dhekeri, Sarkar Dakhinkul and Sarkar Bangalbhum.

152. *Perganas of Sarkar Kamrup.*—The following perganas were under Sarkar Kamrup :—Pergana Kowarbhâg, Pergana Pâtidarang, Pergana Banbhâg, Pergana Basâ amalgamated with Banbhâg, Pergana Bardarang, Pergana Bâhbâri, Pergana Sâtrajiâ, Pergana Chaurâhi-khâtâ, Pergana Kâsimpur, Pergana Barbhâg, Pergana Dehor, Pergana Khetribhâg, Pergana Bajâli, Pergana Bahukhâtâ amalgamated with Bajâli, Pergana Bâusi, Pergana Barnâgar, Pergana Petkatâ amalgamated with Barnâgar, Pergana Barpetâ, Pergana Bejini, Pergana Phulaguri amalgamated with Bejini, Pergana Bâskâ, Pergana Digjal; Kasbe Hajo, Kasbe Gauhâti, Rikâb Mahal, Peshkosh Pândâri or Barag-mahal, Pumbâ-mahal, Gudara-Umananda, Hema-mahal, Maki-mahal, Chetal-bâzi Phara where elephants are captured by Khedda operation, Agâdhubis, Nikâthi-mahal, Paikan-mahal, Kachari-mahal, Chutiâ-mahal, Karkhânâ. There are altogether 41 mahals.

153. *Perganas of Sarkar Dhekeri.*—The following perganas were in the jurisdiction of Sarkar Dhekeri :—Pergana Khutâghât, Pergana Gumâ, Pergana Parbatjowâr, Pergana Kasbe Dhubri, Pergana Jamirâ, Pergana Târiâ, Pergana Ghurlâ, Pergana Jalkar-mahal, Pergana Kasbe Ghilâ, Pergana Châpgar, Pergana Resham-tâti, Pergana Koklar, Pergana Khumâr, Pergana Kâth-mahal, Pergana

Kotwâli, Pergana Dimyâli-mahal, Pergana Dhâmâdi-mahal, Pergana Chulhât, Pergana Destak-mahal. Altogether 19 mahals.

154. *Perganas of Sarkar Dakhinkul.*—The following perganas were under Sarkar Dakhinkul :—Pergana Sambhor, which had 5 *tapas*,—Tape Bagaribâri, Tape Sâmuriâ, Tape Bekeli, Tape Haljal Oza-kheli and Tape Tisimpur ; Pergana Pându had 7 tapâs, Tape Bangeswar, Tape Majhiali, Tape Chayânia, Tape Beltolâ, Tape Bharuâkâtâ, Pergana Dumuriâ, Pergana Bâranti, Pergana Mechpârâ, Pergana Kalmaluapârâ, Pergana Karaibâri, Pergana Pumbâ, Pergana Gâro-mahal and Pergana Gorkâti.

155. *Perganas of Sarkar Bangalbhum.*—The following perganas were under Sarkar Bangâlbhum :—Pergana Baherbandh, Pergana Bhitarbandh, Pergana Gaybari, Pergana Choki-Baretala Chândiâni.

There are 75 mahals in the four sarkars mentioned above.

156. *A Glossary of the names of Perganas.*—Sheik Ibrâhim, coming from the imperial presence, reorganised the country by dividing it into perganas.

Bahbari.—There was in this pergana a clump of red bamboos with five or six joints at intervals of one cubit, watched by the Râja's officers, hence the pergana is called *Bahbari* or orchard of bamboos.

Darang.—The expenses incurred in connection with the amusements of the country [were met from here], hence it is called *Dar-rang* literally, price of amusements.

Kowarbhag.—This place was governed by princes, hence it is called *Kowar-bhag* or princes' portion.

The Darang Pergana was made by combining a couple of villages from other perganas, and a few from Darang.

Kachari-mahal.—It was so called because it was inhabited by the Kachâris.

Chutiya-mahal.—It was so called because it was inhabited by the Chutiâs.

Banbhag.—This was governed by princes who were labourers, hence it is called Ban-bhâg, or the portion of labour.

Chaurabikhata.—Pergana was so called because the Râja had his *khats* or personal estates here.

Barbhag.—It was enjoyed by the Baruâs, hence it is called *Bar-bhag.*

Dehor is so called because there were many *devalayas* or temples here.

Khetri-bhag is so called because it was inhabited by the Khetri sepoys serving under the Râja.

Bajali is so called because it was enjoyed by one Bajalia (?) prince.

Baher-khata was the pergana where the *khats* or estates of princes and princesses were situated.

Phulaguri literally flower-land, is so called because there was a *Kanakchampa* plant here. An officer in charge of the royal revenue was stationed here.

Bausi was enjoyed by a queen-mother, hence (?) it is so called.

Bijini, literally a barber-woman, is so called as it

was inhabited by the queen's barber-woman who used to trim her finger-nails.

157. *Mirza Jahina at Gauhati.*—After this Râja Dharmanârâyan governed the country. Mirza Jâhinâ, Subha of Bengal, fought at Bare-pointa. The Bangâls and the Dhekeris lost a large number of their soldiers, and Mirza Jâhinâ pursued his foes as far as Sâmdharâ, but he had to come back to Gauhati, being unable to stand against the forces of the Swarga-Mahârâja. He sailed down to Bengal, having appointed Allah Yar Khan as Nawab.

APPENDICES

A. PERSIAN ACCOUNTS OF ASSAM

1. *Shah-namah by Firdausi.*—The contest between Shankaladideva, king of Kamarupa, and Bahram Gaur, Sultan of Persia. English translations by Turner Macan, 1829; abridged, J. Atkinson, 1832; A.G. and E. Warner, 1905—1925.

2. *Tarikh-i-Firishta.*—by Muhammad Qasim Hindu Shah. The war between Shankala, king of Kamarupa, and Peeranweisa, the general of Afrasiyab, king of Turan and Scythia, and with Afrasiyab himself. English translation by John Briggs, 1829; reprinted 1908.

3. *Tabaqat-i-Nasiri*—by Minhaj-i-Siraj Jurjani. Muhammad bin Bukhtiyar Khiliji's invasion of Kamarupa in 1198 A.D. The author was at Lakhnauti. English translation by H. G. Raverty, 1873—97, for the Asiatic Society of Bengal, now Royal A.S.B..

4. *Riyaz-us-Salatin.*—by Ghulam Husayan Salim. Invasion of Assam by Muhammad bin Bukhtiyar Khiliji and Hussain Shah. English translation by Abdus Sallam, 1902—1904, for the Asiatic Society of Bengal.

5. *Akbar-namah.*—by Shaikh Abul Fazl. Man Singha's intervention in Cooch Behar caused by the rivalries of Lakshminarayan and Raghudeva. English trnsalation by H. Beveridge, 1897—1921, for the Asiatic Society of Bengal.

6. *Ain-i-Akbari.*—by Shaikh Abul Fazl, being the third volume of the *Akbar-namah*. Divisions of

Kamarupa and the manners and habits of its inhabitants. English translation by H. Blochmann, Vol I, and H. S. Jarrett, Vols. II and III, 1868—1894, for the Asiatic Society of Bengal; earlier version by Francis Gladwin, 1800.

7. *Tuzuk-i-Jahangiri.*—Autobiographical memoirs of Emperor Jahangir, up to the seventeenth year of his reign; continued from the nineteenth year by Mut'amad Khan. The Koch prince Lakshminarayan solicits the aid of Emperor Jahangir against his nephew Parikshit. English translation by W. H. Lowe, 1889, for the Asiatic Society of Bengal.

8. *Padishah-namah.*—Invasion of Assam by Allah Yar Khan, during the reign of the Ahom king Pratap Singha and Emperor Shah Jahan. For the first ten years of Shah Jahan's reign, by Muhammad Amin bin Abul Hasan Quazwini; for the first twenty years, by Abdul Hamid Lahauri; for the third decade of the reign, by Muhammad Waris.

9. *Fathiyah-i-Ibriyah.*—also called *Tarikh-i-Ashan* and *Tarikh-i-Mulk-i-Ashan.*—by Ibn Muhammad Wali Ahmad, surnamed Shihab-ud-Din Talish. Mir Jumla's invasion and the condition of Assam and the Assamese. English translation by H. Blochmann, partly, J.A.S.B., 1872; J. N. Sarkar, partly, J.B.O.R.S., 1915; Lt. James E. Alexander, 1827.

10. *Alamgir-namah.*—by Munshi Muhammad Kazim bin Muhammad Amin Munshi. Invasion of Assam by Mir Jumla and Ram Singha, etc., and the condition of Assam.

11. *Ma'asir-i-Alamgiri.*—by Muhammad Saqin Musta'id Khan. Assam-Mogul conflicts of the Ramsingha and post-Ramsingha period. Bibliotheca Indica Series.

12. *Muntakhab-ul-Lubab* or *Tarikh-i-Khafi*

Khan by Muhammad Hashim Ali Khan, surnamed Khafi Khan. Mogul invasion of Cooch-Behar and Assam, Bibliotheca Indica Series.

13. *Hadiqat-us-Safa*.—By Yusuf Ali bin Ghulam Ali Khan. Mir Jumla's invasion of Assam. English translation of the portion relating to Mir Jumla's invasion was reproduced in the *Calcutta Quarterly Journal* for June 1825.

14. *Risalat-us-Shuhada*.—By Pir Muhammad Shattari. War between Shah Ismail Ghazi and Kameswar, king of Kamarupa. The original Persian text with synopsis in English was printed in the J.A.S.B. 1874, by G. H. Damant, I.C.S.

15. *Maasir-ul-Umara*.—Biographies of Muhammadan and Hindu officers of the Timurid sovereigns of India from 1500 to about 1780 A.D. Life-sketches of several Mogul commanders and generals who participated in the Assam wars, with narratives of their Assam careers. The original Persian is by Shah Nawaz Khan, translated into English, partly, by H. Beveridge, and Baini Prashad 1911—1941 for the Asiatic Society of Bengal.

16. *Baharistan-i-Ghaybi*.—A history of the conflicts of the Moguls with Assam, Bengal, Bihar and Orissa during the reigns of Jahangir and Shah Jahan, by Mirza Nathan, *alias* Shitab Khan, the Mogul Fauzadar of Gauhati. Translated into English from the original Persian copy in the Bibliotheque Nationale of Paris, by the late Dr. M. I. Borah. In two volumes, pages xxix + 938. Published by the Department of Historical and Antiquarian Studies in Assam, Gauhati, 1936.

B. ASSAMESE HISTORICAL LITERATURE

Bibliographical Note

As considerable interest has been roused among students of Indian History in the indigenous chronicles of Assam, known as Buranjis, an indication is given below of the materials for the information of scholars who want to study the subject in an intensive form.

The necessary basic information will be found in Dr. S. K. Bhuyan's paper "Assamese Historical Literature," read at the Fifth Session of the All-India Oriental Conference held at Lahore in November 1928, and published in the "Indian Historical Quarterly," Calcutta, for September 1929. Fuller information can be obtained from Dr. Bhuyan's Prefaces and Introductions in English to the Buranjis edited by him, viz,—

(1) *Assam Buranji.*—By the late Srijut Harakanta Barua Sadar-Amin. A history of Ahom rule in Assam, 1228—1826 A.D., being an enlarged version of *Assam Buranji Puthi* by Kasinath Tamuli Phukan and Radhanath Barbarua. Published by the Department of Historical and Antiquarian Studies, Assam, Gauhati, 1930.

(2) *Kamrupar Buranji.*—A detailed history of the Assam-Mogul conflicts of the seventeenth century, with chapters on ancient Kamarupa. D.H.A.S., 1930.

(3) *Deodhai Asam Buranji.*—A collection of old chronicles dealing with the earlier period of Ahom history, neighbouring tribes, Ahom customs, etc. It includes the chronicle of Assam by Atan Bura-

gohain Rajmantri Dangaria, Prime Minister of Assam, 1662—1679. D.H.A.S., 1932.

(4) *Tungkhungia Buranji.*—A history of the Tungkhungia dynasty of Ahom sovereigns, from 1681 to 1806, by Srinath Duara Barbarua, Head of the Executive and the Judiciary from 1800 to 1817. D.H.A.S., 1932. The original Assamese version.

(5) *Asamar Padya-Buranji.*—Two metrical chronicles of Assam dealing with the events of the period from 1679 to 1826, by Dutiram Hazarika and Bisweswar Vaidyadhipa. D.H.A.S., 1933.

(6) *Kachari Buranji.*—A history of Cachar from the earliest times to the reign of the Kachari Raja Tamradhwaj Narayan and the Ahom king Swargadeo Rudra Singha. D.H.A.S., 1936.

(7) *Jayantia Buranji.*—A history of Jayantia from the earliest times to the reign of the Jayantia Raja Lakshmi Singha and the Ahom king Swargadeo Siva Singha, with sidelights on Jayantia matriarchal system, and the history of the Khasi state of Khyrim. D.H.A.S., 1937. Preface by Mr. S. K. Dutta.

(8) *Tripura Buranji*, or *Tripura Desar Katha.* —A historical and descriptive account of Tripura with special reference to the events of 1710 to 1715, by Ratna Kandali Sarma Kataki and Arjun Das Bairagi, ambassadors of King Rudra Singha deputed to the Tripura court.

From the original manuscript in the British Museum, London. D.H.A.S., 1938.

(9) *Tungkhungia Buranji.*—or a history of Assam from 1681 to 1826, being an English translation of the Assamese text, with an extension of the history up to the British occupation of Assam in 1826. With a glossary of Assamese historical terms and genealogical tables of Ahom kings. Published by the Oxford Uuiversity Press for the D.H. A.S., 1933.

(10) *Assam Buranji.*—Obtained from the family of Sukumar Mahanta. A history of the Ahom kings from the earliest times to the reign of Swargadeo Gadadhar Singha. The Preface and Introduction in English cover 83 pages. The Introduction deals, among other subjects, with the ideology of the Assamese people and cites a number of illustrative anecdotes. D.H.A.S., 1945.

(11) *Padshah Buranji.*—An old Assamese chronicle of the Sultans and Emperors of Delhi, from the defeat of Pithor Raja to Aurangzeb, published by the Kamarupa Anusandhan Samiti, Gauhati, in 1935. This chronicle was described by Dr. Bhuyan in a series of articles in the *Islamic Culture*, Hyderabad, Deccan, in the years 1928-1929, under the heading "New Lights on Mogul India from Assamese Sources," An English translation of *Padshah-Buranji* was

also published in the same journal in 1933-34 under the title "Annals of the Delhi Badshahate."

Reviews of the above Buranjis have been published in the *Journal of the Royal Asiatic Society of Great Britain and Ireland*, *Journal of Indian History*, *Journal of the Bhandarkar Research Institute*, *Islamic Culture*, *Indian Historical Quarterly*, *Calcutta Review*, *History*, *Journal of the Royal Geographical Society*, *Indian Culture*, *Annual Bibliography of Indian Archaeology*, etc.

A few more Buranjis have also been published under the editorship of other authors, *viz.*,—

(1) *Assam Buranji arthat Assam Desiya Itihas.*—A history of Assam, in Bengali, by Haliram Dhekial Phukan, Part 1, from the Pauranic period to the advent of the British. Printed at the Samachar Chandika Jantra, Calcutta, 1829. Reviewed by Dr. Bhuyan in the Journal of the Bangiya Sahitya-Parishat, Calcutta, B.S., 1333, Vol. 33, No. 1. A supplementary note by Pandit Jatindra Mohan Bhattacharya was published in a subsequent issue of the Parishat Journal. A review of this book by Tarachand Chakravarti was published in the *Asiatic Journal and Monthly Register*, Vol. 23, 1837, and an analysis forms part of India Office Library Tract No. 166.

(2) *Assam Buranji Puthi.*—A history of the Ahom kings from the earliest times to the British occupation of Assam, by Kasinath Tamuli Phukan and Radhanath Barbarua. First published in

1844 by the American Baptist Mission, Sibsagar. Reprinted and published by Authority in 1906.

(3) *Darrang-Raj-Vamsavali.*—A metrical chronicle of the early rulers of Cooch-Behar to the time of Samudra Narayan, Raja of Darrang, written about the year 1798 by Suryya Khari Daivajna. Edited by Pandit Hem Chandra Goswami, and published by the Government of Assam, 1917.

(4) *Purani Asam Buranji.*—A chronicle of the Ahom kings from the earliest times to the reign of Gadadhar Singha. Edited by Pandit Hem Chandra Goswami, and published by the Kamarupa Anusandhan Samiti, 1922.

(5) *An Account of Assam.*—Being mainly an English translation of two chronicles, one in Assamese and the other in Ahom, by Dr. John Peter Wade, who stayed in Assam in 1792—94. Edited from the original manuscript in the India Office Library, London, by Srijut Benudhar Sharma of Charing in Sibsagar, and published by Srijut Rameswar Sharma, 1927.

(6) *Ahom Buranji.*—A chronicle of the Ahom kings from the earliest times to Swargadeo Purandar Singha. The original text is in the Ahom language and script, with a parallel rendering in English, by Rai Sahib Golap Chandra Barua. Published by the Government of Assam, 1930.

(7) *Assam Buranji.*—A history of the Ahom kings from the accession of Swargadeo Jayadhwaj Singha in 1648 to that of Swargadeo Gadadhar Singha in 1681, with excerpts from miscellaneous chronicles. Edited by Mr. S. K. Dutta, and published by the D.H.A.S., 1938.

Information about Assamese Buranjis is also available in the following :—

(*a*) Dhekial Phukan, Anandaram.—A *Few Remarks on the Assamese Language*, Sibsagar, 1855, pp. 45-56. A synopsis of this book was published in the *Indian Antiquary* for 1896.

(*b*) Grierson, Sir George.—*Linguistic Survey of India*, Vol. I, Part I, Introductory, p. 156.

(*c*) Gait, E. A., now Sir.—*Report on the Progress of Historical Research in Assam.* Shillong, 1897, pp. 16—24.

(*d*) Gait, Sir Edward.—Preface to his *History of Assam*, Calcutta, 1st edition, 1906; second edition, 1926.

(*e*) Bhuyan, Dr. S. K.—*Ahomar Din*, Jorhat, 1918, pp. 89—92.

(*f*) Bhuyan, Dr. S. K.—*History of the Reign of Rajeswar Singha*, king of Assam from 1751 to 1769. The chapter on the desecration of Buranjis by Kirti Chandra Barbarua. *Banhi*, Gauhati, Vol. XV, No. 2, Jaistha, 1847 *Saka*, pp. 108—111.

There are several Buranjis, yet unpublished, in the library of the Department of Historical and

Antiquarian Studies, Assam, and some of them have been mentioned in Bulletins I, II and III of the Department. Copies of English translations of some Buranjis, prepared under the direction of Sir Edward Gait, are in possession of Sir Jadunath Sarkar in their manuscript form, vide his *History of Aurangzeb*, Vol. III, 1916, Foreword, and Chapters 31-32; and D.H.A.S., Bulletin No. I, 1932, pp. 21-22.

C.—MUHAMMED ALI AT GAUHATI

To my brethren living at Secunderabad I will point out a coincidence of supreme interest. Secunderabad has now become the radiating centre of Indo-Islamic culture and civilisation; and it played a similar role two hundred and fifty years ago when war and conquest were the only medium of cultural contact. The principal informant of the Assamese chronicler was a Secunderabadi Mogul named Muhammad Ali. He has been described as a scholar proficient in Arabic and Persian *loghats*. He was in charge of the education of the sons of Nawab Mansur Khan, Fauzadar at Gauhati, from March 1679 to September 1682, for which he was paid a remuneration of full one hundred rupees per month. He had with him the usual travelling archive and repertory of factlore, written and oral; and the historically-minded Assamese of those days made full use of what Muhammad Ali possessed and knew.

The circumstances which led to the presence of Nawab Mansur Khan and his protégé at Gauhati are of great importance, especially in view of the light which they throw on the *P.B.* chapters devoted to Nawab Mir Jumla, Raja Ram Singha and Sultan Azamtara. By the treaty of 1639 enacted between the Mogul commander Allah Yar Khan and the Ahom general Momai-tamuli Barbarua, Western Assam extending from Gauhati to the Manas river passed into the hands of the Moguls; and Mogul Fauzadars governed the newly conquered territory with their headquarters at Gauhati. During the illness of Emperor Shah Jahàn and the War of Succession, Jayadhwaj Singha, king of Assam, reoccupied Western Assam and overran the whole country up to the neighbourhood of Dacca. Aurangzeb, after having consolidated his position on the throne of Delhi, despatched the veteran general and statesman Nawab Mir Jumla to re-establish Mogul prestige and reputation in Cooch-Behar and Assam. Accordingly Mir Jumla left Dacca in November 1661, marched through the entire length of the country without any effective resistance, and occupied Garagram or Garghaon the Ahom capital in March 1662. After several months of sporadic contests between the two camps which drove them both to unprecendented suffering and hardship, a treaty was enacted in January 1663 which practically restored the terms of the treaty of 1639 as far as jurisdiction was concerned. Jayadhwaj Singha died in November 1663. His successor Chakradhwaj Singha under cover of friendship with the Moguls made elaborate preparations for the reoccupation of Gauhati; and in the middle of the year 1667, Lachit Barphukan, son of Momai-tamuli Barbarua, was sent down at the head of a numerous force to oust the Moguls from Gauhati. In November 1667 the Ahom general succeeded in wresting back Gauhati from the Moguls on which the Emperor despatched Raja Ram Singha of Amber against Assam, his deputation being meant as a punishment for the repeated delinquency which he had evinced in the discharge of his imperial duties, especially by his connivance at the escape of Shivaji Maharaja and the Sikh Guru Teg Bahadur. Ram Singha reached the neighbourhood of Gauhati in March 1668, and he immediately made overtures for peace and the restoration of the territorial limits fixed in 1639 and 1663. The Assamese remained adamantine, and Ram Singha repeated the peace negotiations though without any success. Abortive fighting and peace proposals went on for three long years when things were brought to a head in the beginning of 1671. In the naval battle of Saraighat which took place in the neighbourhood of Gauhati in March 1671 the hopes of the imperialists were dashed to pieces. The forces of the Mogul general were completely defeated, and the Rajput Raja sought refuge in the imperial garrison of Rangamati situated at the frontier of Assam and Mogul India. Having failed to seize another opportunity to invade Assam, Ram Singha returned to Delhi and paid his respects to the Emperor on June 24, 1676. Lachit Barphukan died soon after his memorable victory at Saraighat, and was succeeded in the viceroyship of Gauhati by his brother Laluk Sola Barphukan.

The concentration of the ablest leaders of the country at Gauhati, for the purpose of thwarting any eventual renewed attack of the imperialists, left the Ahom capital in Upper Assam a prey to the machinations and intrigues of self-seeking nobles and ministers. Laluk Sola Barphukan noticed with envy and suspicion the unbridled influence and dictatorship of the Prime Minister Atan Buragohain. Anxious to acquire for himself similar power and prestige, Laluk Sola negotiated with Sultan Azamtara, governor of Bengal, for the evacuation of Gauhati, which the Barphukan promised to effect on the appearance of a few war-boats on the Brahmaputra and a contingent of cavalry on land, led by a Mogul commander. The only condition which the Barphukan imposed was that the prince with the concurrence of his imperial father should make him Raja of Eastern Assam, and confer upon him a reward of four lakhs of rupees.

This proposal had, in the eye of the prince, a double advantage. He would secure a personal triumph which would consolidate him in the fluctuating affection of his exacting father; and would at the same time raise the rank and dignity of his Assamese consort Rahmat Banu Begum to whom he had been married on May 2, 1668, and who happened to be the niece of Laluk Sola Barphukan. The Prince readily acquiesced in the proposal, and despatched Nawab Mansur Khan, Fauzadar of Rangamati, to take delivery of the place. Laluk Sola acted up to his promise, and the Mogul general entered unopposed the fort of Gauhati on March 1, 1679. The elated Barphukan, who surrendered his charge for "a handful of silver" while his father and brother had fought for it at the imminent risk of their lives, now proceeded up to the Ahom metropolis to play the role of a king-maker. This bloodless occupation of Gauhati was magnified at Delhi as a great victory; and Shahrukh, the messenger of Azamtara, who brought the news to the Emperor, was given a reward of Rs. 1,000, a necklace of 19 pearls, and a *turrah* studded with jewels.

The first act of Laluk Sola was the deposition of King Sudaipha, who had been placed on the throne by the Prime Minister, and the installation of a stripling of fourteen years as Sudaipha's successor. The Premier, now a fugitive, was next arrested, imprisoned and killed; and Laluk Sola then turned his attention to the task of disqualifying the princes for succession by mutilating their bodies. Gadapani, the most powerful of the rival princes, deserted his home and wandered from place to place, avoiding the vigilance of Laluk Sola's emissaries. His wife, Princess Jaimati, having refused to give any clue to her husband's whereabouts, was tortured to death under the orders of the puppet monarch which were obviously inspired by Laluk Sola Barphukan. The martyrdom of the Princess roused the nobles to a consciousness of the danger to which their country was exposed. Laluk Sola was killed in his own residence in November 1680; and the nobles placed Gadapani on the throne with the belief that he alone would be competent to oust the imperialists from Gauhati and thus free the major part of his kingdom from the yoke of foreign domination. This took pace in August 1681, and after a year of preparation the new monarch succeeded in recapturing Gauhati from the hands of the Moguls after a decisive encounter at Itakhuli in the neighbourhood of the viceregal headquarters of Assam. Mansur Khan fled with his forces to Rangamati leaving behind a vast amount of provisions and war-materials. The king appointed the Gargayan Sandikai Phukan as his viceroy at Gauhati; and the Ahoms continued to remain in undisturbed possession of Western Assam until the termination of their rule in February 1826.

After the cessation of hostilities Muhammad Ali remained at Gauhati enjoying that immunity from suspicion to which a detached scholar was entitled according to the traditions of the Indians. He found in the new governor of Gauhati, Gargayan Sandikoi Phukan a patron who was as generous and appreciative as his previous master. The Ahom viceroy seized this opportunity of utilizing the scholarship and learning of the Mogul of Secunderabad by arranging for the recording of the narratives of Delhi and other materials which were in his possession: and an old chronicle specifically mentions this fact in connection with the list of the kings of Delhi which was compiled from Muhammad Ali's papers. It is a delightful irony of fate that the gift of a Secunderabadi made to the Assamese at Gauhati two hundred and fifty years ago is now returned to the Secunderabadis by an Assamese from the very same place.—Preface to *Annals of the Delhi Badshahate*, in *Islamic Culture*, Hyderabad, Deccan, for January 1933.

D.—WHO WAS RUNGADDIN PADSHAH?

Who was this Rungaddin Padshah, the vanquisher of Pithor Raja, the last Hindu king of Delhi? Sober history says that the first Muhammadan victor of India and the vanquisher of Pithor Raja was Sultan Shihabuddin Muizzuddin Muhammad Ghori, son of Bahauddin, and the generalissimo of his brother Ghiyasuddin, king of Ghazni and Ghor. After the second battle of Tarain, in which Pithor Raja was defeated and killed, Muhammad Ghori returned to Khurasan leaving his slave-son Qutbuddin Aibak in charge of affairs in India, who occupied Delhi and conducted the government in place of his absentee lord Muhammad Ghori. After the death of Muhammad in March, 1206, Qutbuddin succeeded his master as sovereign of the new Indian conquests as the first Sultan of Delhi, *vide* Vincent Smith's *Oxford History of India*, p. 222. There is no mention in the standard histories of India of any Rungaddin or Ruknuddin Padshah sitting on the throne of Delhi after the defeat and death of Pithor Raja.

The *Tabaqat-i-Nasri* of Minhaj-i-Siraj Jurjani sketches the careers of *twenty* Ruknuddins, of whom only four have the remote chance of being directly or indirectly the original of the Rungaddin of our *Padshah-Buranji* :—

(*i*) *Ruknuddin* Khur Shah, son of Alauddin Muhammad Shah, the last of the Mulahidah rulers of *Alamut* and *Lanbahsar*, Raverty's translation, pp. 1206—1212. The strongest fortress of Alamut was Majmundiz, according to Le Strange's *Lands of the*

Eastern Caliphate, p. 221. Hulaku, the grandson of the Mogul conqueror Chengis Khan, fought with Khur Shah, the former concentrating his forces at Mazamdaran or Tabaristan in Persia. Alamut was taken and dismantled by Hulaku in 1256 A.D., and Ruknuddin Khur Shah was treacherously murdered by Hulaku. The Rungaddin of the *Padshah-Buranji* is the son of one Alamanji Muhammad Shah who ruled at Majitpur in Nako.

(*ii*) ***Ruknuddin*** Ghori Shanasti, son of 'Alauddin Muhammad Khwarazm Shah, Sultan of Iran, and conqueror of Khwarazm or Khiva, Samarkand, 'Irak, Ghazni, Ghor, Kabul, etc., and the formidable antagonist of Chengis Khan. Muhammad Shah occupied the throne of Ghazni and Ghor from Ghiyasuddin and his brother Sultan Shihabuddin Mui'zzuddin Muhammad Ghori, and placed his eldest son Jalaluddin Maugbarni on the newly conquered throne, while Ruknuddin was placed in charge of 'Irak. During the war with Chengis Khan, Muhammad Shah's stronghold was *Ilal* in *Mazamdaran, vide Tabaqat*, p. 279. Muhammad Shah died in 617 A.H. and was succeeded by Jalaluddin, and then by Ruknuddin. The latter was also called *Ghori-Shanasti* or the Ghori-breaker, as he was born "on the night preceding the day on which Sultan Shihabuddin Muhammad Mui'zzuddin Ghori retreated from before the gates of Khwarazm in the year 601 A.H.", p. 281.

(*iii*) ***Ruknuddin*** Hamzah Kiwan-ul-Mulk, the Kazi of Muhammad Ghori, who was sent as an envoy with an ultimatum to Pithor Raja, *Tabaqat*, p. 466.

(*iv*) ***Ruknuddin*** Sar, Malik of Kidan in Ghor, whose name figures in the list of kinsmen and relatives of Sultan S. M. Muhammad Ghori, p. 491, and who probably accompanied his relative in the latter's victorious campaign in India.

Firishtah's history does not throw any light on the Rungaddin problem. Probably, the exploits of one of the above Ruknuddins, which must have been stock themes of gossip, have been extended to the defeat of Pithor Raja, and the real hero S. M. Muhammad Ghori has been eclipsed or partly transformed into Rungaddin. The *Alamanja* and *Majitpur* of our narrative might be perversions of Alamut, Ilal-Mazamdaran and Majmundiz. Nako may be Lako, a liquid variation of the cerebral *'Irak*, which is however written correctly in the classes of horses mentioned here and there, *viz.*, "Arbi, Turki, Sujarni and 'Iraqi". According to the *P.B.* Rungaddin's successor on the Alamanji throne was his son Sultan Muhammad M'azum. We get the names of some of the generals of the expedition,—Farteijang-khan, the commander-in-chief of Rungaddin; Shah 'Adil Khan, son of the former; Adam, Rungaddin's brother; Jambur Khan, Hurzabbar Khan, Hazur Khan and Rahlol Khan. Pithor Raja's commanders were,—Unmatta Singha, Suranga Singha, Kumud Singha, Rana Singha.

The most reasonable explanation of the problem will be if we take Rungaddin to be Qutbuddin himself; Muhammad Shah, Rungaddin's father as Muizzuddin Muhammad Ghori; Rungaddin's successor on the Alamanji throne, Muhammad M'azum as Al Mu'izz-us-Sultan Taj-ud-din-Yildiz. The dynasty of Ghaznivite rulers to which Muhammad Ghori belonged was known as the Shanasabaniah dynasty, but after the death of Muhammad Mu'izzuddin Ghori, it came to be known as Al-Mu'izzi-us-Sultani from Muhammad Ghori's name Mu'izzuddin, *Tabaqat*, p. 496; this title was applied to Muhammad's successors Qutbuddin-Aibak in Delhi, and to Taj-ud-din Yildiz in Ghazni. We thus find an explanation for the title *Alamanji* used in the *P.B.* and the Assamese chronicler's application of the title to Muhammad Mu'izzuddin Ghori himself is excusable, as it formed an important bead in the great conqueror's string of epithets. According to Minhaj, Sultan S.M.M. Ghori "was wanting in children, and one daughter was all he had by his wife", p. 496-7. This fact was pointed out to him by a confidential favourite, to whom the Sultan replied, "Other monarchs may have one son, or two sons: I have so many thousand sons, namely my Turk slaves." The Sultan did not deviate from his word, and placed the crowns of Ghazni and Delhi on his Mamluk sons Taj-ud-din and Qutbuddin. According to the *P.B.*, Alamji Muhammad Shah also has no son, by any of his 300 wives. In the multiplicity of Ruknuddins and Muhammad Shahs, and the acceptance of slave-sons as natural heirs, our Assamese chronicler's confusion with regard to certain *names* figuring in the history of a region noted for its innumerable principalities and chieftains, is certainly pardonable. That he has been able to steer clear through this labyrinth of names and personages by giving us facts the *essence* of which is in entire agreement with standard histories, is a matter for congratulation.

E. SECUNDERABAD

The description of Secunderabad as given in the *P.B.* amounts almost to a condensed gazetteer. I note the salient points which may be helpful in identifying the place:—

Geographical.—Secunderabad or Hiranagar is situated on the south, at a distance of nearly three months' journey from Delhi. Sec. was formerly a wilderness whch was reclaimed by Sekendar Padshah of Iran. The Sultan invited men from all quarters to settle at Sec. till it yielded an annual revenue of Rs. 40,50,000. The kingdom measured 220 *kos* by 103 *kos*, and was surrounded on all sided by sea-water, having a moat as wide as a river on three sides and the sea on the fourth. The moat could be traversed longitudinally in about ten hours. The dike had no mooring place for boats, and it was filled with monstrous crocodiles and sea-horses. The latter, known as *Dariai Ghora*, came out of the waters occasionally to bask on the bank where they were seized by men and sold for Rs. 1,000 to Rs. 1,500 each. The inhabitants were all Muhammadans, and there was not a single Hindu there. They lived on maize and eggs of China ducks. Rice or paddy could not be had at Sec., unless it was taken there by merchants from other places, in which case its price used to be Rs. 3 to Rs. 4 per seer. The articles sold in the shops were diamonds, pearls, emeralds, rubies, amber, corals, etc. Sec. had an army of 60,000 horse, in which Arabian, Turuki, Tazi and Suzarni ponies were used. It had also a large Nawarrah or flotilla of Suluf (Salb), Batel (Patil) and other classes of war-boats. There was a rampart on all sides of Sec. barricaded with natural trees and thick bamboo-clumps whose trunks touched each other. The forts were constructed with brick and stone, and trained soldiers were employed in the navy.

Historical.—After the establishment of Sec., Sekendar Padshah returned to Iran, leaving Nawab Ghalib Khan, a commander of 9,000, to rule over the place as viceroy. Siliman Padshah of Farrang intending to occupy Sec., employed several devices including the despatch of soldiers to live in Sec. as peaceful citizens and merchants. Ghalib Khan was murdered by a woman presented to him by Siliman. After a series of contests Sec. was conquered by Siliman Padshah, and it remained in his possession till Muhammad 'Ali narrated the story to the Assamese chronicler. Nasir Muhammad Padshah ruled at Sec. during the reign of Emperor Jahangir. The Emperor marched against Sec. and after a very hard struggle succeeded in conquering that kingdom. Jahangir established a court and a garrison at Sec. with Amir-ul-Omara Sher Khan 'Ali Haft-hazari as head. Muhammad Ali was a Mogul hailing from Sec., which he knew most intimately, this being the reason why we have such an unusually elaborate description of that kingdom.

Is this Sec. the modern Sec. in the dominion of His Exalted Highness the Nizam of Hyderabad? Golconda was established in 1512 A.D. by Sultan Kuli Qutb Shah who was supposed to be the grandson of Mirza Jehan Shah of Persia, *vide Firishta*, tr. Briggs, vol. 3, p. 322. According to the *Tarikhi-Qutb-Shah*, a translation of which has been appended by Briggs, Qutb Shah was fifth in descent from Amir Iskandar. The gold and diamond mines of Golconda were proverbial even in Europe. Siliman Padshah of Farrang might be a Firinghee adventurer; the strategy employed by him in the conquest of Sec. seems to be of an occidental character. Farrang or Afranj is the name by which Muhammadans designated Franks or Firinghees or Europeans, even so early as Minhaj-i-Siraj Abu 'Umr-i-'Usman Al-Jurjani, the author of the *Tabaqat-i-Nasiri*. The author of the *P.B.* has clearly distinguished between the two words *Siliman* and *Sulaiman*. There are many instances of Firinghee conquests in the Deccan during the Mogul period. One will be tempted to identify Sekendar Padshah with the Macedonian conqueror Alexander the Great who founded, in the East, Alexandria, or Iskenderia of the Arabians, Herat, Nikaia or modern Jalalabad, and Boukephala or Jhelum. The island state of Hormuz, the Ormus of Milton, was conquered in 1515 A.D. by Alfonso D'Albuquerque, the Governor of the Portuguese Settlements in India. But these places do not answer in all points the description of Sec. as given in the *Padshah-Buranji*.

About the year 1696, Sulaiman Khan, the youngest brother of Daud Khan Panni, was the governor of Porto Novo, a town on the sea-coast, fifteen miles south of Cuddalore. His dealings with the English merchants of Madras were like the methods adopted by Siliman Padshah of the *Padshah-Buranji*. In the English records of the period he figures under the name "Selimon Cawn," *vide* Manucci's *Storia do Mogor*, tr. Irvin, Vol. III, pp. 370—381; and *Maasir-ul-Umara*, tr. Beveridge, pp. 458—460.

F.—SIGNIFICANT CONFIRMATIONS AND DEVIATIONS

A few instances are cited below, to illustrate from the *Padshah-Buranji*, reaffirmations of hitherto accepted facts, corroborations of doubtful issues, deviations from settled conclusions, as well as fresh revelations of a significant character:—

(1) The Muhammadan victor of the Rajput prince Pithor Raja is given in the *P.B.* as Rungaddin Padshah, son of Muhammad Shah of Alamanja, king of Nako, whose capial was at Majitpur. The author specifically mentions that *Hinduan* or Hindu rule ended with Pithor Raja. The establishment of Muhammadan supremacy in India is ascribed to the *saka* era 843, or 921 A.D., the only date recorded in our chronicle. This contradicts the universally accepted conquest of Delhi by Muhammad of Ghor in 1192 A.D. after the defeat and execution of Pithor Raja, the Chauhan prince.

(2) The first Muhammadan conqueror of India, according to the *P.B.*, divides his palace into several compartments, *viz.*, Mardana-mahal, Zanana-mahal, Dewan-khas, Roz-dewan, Khansama, Roz-adawalat; each of the seven days in the week has a particular function allotted to it. This division was kept up by subsequent Muhammadan rulers of India.

(3) The Mansabdari system was first introduced by the victor of Pithor Raja, according to the *P.B.* His army consisted of 600,000 horse, which were placed under properly graded Mansabdars and Fauzadars in command of 7,000, 6,000, 5,000, 4,000, 3,000, 2,000, 1,000, 800, 500 and 150: and contingents were stationed in several parts of the kingdom. Mansabs indicated actual commands, and not mere titular ranks into which some of them dwindled under the successors of Akbar. Vincent Smith, in his *Akbar*, p. 362, says that the earliest mention of the grading of Mansabdars was in the time of Babar.

(4) A hospitable old woman instructs Sher Khan as to the proper method of attacking the enemy from the analogy of a dish of rice which should be eaten from one side only. This story is attributed to Timurlane with precisely the same details, by Manucci, tr. Irvine, Vol. I. pp. 99-100.

(5) No seat was offered to Humayun when he appeared as a fugitive before the king of Persia. Humayun's attendant, according to the *Padshah-Buranji*, laid a shield on the floor and covered it with a cloth whereupon sat Humayun. This story is repeated by Manucci though the proviso seat was "by cutting open the covering of a quiver and spreading it in front of the royal seat. On this Humayun at once sat down."

(6) The quick intelligence and loyalty shown by Humayun's attendant struck the king of Persia with

amazement and surprise as to how he could lose his sovereignty at Delhi fortunate as he was in the services of such faithful and devoted followers like that attendant. This mild admonition is to be found both in the *P.B.* and Manucci, Vol. I, pp. 114-115. Manucci's passage runs as follows: "The Persian King asked king Humayun how he could lose his kingdom when he had such attentive and well-affected servants." To this may be compared the *P.B.* passage "Why did you flee from Delhi fortunate as you were in the enjoyment of the services of faithful servants like this one?

(7) According to the *P.B.*, the sons of Shah Jahan had the following mansabs, Dara, mansab 20,000 and sawar 20,000; Shuja, mansab 15,000, and sawar 15,000; Aurangzeb, mansab 15,000, and sawar 15,000. After the subjugation of Bengal, Raja Man Singha was allowed by Jahangir to retain his mansab of 8,000. But Prof. Beniprasad, in his *History of Jahangir*, p. 119-n., says "Man Singha, Mirza Shah Rukh and Aziz Kokah the Khan-Azam were the three personages who attained to 7,000."

(8) Prof. Beniprasad in his *Jahangir*, pp. 97-98, gives a brilliant description of the Nao-roza festivities, which materially agrees with that of the *P.B.* In the latter version the Emperor is mentioned in unambiguous terms as the only man who has access to the fancy bazaar, whereas no such prerogative is hinted at in Prof. Beniprasad's account, where from the pitching of the tents of the Nawabs in the vicinity of that of the Emperor, and the flowing of wine in rivulets, the uncritical reader may think that other men were also not denied access to the ladies' bazaar. Prof. Beniprasad believes that the Nao-roza festivities continued for nineteen days; but the *P.B.* corroborates the supposition of Sir Thomas Roe, Man-

delslo and Terry that Nao-roza meant nine days, and that its celebration continued for nine days.

(9) The *P.B.* is precisely accurate in occasionally designating Mir Jumla as Mazum Khan and Mirza Mulla, and Prince Azam as Azamtara, and in this he follows the nomenclature adopted in other Assamese chronicles. We learn from Bernier's *Travels*, Constable, p. 16-n, that Muazzam Khan was Mir Jumla's surname; while Irvine in his *Later Mughals*, vol. 1, p. 2, says that Prince Azam is usually styled Ali-jat and often Azamtara. But we have not been able to know why Man Singha is always referred to in the *P.B.* and in other Assamese chronicles as Mandhata, and sometimes as Makunda.

(10) In the *P.B.* Mir Jumla is described as the son of Mirza-Hazaru: the general's son Masudami Khan is left at Dacca, when Mir Jumla marches against Cooch-Behar and Assam. He must be the same as Muhammad Amin Khan, to whom, according to Bernier, Aurangzeb wrote the famous letter mingled with tears of joy and sorrow.

(11) The waqaynavis plays a very important part in the *P.B.* He reports to the Sultan of Delhi when Timurabad is strewn with gold mohurs. He accompanies Ram Singha as an imperial reporter on the activities of the suspected Raja. Sultan Azamtara tries to gag the waqaynavis so that his unrelenting father may not hear of his misrule in Bengal.

(12) The Rajas of Amber were powerful Hindu adherents of the Mogul throne. Man Singha fights the Emperor's battles: but he is clever enough to see through the Emperor's perpetual preference of himself for the leadership of military expeditions. Jai Singha's Rajput stalwarts propose to seize the person of Shah Jahan, and place the Kuchchwa Raja on the throne; but Jai Singha does not intend to deviate an

inch from hereditary loyalty to the Mogul *satrapy*. Ram Singha directly or indirectly allows Sewa-raja and the Sikh Guru to escape from captivity and surveillance.

(13) According to Vincent Smith, *Oxford History of India*, p. 395, Mumtaz Mahall, died in June 1631, in childbirth. But the *P.B.* makes her swallow poison to avert the sight of her sons' fratricidal conflict.

(14) Aurangzeb deputes Nawab Sulati-fat Khan, Bahadur Khan and Shamser Khan against the Sewa-raja Kandarpa Singha, but they do not attain any success. The Amber Raja is next despatched, who defeats the Sewa-raja, and cajoles him to the presence of the Emperor, from whose confinement he escapes. The career of the Sewa-raja of our *P.B.* corresponds exactly with that of the great Mahratta hero, Shivaji Maharaj. If our author had used only the word Sewa-raja we would have taken it to mean Shiwaraja, Shivaraja or Shivaji, but the specific mention of Kandarpa Singha, as the antagonist of Ram Singha and the subsequent guest of the Emperor, gives us a hard nut to crack.

(15) Sir Jadu Nath Sarkar writes in his *Aurangzeb*, III, pp. 213-214, "Service in Assam was extremely unpopular, and no soldier would go there unless compelled. Indeed, there is reason to believe that Ram Singha was sent to Assam as a punishment for his having secretly helped Shivaji to escape from captivity at Agra". This is materially corroborated in the *P.B.* where Ram Singh's deputation to Assam is described as a punishment for his connivance at the flight of the Sewa-raja and the Sikh Guru from captivity. Ram Singha's support of Teg Bahadur, as narrated in the *P.B.* is confirmed by Cunningham in his *History of the Sikhs*, 1903, p. 79.

(16) In the *P.B.*, Nawab Shaista Khan warns Raja Ram Singha of the poisonous airs of Assam and the irresistible charms of Assamese women, and asks him not to admit the latter into his camp. This impression of Assam is to be found in popular traditions spread all over India. According to a manuscript note in possession of the Mahanta of the Sikh shrine at Dhubri, Man Singha, the grandfather of Ram Singha, was poisoned by one of his Assamese mistresses who imparted the poison to her lord to prevent his proposed invasion of Assam. What the Moguls thought of the women of Assam is recorded in the *Khulasat-ut-Tawarikh* compiled in 1695 : "The beauty of the women of Kamrup is very great; their magic, enchantment and use of spells and jugglery are greater than one can imagine. . . . . They conquer the heart of whomsoever they like and bring them under their command". The same imputation of sorcery and witchcraft is made in the *Fathiyah-i-Ibriyah* and *Ain-i-Akbari*. See the story of Jamila and Hamid in the Urdu book *Kamrup-ki-jadu* by Syed Golam Hyder Khan Sahib of Rai Barelli, where references are made to Kamrupi magic, p. 27. The *Alamgirnamah* thus remarks on the unhealthy climate of Assam,—"Kamrup is remarkable for bad water, noxious air and confined prospects".

(18) According to the *P.B.*, Sultan Muazzam accompanies Mir Jumla in the expedition against Prince Shuja; Muazzam goes over to his uncle's side being fascinated by the beauty of Shuja's daughter Fatima. The Prince concerned is Sultan Muhammad, Aurangzeb's eldest son; and not Sultan Muazzam, the second son. The story of Sultan Muhammad's desertion is related by Bernier, Tavernier, Manucci and by Sir Jadu Nath Sarkar. Bernier and Tavernier are silent about Shuja's daughter; while Manucci gives her name as Mah-Khanum, and Sir Jadu Nath as Gulrukh

Banu. Sultan Muhammad returned subsequently to Mir Jumla's camp, but he was sent up to Delhi closely guarded. He had to pass the remaining days of his life as a prisoner in the fortress of Gwalior till his death in 1676, though he gained a limited amount of liberty two years before his death when he was transferred to Salimgarh.—*Vide*, Bernier's *Travels*, ed. Constable, pp. 82-83; Tavernier's *Travels*, ed. Ball. I, pp. 287-289; Manucci's *Storia*, I, pp. 336-338; and Sarkar's *Aurangzeb*, II, pp. 260-261, 275.

NOTES

1. Shankal, king of Kamarupa :—Gait's *History of Assam*, 1906, pp. 19-20 : Mr. L.N. Bezbarua's address at the Seventh Session of the Assam Literary Conference, Gauhati, p. 5 ; Dowson and Elliot's *History of India*, Vol. 6, p. 533 ; Preface to Firishta's *History*, tr. Briggs, pp. 64-76 ; Firdusi's *Shah-namah* ; *Riyaz-us-Salatin*, tr. Salam, p. 56 ; *Banhi*, Assamese magazine, Gauhati, Vol. 13, pp. 15-16 ; Sykes's *History of Persia*, Vol. 1.

2. Muhammad bin Bukhtiyar Khiliji's invasion :—Stewart's *History of Bengal*, Bangabashi edition, 1910, pp. 56-69 ; P.R.T. Gurdon, A Rock inscription at North Gauhati, in the Report on the work of the Kamarupa Anusandhan Samiti, 1920, pp. 33-35 ; *Tabaqat-i-Nasiri*, tr. Raverty, A.S.B ; S.F. Hannay, *Notice of the Stone Bridge in Kamrup*, J.A.S.B., Vol. 20, p. 291 ; K.L. Barua, *Early History of Kamarupa*, 1933, pp. 205-211 ; S.K. Bhuyan, *A pre-Ahom Rock inscription near Gauhati*, written for the late Mr. C.E.A.W. Oldham, awaiting publication.

3. Ghiyasuddin's invasion :—Gait, *Koch Kings of Kamarupa* J.A.S.B., 1893, p. 280 ; Gunabhiram Barua, *Assam Buranji*, 1901, p. 43.

4. Yuzbek's invasion :—Gait, *Koch Kings*, p. 280 ; G. Barua, *Assam Buranji*, p. 74 ; *Tabaqat*, p. 263.

5. Gushtasib's treasures :—Tughril Khan, who invaded Assam some years after Muhammad bin Bakhtiyar Khiliji came upon "1,200 hoards of treasure, all still sealed as when left there by Gushtasib, which fell into the hands of Muhammadans",—*Tabaqat*, p. 561. Gushtasib was the son of Zan and fought with Arzasib, son of Afrasiyab, the vanquisher of Shankal, Raja of Kamarupa. Minhaz says that Gushtasib returned from China through Kamarupa. The Iranian records do not refer to any Indian exploit of Gushtasib ; but his son Isfandiyar reduced the sovereign of Hind to submission, and also invaded Chin,—Raverty's Notes.

6. Muhammad Shah's invasion :—H. Blochmann, *Kuch Bihar and Assam*, J.A.S.B., 1872, p. 79-*n* ; Muhammad Kazim, Alamgir-namah, B.I. Series, p. 731.

7. Saint Jalaluddin in Assam :—Ibn Batutah, tr. Lee, p. 195 ; H. Beveridge, *Khurshid-zaban-namah of Sayyid Ilahi Baksh al-*

Hussaini Angrizabadi, J.A.S.B., 1895, p. 230 ; Dr. J. Wise, *Note on Shah Jalal, the patron saint of Sylhet*, J.A.S.B., 1873, p. 278, with Blochmann's postscript, p. 281 ; Sachau, *Alberuni's India*, Vol. I, p. 201 ; Mm. Padma Nath Bhattacharyya, *Faquir Shah Jalal*, Pradip, 1312 B.S. See also J.A.S.B., 1873, part 3, p. 260.

8. **Sikandar Shah's invasion :**—Vincent A. Smith, *Catalogue of the Coins in the Indian Museum*, Calcutta, Vol. II, p. 152 ; S.N. Bhattacharyya ; *Mogul North-East Frontier Policy*, 1929, pp. 62-63.

9. **Ismail Ghazi's invasion :**—Gait's *History*, p. 43-n. ; Damant, *Notes on Shah Ismail Ghazi*, J.A.S.B., 1874, pp. 215-240 ; Gait, *Koch Kings* ; S.K. Bhuyan, *Kamrupar Buranji*, p. 3.

10. **Hussain Shah's invasion :**—Stewart's *Bengal*, pp. 132-138 ; *Fathiyah-i-Ibriyah*, tr. Blochmann, J.A.S.B., 1872, p. 79; tr. J.N. Sarkar, J.B.O.R.S., 1915, pp. 188-189 ; *Riyaz-us-Salatin*, tr. Salam, pp. 132-133 ; C.J. Brown, *The Coins of India*, p. 80.

11. **Turbak's invasion :**—Haliram Dhekial Phukan's *Assam Deser Itihas*, 1829, p. 54 ; G. Barua, *Assam Buranji*, p. 75 ; S.K. Bhuyan, *Deodhai Asam Buranji*, pp. 27-28 ; S.K. Bhuyan, *Assam Buranji*, obtained from Sukumar Mahanta's family, pp. 18-22.

12. **Kalapahar's invasion :**—Gait, Blochmann, Gunabhiram Barua.

13. **Abu Bakar's invasion:**—Gait and Blochmann ; *Tuzuk-i- Jahangiri*, p. 147 ; *Padishah-nama*, II, pp. 64 ff. ; M.I. Bora, *Baharistan-i-Ghaybi*, D.H.A.S., Vol. I, pp. 364-394, Vol. II. P. 488.

14. **Islam Khan, governor of Bengal:**—There were two Islam Khans who ruled over Bengal,—(1) During the reign of Emperor Jahangir. Islam Khan Chisti Faruqi, grandson of the celebrated saint Shaikh Selim Chisti. In 1612 A.D. Islam Khan founded Dacca or Jahangirnagar. Jahangir wrote,—"Islam Khan was a brave man of most excellent disposition, in every respect distinguished above his tribe and family,"—*Echoes from old Dacca* by Mr. Syed Hossain, pp. 2-3. (2) During the reign of Emperor Shah Jahan, Islam Khan Mashhadi, his actual name being Ikhtesis Khan. A. Salam, tr. of *Riaz-us-Salatin*, says that Islam Khan succeeded his brother Mukarram Khan in the governorship of Koch Hazo, p. 211 ; "In the 11th year of Shah Jahan's reign, Islam Khan, governor of Bengal, achieved several notable triumphs,—chastisement of the Assamese, capture of 15 Assamese forts, capture of Srighat and Pandu, capture of the son-in-law of the Assam Raja, and the successful establishment of imperial military

outposts or thanas in all the mahals of Koch Hazo, etc." The first, Islam Khan Chisti, plays a very important part in Mirza Nathan's *Baharistan-i-Ghaybi.*

15. Allah Yar Khan's invasion:—Blochmann; *Padishah-namah*, II, p. 94; H.C. Goswami, *Purani Assam Buranji*; S.K. Bhuyan, *Assam Buranji*, obtained from S. Mahanta's family, pp. 73-75.

16. Mir Jumla's Assam expedition:—According to the *Padshah-Buranji*, Aurangzeb reported to Shaista Khan that Mir Jumla had proceeded to Assam without the Emperor's orders, to which Shaista Khan replied,—"Mir Jumla has no bread in this country, he is doing all this to procure a status for his descendants in India." The Emperor's confirmatory orders were received by Mir Jumla in the *firman* referred to by Sarkar in his *Aurangzeb*, Vol. III, p. 179. The *Riyaz-us-Salatin* says that the Emperor on hearing of Mir Jumla's occupation of Cooch Behar directed him to march to Arrakan to rescue the family of Shuja,—"The Khan in reply to this Imperial order represented that the Imperial troops were busy in fighting to conquer the province of Kuch Bihar and Assam, and that to mârch to Arrakan, without accomplishing the conquest of these two provinces, was opposed to expediency, and that he would postpone the expedition to Arrakan to next year, and that this year he would set about subjugating the provinces of Kuch Behar and Assam"—tr. Salam, pp. 224-225.

17. Mir Jumla's invasion :—J.N. Sarkar, *History of* Aurangzeb, Vol. III, Chapter 31; *The Assam and the Ahoms in 1660*, J.B.O.R.S. 1915; S.K. Bhuyan, Mir Jumla's letter to Aurangzeb, *Sadhana*, Vol. I; *Fathiyah-i-Ibriyah*, Assamese translation in *Ahomar Din*; *Mir Jumla and Ram Singha in Assam*, J.I.H., December 1926; Nawab Mir Jumla's Expedition to Assam, in Assamese, *Avahan*, Calcutta, Vols 7 and 8; *Hadiqat-us-Safa*, Calcutta Quarterly Journal, June 1825; *Alamgir-namah*, Description of Assam, tr. Vansittart, Asiatick Researches, Vol. II, p. 176; Glanius, *Unfortunate Voyage into the Kingdom of Bengala*, 1682; *Fathiyah-i-Ibriyah* by Shihabuddin Talish, translator, T. Pavie in French, B.A. Husayni in Hindi, Blochmann in English J.A.S.B., 1872; S.K. Bhuyan, *Kamrupar Buranji*, pp. 62-73; *Assam Buranji*, from S. Mahanta's family, pp. 90-104; almost every old Assamese Buranji.

18. Ram Singha's invasion :—Sarkar, Blochmann, Gait, Bhuyan, works mentioned *ante*; *Col.* Brooke, *Political History of Jeypore*, p. 14; Blochmann, *A Chapter from Muhammadan History*, Calcutta Review, 1870; Tod, *Annals of Rajasthan*, Vol. II, The Annals of Amber; J.D. Cunningham, *History of the Sikhs*; Macauliffe, *Sikh Religion*, Vol. IV; S.K. Bhuyan, *Lachit Barphukan*, and *Atan Buragohain and His Times*, shortly to be published; Assamese Buranjis.

19. Mansur Khan :—S.K. Bhuyan, *Assam Buranji*, obtained from S. Mahanta's family, pp. 139-148; Gait, Blochmann, Gunabhiram Barua; William Robinson, *Descriptive Account of Assam*, 1841.

20. Rudra Singha's plan to invade Bengal :—J.P. Wade, *An Account of Assam*, edited from an India office manuscript, by Srijut Benudhar Sharma, pp. 130-137; S.K. Bhuyan's *Review of* Wade's *Account of Assam*, Cotton College Magazine, January, 1925, Stewart's *Bengal*, p. 405; S.K. Bhuyan, *Assam Buranji by* Hara Kanta Barua, pp. 67-68; Maniram Dewan's *Assam Buranji*, in manuscript, with D.H.A.S.; S.K. Bhuyan, *Tripura Buranji*, from a British Museum ms., published by D.H.A.S. in 1938, pp. 1-2, 15-16.

21. Rudra Singha's message :—King Rudra Singha despatched the following ultimatum to the "Nobobs and Princes of Bengal," "We formerly possessed the provinces on this side of the Corotea river and we are now desirous to resume them. Do not prove inimical to us. If we remain friendly everything will succeed. Be yours the countries, the Government and the Revenue; mine the name. Act in a manner to preserve peace. Fear not our approach; send friendly answers respecting your welfare without delay"—Wade's *Account of Assam*, p. 131. The deliberations in Rudra Singha's cabinet are recorded in S.K. Bhuyan's *Tungkhungia Buranji*, paragraph 65, Assamese version published in 1932, English version published by O.U.P. in 1933.

22. Assam and Muslim invasions :—Pringle Kennedy in his *History of the Great Mughals*,—"Assam had been almost absolutely unaffected by the Muhmmadan invasions of India. Situated in the far East on the banks of a great river, with impenetrable forests, wooded hills, and abnormal rain-fall, and there being almost no means of communication, its people had worked out a distinct national existence in which an adapted form of Hinduism found its place",—Vol. II, pp. 94-95.

23. Assamese magic :—J.N. Sarkars' translation of *Khulasat-ut-Tawarikh* given in his *India of Aurangzeb*, 1901, p. 43. The Mogul reporter, on whose testimony the above account was based, certainly mistook the wooden pillars carved to look like men, used extensively in the monasteries and potentates' houses even up to this day. Cf.,—"Probably nowhere else in the whole world are wooden houses built with such decoration and figure-carving as by the people of this country, Assam"—*Fathiyah-i-Ibriyah*, tr. J.N. Sarkar, J.B.O.R.S., 1915, p. 194.

24. Mir Jumla dies of sorcery :—Even Mir Jumla is said to have died of " the well known sorcery of the Assamese" *Riazus* p. 226. Shihabuddin Talish states that Mir Jumla's fatal " Sickness was the result of witchcraft practised by the Rajah of Assam."

25. Muslim pirs in Assam :—Ms. document in possession of the Mahanta of the Gurudwar Damdame at Dhubri where Teg Bahadur halted for some time. References to Kamrupi magic are made in the accounts of Teg Bahadur's stay in Assam in *Suryya-Prakas*, and in *Tawarikh-Guru-Khalsa-Bartak*. See Macauliffe, *Sikh Religion*, Vol. IV, p. 354. There is a Muslim shrine at Dhubri, known as *Panch-pirar-Darga*, where the remains of Shah Akbar, one of the Darvishes who accompanied Ram Singha, are buried.

26. Bhaskaravarma :—Bana's *Harsh-charit*, tr. by Cowell and Thomas, Chapter 7; Nidhanpur Copper-plate Inscription of Bhaskaravarma, by Mm. Padmna Nath Bhattacharyya, Epigraphica Indica, Vol. 12, Part 2; *Kamarupa-Sasanavali*, by Mm. Padmanath Bhattacharyya, 1931, pp. 1-43; *Travels of Hiuen-Tsang*, tr. Watters, Beal; Life of King Harsha by Radhakumud Mookerji, K.M. Panikar; K.N. Dikshit, The Nalanda Seal of Bhaskaravarma, J.B.O.R.S., 1920, p. 151.

27. Harshadeva :—Bhagavanlal Indraji, *Inscription of Jayadeva of Nepal*, dated 769 A.D., Indian Antiquary, Vol; 9, C.V. Vaidyas *Mediaval Hindu India*, Vol. I, p. 332; S. Krishnaswami Aiyangar, *Forgotten Episodes in the History of Mediaval India*, J.I.H., December 1926; *Gauravaho* of Vakpatiraja, Bombay Sanskrit Series.

28. Assamese patriotism :—Prof. S. Khuda Bukhsh, after visiting Assam in December 1927, summarised his impressions as follows,— "I was deeply struck by two things: the seriousness that pervades the atmosphere of Assam, and the love of the province which marks its inhabitants. They are patriotic, self-sacrificing, entirely devoted to its interests, and their devotion is the devotion of a lover who is always alert, and never neglectful of his mistress's interests."—*The Times of Assam*, Dibrugarh, January 7, 1928, p. 6.

29. Assamese Muhammadan commanders :—This statement is based on the story of the Muhammadan commander Bagh Hazarika whose military genius was partly responsible for the success of Lachit Barphukan's operations against Ram Singha. It was heard from Maulavi Mufizuddin Ahmed Hazarika, author of *Jnan-malini*, and Government Literary Pensioner, Dibrugarh, a descendant of the said Bagh Hazarika.

30. Sympathy of Assamese Muslims :—J. N. Sarkar, *Assam and the Ahoms in* 1660, J.B.O.R.S., 1915, p. 193.

31. Assamese and Kalitas:—The author of the *Fathiyah-i-Ibriyah* made a distinction between the hardy and the gentle sections of the people of Assam, though he adopted a misleading nomenclature, the former being designated as *Assamese* and the latter as *Kulitas* : " The ancient inhabitants of this country belong to two nations, the Assamese and the Kulita. The latter, in all things, are superior to the former, except where fatigues are to be undergone, and in warlike expeditions, in which the former are better,"—Tr. Blochmann, J.A.S.B., 1872, pp. 81-82. Blochmann quotes from a letter by Col. Dalton, author of *The Ethnology of Bengal* : " What the Persian says of the physical superiority of the Assamese over the Kolitas was, no doubt, quite true at the time; for the Assamese were then a hardy, meat-eating, beer-drinking, fighting race, and the Kolitas were effeminate subjected Hindus",—footnote on p. 82. The Ahom monarch Gadadhar Singha, 1681-1696, realised the " evils " of non-flesh-eating, and he made a systematic attempt to suppress the influence and power of the Vaisnava preachers,—S.K. Bhyuan, *Oppression of the Vaisnavas*, Assam Bandhab, Nowgong, Vol. I, and *Tungkhungia Buranji*, paragraphs 49-50.

32. Ahoms and Hinduism :—Gunabhiram Barua says,—" By the adoption of Hinduism the customs and manners of the Ahoms underwent complete transformation. Gradually they imbibed the traits of the lip-strong Brahmans in place of the warlike habits of the arm-strong Kshattriyas",—*Assam Buranji*, p. 134.

33. Assamese invincibility :—The passage is taken from *The Religious History of Assam*, Calcutta Review, 1867, Vol. XLVI, p. 78. The author's name is unknown.

34. War against the Assamese :—The first passage is taken from *A Description of Assam from the Alamgir-nama*, tr. Henry Vansittart, *Asiatick Researches*, Vol. II, 1807, pp. 179-180 ; and the second from *Fathiyah-i-Ibriyahi*, tr. Sarkar, J.B.O.R.S., 1915, pp. 188-189.

35. Ram Singha's eulogy :—S.K. Bhuyan, *Assam Buranji*, obtained from S. Mahanta's family, p. 123.

36 Qasida on Assam :—Sarkar, *Assam and the Ahoms in 1660*, J.B.O.R.S., pp. 182-184. The first few lines of Mulla Darvish's poem may be reproduced,—

" Through the force of Fate and the aid of the Divine will,
Took place [our] journey in Assam, which lies on the border of China and Cathay.

It is another world, another people and other customs ;
Its land is not like [our] land, its sky is not like [our] sky.
Its sky sends rain down without the [originating] cause of clouds ;
On its ground the green grass sprouts up without any aid from the soil.
It stands outside the circle of the Earth and the bowels of the [enveloping] sphere.
It has been separated from the world, like the letter *aliph.*
The seasons all begin [here] at the time of their conclusion [elsewhere];
Here there is heat in [our] winter and chill in [our] summer.
......The Rajah of Assam brought to the field an army
Whose large number became a cage on earth ;
[They are] tumult-raising and sudden [in attack] like the eyes of the fair sex,
Hurling arrows and [other] missiles, and making a [firm] stand in the battle-field."

37. Khaunds and Bairagis :—S.K. Bhuyan, *Assam Buranji*, by Harakanta Barua, p. 64.

38. Muslim officers :—The following Muslim officers were attached to the Ahom court,—12 Dewans, 1 Nawab Dekah, 2 Persian Readers, 1 Engraver, according to Mills's Report on Assam, Sibsagar, Appendix, p. 73. For Persian coins of Ahom sovereigns, see J.A.S.B. Numismatic Supplement, 1904, pp. 113-114 ; and *Oroonadoi*, Sibsagar, January 1853.

39. Grant to Anwar Hazi Faqir :—The grant is dated Aswin 10, 1702 *saka*, or 27th September 1780 A.D. or near about. Maulavi Sayiid Keramat Ali of Hazo obtained the sanad from the Faquir's descendants, Dr. Bahar Ali and Maulavi Mohammad Yar Ali Shah of Jorhat, and published it in the *Batari* of 27th January, 1934.

40. Ahom kings' Muslim priests, etc. :—Dr. J.P. Wade's *Geographical Account of Assam*, India Office Library manuscript. It has been edited by S.K. Bhuyan, and published serially in the *Assam Review*, Silchar, from December 1928 to August 1929. The passage occurs in the issue for March 1929, Vol. II. Emperor Aurangzeb's sanad to the Umananda priests was deciphered by Maulavi Sayiid Abdul Quddus of Maskhowa, Gauhati ; *vide*, Mr. S.C. Goswami's article on the subject in the Journal of the Assam Research Society, Vol. II, Nos. 1 & 2. The Poa-Macca inscription and the sanad to the Kamakhya priests have been deciphered by Professor Abdul Hye of Cotton College, Gauhati, and Mr. Quddus.

41. Story of Kalapahar :—A chapter appended to *Assam Buranji* obtained from S. Mahanta's family, not inserted in the published edition.

42. Mir Jumla sent to Assam :—S.K. Bhuyan, *Assam Buranji*, from S. Mahanta's family, p. 91.

43. Assamese envoys at Delhi :—S.K. Bhuyan, *Kamrupar Buranji*, pp. 75-76. The two Assamese envoys Sanatan and Chandra Kandali, left the Ahom capital on 25th December, 1663, in the company of the Mogul ambassadors Dor Beg and Rustom Beg. The account of their journey to Delhi and stay there deserves reproduction,—" Then our Katakis or envoys left their boats at Rajmahal in charge of seven of their attendants. From there they continued their journey in an imperial Rahegari [Rahdari ?], and arrived at Delhi after a four days' halt at Agra. The Ahadis [Dor Beg and Rustom Beg] having reported their arrival to the Emperor, they were lodged in the quarters of Nawab Hasan Ali situated on the bank of the Jamuna. The Nawab was absent on war duty. Sanatan Kataki said to Dor Beg and Rustom Beg,—" We are Brahmans and how will it be possible to arrange for our food and residence in this place ? " Dor Beg then informed the Dewan, brought some workers, and constructed separate houses for the two Katakis near the river Jamuna. Two days later, the Dewan sent to the two Katakis the following *Siddha* or present of food articles,—Rice 600 maunds, fine rice 80 maunds, *mug dal* 40 maunds, *Kalai dal* 20 maunds, *masur dal* 20 maunds, *mah* 60 maunds, *ghee* 40 seers, pepper 8 seers, turmeric powder 4 seers, asafoetida half a seer, ginger 10 seers, milk 8 mathis, salt 20 maunds, sugar 20 maunds, bay-leaf one load of two baskets, *tatar* 7 baskets, *bilati pan* or betel-leaf 8 baskets, and 3 deer. Then after five days came the *Siddha* from the Emperor. The Katakis were given 500 rupees, and their men rupees 200. Then after an interval of eight days our two Katakis were presented before the Emperor. The Padshah was sitting on the throne.............Men were busy in their work sitting under roofs with golden streamers fluttering above. Then the Padshah, Sri Sri Lord of Delhi. Sri Srijut Maharaja Srijut Amir-ul-Omrao Alamgir Padshah heard the letter and said,—" I will relinquish the territories occupied in excess of the Koch boundaries, and I shall also make over those subjects [of Assam] who have been captured by our men." An epistle was made over, but no envoy was sent. Sanatan and Chandra Kandali were given a present of 1,000 rupees in cash for eating *pan* and *tamol*, and were sent off by the Dewan from Delhi; and they also received the following articles,—two pairs of silver trays, 2 *jamas*, 2 *pags*, 2 *patukas*, 2 *chit-pamarus*, and 2 *pesgasis*; no present was given from the Emperor's place. The Nawab of Dacca, Shaista Khan, despatched his envoy Panditrai to the Swargadeo in the company of the two Assamese envoys."

44. Beating of Nahbat :—S.K. Bhuyan, *Assam Buranji*, obtained from the family of S. Mahanta, p. 115.

45. Rahmat Banu's letter :—Rahman Banu Begum's letter to Laluk Sola Barphukan has been found in an old Assamese manuscript Buranji obtained by the D.H.A.S. from the family of the late Pandit Hem Chandra Goswami, still unpublished.

46. Grierson's testimony :—Linguistic Survey of India, Vol. I, Part I, Introductory, p. 156.

47. Burdwan chronicle :—An Assamese manuscript chronicle of Burdwan was exhibited by the late Pandit Hem Chandra Goswami in the Bengal Literary Conference held at Burdwan, where it was lost.

48. Tripura Buranji :—A chronicle of Tripura written by King Rudra Singh's two ambassadors to that country, Ratna Kandali and Arjun Das Bairagi, has been published by the Department of Historical and Antiquarian Studies, Assam, edited by S.K. Bhuyan. His Highness the Maharaja Manikya Bahadur of Tipperah has pronounced it to be "a wonderful book", and is translating it into English himself.

49. Tribute paid to Mir Jumla :—In his Report on the Progress of Historical Research in Assam, 1897, p. 17, Sir Edward Gait refers to a manuscript "containing an account of the tribute paid by the Ahoms to the Mussalmans after the defeat of the former by Mir Jumla in 1663 A.D." Two short Chutiya chronicles have been incorporated in *Deodhai Asam Buranji*, edited by S.K. Bhuyan.

50. Assamese prose literature :—The antiquity of Assamese prose literature in contrast to its total absence in Bengal was elaborately discussed by Sir P.C. Roy in an article in the *Prabasi* in 1919-20.

51. Assamese historiography :—For full information about Assamese historical literature, see Appendix B.

52. Preamble to Tungkhungia Buranji :—compiled in 1804 A.D. by Srinath Duara Barbarua, the Chief Executive Officer of the Ahom government,—"Salutation to Sri-Krishna!

Salutation to Ganesa! Salutation to Parvati! This is the Buranji written in *saka* 1725, under the orders of the Duara Barbarua. Keep it secretly. Do not give it to your son if you have no confidence in him. Show it to your friend if he is not hostile to you. Pandits have prohibited the betrayal of Princes; and if trust is violated it amounts to an indecent gesture shown to one's mother. So keep it in confidence. More specially it is an unfathomable Sashtra, who does ever find its bottom? Even great sages have become victims of mistake: so Pandits should not at random find fault with the book. If one is bent upon detecting blemishes he will find many. This Buranji of the Tungkhungia Dynasty is written on Thursday on *Panchami tithi*, on the 22nd day of Phalguna." In a chronicle written by Atan Buragohain Rajmantri Dangaria, Prime Minister of Assam from 1662 to 1679, it has been enjoined,—" Keep this book secretly. Show it privately to one who is unhostile and friendly to you. The disclosure of the mysteries of monarchs has been prohibited by Pandits."

53. Training of Katakis :—Very astute and learned men were appointed Katakis, and they were generally Brahmans. One Ramchandra, an envoy from Jayantia, being accused of unprofessionnal conduct as a diplomat, said to the Barbarua, Srinath Duara,—" We are Brahmans: and we do not understand the old-time relations of kings and states. You have here Katakis who have been systematically organised and trained from ancient times. But we are not envoys of that description. We admit our fault."—S.K. Bhuyan, *Tungkhungia Buranji*, paragraph 334.

54. Where is Nako? The author of the *Padshah-Buranji* refers to *the land of the Nakos.* This country is famous for its fabulous birds, *viz.*, Hurma, Sarol, Serengi, and Murta-khuras. The *hurmas* lived on the flesh of elephants and rhinoceros; the *sarols* like the phoenix flapped their wings and produced fire in which they were consumed; the *serengis* assumed several colours during the course of the day; and the *murtakhuras* or *swikars* swallowed live charcoals of bamooo fuel without any injury to themselves. This *Nako* may be a variation of the fabulous bird Lokheh mentioned by Emperor Babar in his autobiographical memoirs as believed to have existed in Afghanisthan or near about that kingdom in Transoxonia. Pringle Kennedy writes in his *History of the Great Mughuls*, Vol. 1, p. 134,-' Another curious fable Babar mentions as regards a bird which he called Lokheh or Chameleon-bird, to wit, that if it flies across a vine-yard, it falls down'. In another text we get Thana Panjar, Muhammad Ali, and Rukundin, in place of Alamanja, Marda Sher Khan Ali, and Rungaddin respectively.

55. Sujarnis is obviously a misnomer for *Sumarnis*, the name given to ponies imported from Smyrna; *Mujaannnas* occurs in *Ain-i-Akbari*; see *Hobson-Jobson*, under *Toorkey*.

56. In another text,—"During the conflict I could not recuperate myself, being a victim of dire misfortune."

57. The name **Rungaddin** or **Rukundin** is found in the list of the rulers of Delhi from Judhisthir to Aurangzeb inserted in some Assamese chronicles. According to one list Rungaddin vanquished the Rajput Raja Udaymalla; according to another he defeated Pithor Raja. The period of his reign, *viz.*, 23 years, 9 months and 8 days is uniform in all Buranjis; though the starting date varies, 1st Ashar, 787 *saka*, in one; and 11th Ashar, 764 saka, in another. This, I believe, is a scribal mistake as 764 *plus* 23 makes 787. The Kali era when he commenced his rule at Delhi is given as 3,944. Rúkundin's successors in Delhi according to these lists are Bahauddin, 25 years; Samruddin, 29 years; Kutubuddin, 27 years, Shahabuddin, 21 years; Bibi Rabiya, 7 years 3 months, 10 days from 891 *saka*.

58. Daigati.—I was almost tempted to say that the *Daigati* of the *P.B.* was a variation of *Chaigati* or *Chaghatai*, bút it may be also a corruption of the Mongol word *Darugachi*, meaning a governor. See *Ser Marco Polo* by Henri Cordier, p. 6. The *P.B.* statement that Timur was the son of a Daigati Nawab corresponds to what Lieut.-Col. Sykes says,—"Timur was descended from a certain Karachar Khan, a vizier in the service of Chagatay", *Persia*, II, p. 19. *Daighati* may also be a corruption of the word *Dughlat* which figures as a toponomous appellation of several personages of the Chagatai clan in Gulbadan Begum's *Humayun-nama*, tr. Mrs. Annette Beveridge.

59. Loha-langa faquir:—It is curious to note that the two words *Loha-langa and Timur-langa* mean exactly the same; *langa*—lame, and *Timur* and *Loha*—iron. The remains of Timur's spiritual leader are entombed in a white cenotaph at the portāls of the great Tartar's mausoleum at Samarcand, Sykes's *Persia*, picture facing p. 214. The Loha-langa order of faquir are probably those described by Tavernier,—"Some of the faquirs or Dervichs were armed with a sort of weapon which we have not in Europe; that is to say, a sharp piece of iron like the side of a platter without a bottom, which they wind eight or ten times about their necks, and carry like a calve's chaldron. They draw out these iron-circles as they intend to make use of them; and they will throw them with such a force against a man, that they shall fly as swift as an arrow, and go very near to cut a man in two in the middle", *Travels*, Bangabasi edition, p. 65. A manuscript on 'Farlanger Fakir' was exhibited at Lucknow in connection with the 9th meeting of the Indian Historical Records Commission in December 1926. The story of Timurlane's rise through the instrumentality of a faquir, as given in the *P.B.*, used to be related by the late Maulavi Karamjan Hajarika of Lakhtakia, Gauhati, who was reported to have come upon it in a Persian history.

60. Bhang has been described by Manucci, tr. Irvine, Vol. II, page 7, as a "beverage made of the leaves of dried hemp ground down which intoxicates as soon as taken. Aurangzeb wanted to suppress this disorder".

61. Jalal Husain :—The Sultan of Delhi during whose reign Timur invaded India in 1398 A.D. was Muhammad Tughlak, and *not* Jalal Husain. Jalaluddin Muhammad was the Keiani prince of Sistan whose army was routed by Timur, during which engagement the conqueror received a wound in his feet which was permanently crippled for which Timur was called Timur-langa, or Timur the Lame, or Tamerlane,—Sykes's *Persia.*

62. Sak in Assamese would mean vegetables, in Persian wine. To the chronicler who has used so many words of Persian origin the latter sense would not be unknown. I have retained the vernacular word not knowing definitely which of the two was in the mind of the writer, though I am somewhat inclined towards the first meaning.

63. Sewa was most likely Bijapur, *Sabai* or *Savai* being the surname of the first Adil Shahi Sultan Abdul Muzaffar Yusuf. See *Hobson-Jobson* under *Sabaio*, and also Ain-i-Akabri Vol. 1., pp. 586, 600.

64. The story of acquiring the correct method of military operations from the analogy of a dishful of rice is attributed to Timurlane, with precisely the same details, in Manucci, tr. Irvine, Vol. 1., pp. 99-100.

65. Rum means Asia Minor, but the Assamese always applied it to Persia; they designated China as *Kheh*, and a non-Assamese as a *Bangal*; they called a European *Baga Bangal* or White *Bangal.* The *P.B.* reproduces the conversation of Humayun and Shah Tahmasp of Persia on the political situation of India which is supported by *Maasir-ul-Umara*, tr. Beveridge, p. 125,—"Shah Tahmasp in conversation with Humayun discussed the question in India, and the loss of sovereignty. He said,—"It appears that there are in India two parties who are distinguished for military qualities and leadership, the Afghans and the Rajputs. At present you cannot get the Afghans on your side for there is no mutual confidence. Make them traders instead of servants, and arrange with the Rajputs and cherish them." There is a very beautiful picture of Shah Tahmasp entertaining Humayun at his court in Sykes's *History of Persia*, vol. II, p. 248. It was during Humayun's stay in Persia that the *Kohinoor* passed from his hands to the Sultan of Persia, *Babar's Diamond* in *Asiatic Quarterly Review*, for April, 1899, though Catrou claims the large diamond as the gift of Mir Jumla to Shah Jahan, Bernier's *Travels*, Constable, 469-ff.

66. She was no other than **Hamida Banu Begum** or the Miriam-Makkani of the *Maasir-ul-Umara*, of whom Sykes writes in his *History* of Persia, Vol. 2, p. 248,—" Humayun was married to a daughter of the Shaykh of Jam, who bore him the famous Akbar." A memorial inscription at Turbat-i-Shaykh Jam, dated A.H. 952 or A.D. 1544, describes Humayun as "A Wanderer in the Desert of Destitution." The *Humayun-nama* written by the Emperor's sister Gulbadan Begum says that Akbar and his mother accompanied Humayun in his exile in Persia.

67. This story is repeated in Manucci, I, page 114, though the proviso seat was made " by cútting open the covering of his quiver and spreading it in front of the royal seat. On this cloth Humayun at once sat down."

68. It is curious and surprising that this statement of the chronicler writing in an obscure corner in Eastern India, is an exact repetition of what we find in Manucci, I, pp. 114-5. " The Persian King asked King Humayun how he could lose his kingdom when he had such attentive and well-affected servants.

69. Ise Khan Masandali.—Ise Khan Masandali, whom Man Singha placed on the *masnad* of Bengal, should be distinguished from Alauddin Islam Khan Chisti Faruqi and Islam Khan Mashhadi who became governors of Bengal in 1608 and 1637 respectively. Man Singha was withdrawn from Bengal in 1606 to quell disturbances at Rohtas in Bihar, see Burgess' *Chronology of Modern India* and Prof. Beniprasad's *Jahangir*. Ise Khan Masandali is described in the *P.B.* as an influential Zemindar who refused to aid the Bengal rebel on the principle,—" We are Zemindars and are unconcerned as to who wields the sovereign power in the state." There was one Ise Khan Masand-i-Ali, the Bhuyan king of Khizarpur, built aboút 1584 the Mogul garrison at Rang [illegible] His grandson Manawar Khan, the Menorca [illegible] Glánius, naval commander attached to Mir Jumla [illegible] See *Mir Jumla's Invasion of Assam*, in [illegible] No. 57.

70. Man Singha's antagonist Husain Shah.—Husain Shah, Sultan of Bengal, who invaded Assam in 1498 could not be the ruler of that name whom Man Singha subdued during Jahangir's reign. Man Singha was withdrawn from Bengal in 1606, and he died in 1614. Man Singha had a tough fight with the rebellioús Usman Khan of Bengal in 1599 during Akbar's reign, *vide Baharistan-i-Ghaybi*, tr. Dr. M. I. Borah, Notes, Vol. II, p. 794-795. Alauddin Húsain Shah was king of Bengal from 1489 to 1520 A.D., *vide* Stewart's *History of Bengal*, pp. 133-138, and H. Blochmann's *A New Ruler of Bengal*, J. A. S. B., 1872, Part IV, pp. 333-336. See Cunningham's note on p. 63 of his *History of the Sikhs*, ed. Garrett,—"It is not unusual in India to talk of eminent men as living, although long since dead, as a Sikh will now say he is Ranjit Singh's soldier."

71. Muhammad Ali.—Mansur Khan remained at Gauhati from March 1679 to September 1682, till the battle of Itakhuili when the Ahoms reoccupied Gauhati, and Gaugayan Sandikai Barphukan was appointed Ahom viceroy at Gauhati. A chronicle mentions that the Ahom viceroy employed Muhammad Ali in supplying information about Delhi, etc., for being recorded by Assamese chroniclers. The list of the Kings of Delhi was compiled from the records in possession of Muhammad Ali. See Appendix C.

72. Akhun.—The word used in the *P.B.* in connection with the scholarship of Muhammad 'Ali is Akhun, of which we read in the *History of the Rosheniah Sect and its founder Bayezid Hussain*, "*Akhun*, a religious instructor, a doctor in theology, is used in Afghanisthan as synonymous with the term *Mulla*, a judge, a doctor in Laws; both terms are applied indiscriminately to a man of learning,"—*Asiatick Rasearches*, Vol. II, p. 365.

73. Manucci relates a similar experience of Shah Jahan when he proposed to pay Raja Chattrasal Rae a visit to his country, Manucci, II, pp. 432-433; Aurangzeb was thrown into a similar predicament when he met Jai Singha in Lakhi jungle the latter being attended by "three thousand well-armed horsemen—all Rajputs,"—*ibid*, I, pp. 330-32.

74. Naranarayan, king of Cooch-Behar, was a contemporary of Akbar and he died about 1584. It is not unusual to attribute the name of a famous king to his descendants as well.

75. Prithivi Shah. The description of Kandor as given in the *P.B.* agrees with the district of Baglana, between Khandesh and the Surat coast, having prosperous valleys and hill-slopes, smiling with cornfields and gardens, ruled by a Rathor family in unbroken succession for fourteen centuries, whose Rajas styled themselves as *Shah*. Sarkar's *Aurangzeb*, I, p. 51. According to the *Maasir-ul-Umara*, tr. Beveridge, Kandour is 30 *Kos* from Ahmadabad, p. 53: Baglana lay between Guzrat and Deccan, p. 353. Baglana was annexed to the Mogul territory in 1638 by Prince Aurangzeb, during Shah Jahan's reign, perhaps as a result of the diplomatic interview recorded in the *P.B.* Cp. the Persian proverb,—"*Do badshay dar aqlime na gunjund*," i.e., two sovereigns cannot live together in the same kingdom. Shah Jahan's contemporary Prithivi Singha, the Raja of Srinagar, gave shelter to Sulaiman Shúkoh, the fugitive son of Dara Shukoh.

76. Shah Safi or Safavi II, was the Sultan of Persia, 1629-1642, being the grandson of Shah 'Abbas the Great, and 'Ali Mardan Khan was the governor of Kandahar under Shah Safi. Quliz Khan, the Galiz Khan of our narrative was first governor of Lahore and then of Kandahar. 'Ali Mardan joined the Moguls and became governor of Kashmir and the Punjab. See *Maasir-ul-Umara*, p. 187; Sykes, *Persia*, Vol. 2, p. 297. See also Bernier's *Travels*, O. U. Press, II, p. 6. About Prince Shuja's expedition aganist Shah Safi, see *Maasir-ul-Umara*, Beveridge, p. 233.

77. Shah Jahan and Bijapur.—This is probably the letter addressed by Shah Jahan to the 'Adil Shahi Sultan which was discussed by the latter in full court, when the captains of Bijapur cried out words of defiance, ending in the delivery of a haúghty reply to the Delhi envoy, Sarkar's *Aurangzeb*, Vol. I, p. 256.

78. Cooch Behar.—From the time of Akbar, Cooch Behar was under Mogul vassalage. During the War of Succession it assúmed independence and stopped paying the stipulated tribute to the Moguls.

79. Mashud-ami Khan.—This Mashud-ami Khan, son of Mir Jumla, was no other than Mir Muhammad Amin Khan whose life-sketch is given by Shah Newaz Khan, p. 241. His rollicking drunkeness caused the imprisonment of the Nawab's family by the Sultan of Golconda. He rose to be the governor of Guzrat and was offered the Grand-Viziership by Aurangzeb. According to Tavernier, p. 134, "Mirgimola had several daughters, but only one son, who had a great train, and made a great noise at court."

80. Dilir Khan.—Dilir or Dilal Khan's chivalrous and successfúl attack on the impregnable Assamese fort of Shamlagarha is picturesquely described in the *Maasir*, tr. Beveridge, 498-500.

81. Deccani Sultan Muhammad Shah.—The Sultan of Golconda who resented Mir Jumla's growing power and disloyalty was Abdúlla Qutb Shah who died in 1674 A.D. Muhammad Shah was the 'Adil Shahi Sultan of Bijapur, his consort being Bari Sahiba, sister of the Golconda Sultan. Muhammad Shah died in 1656, his nominee on the throne being 'Ali Adil Shah II whose parentage and authority were questioned by many. Our chronicler seems to have confused between the incidents of Golconda and Bijapur. His use of *Khan* instead of *Shah* after the name of Muhammad is significant, as we know that Bijapuri Sultans were addressed as *Khans*, and not as *Shahs* by Delhi Emperors before Shah Jahan,—Sarkar's *Aurangzeb*, I. p. 255.

82. In another chronicle Mir Jumla has been described as the son of Mirza Hena.

83. Sewa-raja.—This story is unmistakably the one of Sivaji. Jai Singha was sent to subdue the Mahratta chief, and Ram Singha accompained his father to the Deccan, and was subsequently appointed to be the custodian of the prisoner. At the conclusion of the wars Jai Singha assured Sivaji of his freedom and safety. The Maharatta chief was allowed by Emperor Aurangzeb to sit among the Panch-hazari Omraos, and Shivaji expressed his vehement dissatisfaction to Ram Singha and reminded him of his father's promises. Our chronicler mentions Sewa as a place against which the Rajput Raja was despatched: this may be Sivapur which was built by Sivaji. Two expressions are used in the *P.B.* to designate the hero,—*Sewa-raja* and *Raja of Sewa*. Kandarpa Singha is inexplicable, unless we take it as a palpable mistake arising out of confusion of names like Kankana and Kandana so intimately associated with the heroic exploits of the Mahratta leader.

84, Multafat Khan, the qiladar of Ahmadnagar fort, figures prominently in the campaigns against Shivaji. Sulatifat Khan of the *P.B.* is obviously a scribal mistake for Multafat Khan, as in Assamese manuscripts the letters representing *S* and *M* can be distinguished only by long practice and training.

85. This story is applicable to Raja Karan Bhurtiyah of Bikanir against whom Jai Singha was sent. Rao Karan himself joined Jai Singha's campaign against Shivaji.

86. Teg Bahadur and Ram Singha.—That Teg Bahadur the ninth Sikh Guru accompanied Ram Singha to Assam is mentioned in all contemporary Sikh chronicles. Cunningham on the authority of a manuscript Gurmukhi summary of Teg Bahadur's life says that the Guru meditated on the banks of the Brahmaputra, and convinced the heart of the Raja of Kamrup who become a believer in his mission. The Guru retired from Assam on hearing of the birth of his son Govinda.

87. Black arts practised by Kamrupi women.—According to popular traditions in Assam, and recorded in the manuscript note in possession of the Mahant of the Sikh shrine at Dhubri, Man Singha the grand father of Ram Singha was poisoned by one of his Assamese mistresses who imparted the poison to her lord to prevent his proposed invasion of Assam. What the Moguls thought of the women of Assam is recorded in the *Khulasat-ut-Tawarikh*, compiled in 1695,—"The beauty of the women of Kamrup is very great; their magic, enchantment and use of spells and jugglery are greater than one can imagine, ... They conquer the heart of whomsoever they like and bring them under their command." The same imputation of sorcery and witchcraft is made in the *Fathiyah-i-Ibriyah* and *Ain-i-Akbari*. See the story of Jamila and Hamid in the Urdu book *Kamrup-ki-Jadu* by Syed Golam Hyder Khan Sahib of Rai Barelli where references are made to Kamrupi magic, p. 27. The *Alamgir-namah* thus remarks on the poisonous climate of Assam,—"Kamrup is remarkable for bad water, noxious air and confined prospects."

88. Manowar Khan was the great-grandson of Ise Khan. He was a Zemindar and an owner of numerous war-boats, and was commonly known as the "cruising admiral." He was attached to Mir Jumla's expedition to Assam, and held charge of the Mogul fleet at Lakhaugarh. A bazaar near the Dacca railway station is known as Manowar Khan's Bazaar.

89. Laluk Barphukan—This Barphukan was Laluk Sola, who surrendered Gauhati to Mansur Khan without fighting in lieu of a promise that Azamtara should make him Raja of Assam. Baduli Phukan was Mir Jumla's chief ally. He went to Bengal along with Mir Jumla and became the medium of the treasonable correspondence between Laluk Barphukan and Sultan Azamtara. See Appendix C.

90. This table can be compared with "Tables of distances in Hindustan" in British miles, from Agra, Delhi, Hyderabad, etc, in Rennell's "Memoir of a Map of Hindustan,"

91. Masalanda Gazi.—James Prinsep in his *Useful Tables*, Thomas edition, p. 293, mentions against the date 1498:—"Assam invaded by Dalal Gazi, son of Husain Shah, Masalandar

Gazi, Sultan Ghiyasuddin." Blochmann comments on this passage in his paper *On a new king of Bengal*, J.A.S.B., 1872, p. 336.—"It is not said who Masalanda Gazi or Sultan Ghiyasuddin are, whom Prinsep mentions as having gained a footing in Assam," nor does the *P.B.* beyond giving the mere names.

92. Viswa Singha, the founder of the Cooch Behar dynasty, on ascending the throne in 1527 A.D. appointed his twelve principal followers as Karzis,- Bhakhura Karzi, Paro, Nichila, Churchal, Satananda, Megha, Purandra, Bhota, Biru, Sharanam, Harishchandra, and Ripunjoy Karzi. Their descendants also enjoyed the Karziship.

93. In Ain-i-Akbari, Blochmann, Lakshminarayan gave his daughter to Man Singha, Vol. I. 340; also J.A.S.B. 1872, p. 53.

94. For **Parikshit's** imprisonment of the family of Raghunath and the latter's complaint, see *Padishah-namah*, quoted in J.A.S.B. 1872, p. 53.

95. According to the **Padishah-namah,** the articles offered by Parikshit to Mukarram Khan were 100 elephants, 100 tanghans (ponies) and 20 maunds of lignum aloes, J.A.S.B., 1872, page 54.

96. "**Koch Hazo** almost coincides with the modern district of Goalpara, Lower Assam, extending from above Hatisalah in the Karaibari Hills and Pergana, on the left side of the Brahmaputra, along the bend of the river to Goalpara. On the right side, it commenced north of the Pargana of Bhitarband and contained the district along the angle of the river as far as Parganah Khoontaghat inclusively, with the towns of Dhubri and Rangamati. On the east Koch Hazo bordered on Kamrup, or that part of Assam which lay between Goalpara and Gauhati on both sides of the Brahmaputra," J.A.S.B., 1872, p. 50. But from the text it appears that from the time of Ibrahim Karori, Koch Hazo included Kamrup which formed a separate sarkar. Sarkar Dakhinkul also included several perganas of Kamrup.

THE END

GOVERNMENT OF ASSAM

DEPARTMENT OF HISTORICAL AND ANTIQUARIAN STUDIES

PUBLICATIONS FOR SALE

ASSAMESE

1. **Assam Buranji,**—1228-1826 A.D., by Harakanta Barua Sadar-Amin. Cloth, Rs. 2-8 ; Paper Cover, Re. 1.
2. **Kamrupar Buranji.**—Containing details of the Assam-Mogul conflicts. Cloth, Rs. 2-8 ; Paper Cover, Re. 1.
3. **Deodhai Asam Buranji.**—An earlier Ahom history. Cloth, Rs. 3.
4. **Tungkhungia Buranji.**—1681-1806 A.D., by Srinath Duara Barbarua. Cloth, Rs. 2-8.
5. **Asamar Padya-Buranji.**—Two metrical chronicles by Dutiram Hazarika and Bisweswar Vaidyadhipa. Cloth, Rs. 3.
6. **Kachari Buranji.**—Assam-Cachar relations up to 1714 A.D. Re. 1-8.
7. **Jayantia Buranji.**—Assam-Jayantia relations up to 1744 A.D. Re. 1-8.
8. **Tripura Buranji.**—Detailed account of Tripura by two Assamese envoys deputed to the Tripura Court. From a manuscript in the British Museum. Re. 1-8.
9. **Assam Buranji.**—1648-1681 A.D. Re. 1.
10. **Ankia Nat.**—Containing the extant dramas of Sankardeva, Madhabdeva and Gopaldeva. Rs. 3.
11. **Nitilatankur.**—A treatise on politics and warfare. Re. 1.
12. **Assam Buranji.**—1228-1696 A.D., recovered from the family of the late Srijut Sukumar Mahanta of North Gauhati. Rs. 3.

N.B.—All the above books contain Introduction in English. A Synopsis or Analysis in English has also been inserted in publications Nos. 5, 6, 7, 9, 10 and 12.

ENGLISH

13. **Tungkhungia Buranji.**—Or a History of Assam, 1681-1826 A.D. With Genealogical Tables, Bibliography, Glossary and Index. Published by the Oxford University Press. Rs. 11.
14. **Baharistan-i-Ghaybi.**—Conflicts with the Moguls in Assam, Bengal, Bihar and Orissa in early seventeenth century. Translated from the original Persian. In two volumes. Cloth, Rs. 10 per set.
15. **Bulletin No. I.**—With an Introduction by His Excellency Sir Laurie Hammond. Governor of Assam. 1927-1932. Re. 1.

16. **Bulletin No. 2.**—With an Introduction by His Excellency Sir Michael Keane, Governor of Assam, 1932-1937. Re. 1.

17. **Bulletin No. 3.**—A souvenir of the Opening Ceremony of the Narayani Handiqui Historical Institute. Re. 1-8.

18. **Bulletin No. 4.**—A souvenir of the Unveiling Ceremony of the portrait of the late Mrs. Narayani Handiqui. Re. 1.

19. **Assamese, Its Formation and Development.**—A treatise on the history and philology of the Assamese language. Rs. 10.

20. **Account of Assam.**—Compiled in 1807-14 by Dr. Francis Hamilton, formerly Buchanan. Re. 1-8.

21. **Lachit Barphukan and His Times.**—Or a history of the Assam-Mogul conflicts of the period 1667-1671, with a life-sketch of Raja Ram Singha of Amber; notable utterances of Assamese kings, ministers and commanders; diplomatic epistles; and a Bibliography. Cloth, Rs. 4.

22. **Annals of the Delhi Badshahate.**—Being a translation of the Assamese chronicle *Padshah-Buranji*, with Notes. The Introduction deals with Assam's contact with the Muslim world, Padshah-Buranji manuscripts, etc. Rs. 5.

23. **Anglo-Assamese Relations.**—From the earliest contacts to the beginnings of British administration in Assam; based on the original records of the East India Company, etc. *In the Press.*

NB.—*Of the above books*:—

Nos. 1 to 8, 12 and 13, 15 to 18, and 20 to 23, have been edited or compiled by Rai Bahadur Dr. S. K. Bhuyan, M.B.E., M.A., B.L. (Cal.), Ph.D. (Lond.), Director of Historical and Antiquarian Studies in Assam. No. 13 is an English translation, by Dr. Bhuyan, of No. 4, with extension of the history from 1806 to 1826.

No. 9 has been edited by Mr. S. K. Dutta, B.A. (Cal.), B.Sc. (Lond.), Barrister-at-Law, Honorary Deputy Director of D.H.A.S.

No. 10 has been edited by Srijut Birinchi Kumar Barua, M.A., B. L., Honorary Assistant Director, D.H.A.S.

No. 11 has been edited by the late Srijut Sarat Chandra Goswami, I.S.O.

No. 14 is an English translation of the original Persian chronicle by the late Dr. M. I. Borah, M.A., B.L. (Dac.), Ph.D. (Lond.), Head of the Department of Persian and Urdu in the University of Dacca.

No. 19 is by Dr. Banikanta Kakati, M.A., Ph.D., Professor, Cotton College, Gauhati.

To be had of

Office of the Department of Historical and Antiquarian Studies,
Narayani Handiqui Historical Institute,
GAUHATI, ASSAM, INDIA.